The Vancouver Guide Book

The Vancouver Guide Book

Ginny and Beth Evans

Chronicle Books
San Francisco

THE VANCOUVER GUIDE BOOK
©1986 Eve Publishing
and Ginny and Beth Evans

ISBN 0-87701-382-9

Cover Photograph:
Stefan Schulhof
Schulhof Photography

Graphics:
Ina Lee

Maps:

Ian Thomson and Philip Michalchuk
Base maps courtesy of:
  Department of National Defence, Ottawa
Map Production:
  B.C. Ministry of the Environment
Granville Island, Hotson Bakker

Printed and bound in Canada by
Hignell Printing Limited, Winnipeg

Typeset by
The Typeworks, Vancouver

First Published in the United States 1986 by
CHRONICLE BOOKS
ONE HALLIDIE PLAZA
SAN FRANCISCO, CA 94102

Photography

Acknowledgements

In 1979, when we put together the first *Vancouver Guidebook,* we found that we owed our biggest debt of thanks to all those who, on the other end of the telephone, were so readily hospitable and helpful. This has again been the case in updating the guide and has made research a process of getting to know people as well as prices and places.

Specifically, we would like to thank Betty Campbell, the inspiration and publisher of the first guide, and contributors to it—John Rodgers and Lee Straight—who took pains to revise their knowledgeable articles for this version. Fedor Frastacky, Beth's husband, had, this time round, to contend with parenthood as well as hiking (his specialty) and the general upheaval of his life. Other Vancouver informants—Ina Lee (also creator of the book's graphics), Meg Best, Mare and Bruno Christiansen, Suzanne Fong, Ross MacDonald, Andrew Mason, Pip Steele and Emily Waddingham—generously shared with us their experience. Charlie Binks took the time and trouble to find some new angles on the city as we were seeing it; regrettably there was not enough room to print more of the pictures he took. We would also like to thank Rosemary Emery, Kate Sirluck and Teresa Trivett for their editing help and Kasandra Maidmentt for invaluable research assistance.

That just leaves the family, who launched Eve Publishing, babysat, kept the accounts, and supplied the expertise we were lacking. Thank you grandmothers Evans and Frastacky, our father W.W., our sister Eleanor, and Uncle Don.

And good luck Vancouver in your Expo year.

Table of Contents

Hyak, at Vancouver Public Aquarium

1 *Vancouver*

WELCOME TO THE CITY

Having heard of Vancouver, you've probably heard that it rains a lot here. It is said that long-time residents get so used to the rain that they water their lawns as soon as the sun comes out. You might even hear the winter's weather called "perma-grey". But behind the fog, mist and ample annual rainfall lies one of Canada's great open secrets—an evergreen city of unpretentious vitality.

Protected by an ancient chain of cloud-catching mountains, the surrounding sea, and a low-key reputation, Vancouver cloaks its westcoast sophistication in natural tones. Interior decorators go mad with wood, restauranteurs bring the outdoors inside, and local artists and craftsmen take flight into fanciful or earthy odes to the environmental beauty of the region.

When the sun shines and the mountains appear, the city can turn your head. Its compass directions may turn you around too. Montreal faces the south, the U.S. and the sun—its "mountain" at its back. Toronto fronts on the lake to its south. Vancouver, however, looks at the mountains along its North Shore. In housing everywhere, whimsical terraces, windows, abutments, additions, porches, and decks reach for a glimpse of the spectacular scene.

Given such heightened beauty, it is not surprising that visitors may overlook the more typically urban experiences of such a large centre. Not only does Vancouver continually draw one's spirit away from the congestion, hustle, and anxiety associated with the modern city, but it is ridiculously easy to take one's body to the hills as well. Mountain parks lie at Vancouver's doorsteps, front and back; thousands of acres of garden and forest reside within and around the city itself. From any number of vantage points on the seashore or atop downtown skyscrapers, one can witness the whole—city, sea, and mountain mystery—in a nutshell.

Vancouver's own brew of salty savoir-vivre and enterprise has always made it a haven for easterners, outdoor sportsmen, and birds of every sort. More recently, the city has become an esteemed centre of the visual arts, dance, music, urban architecture, and eating. While no one seems to hurry in their day-to-day life, things are always openly on the move. The law courts moved under glass, the art gallery has moved into the old courthouse, and False Creek has undergone a face-lift. Between four and six o'clock scores of joggers are on the move everywhere.

Despite its relative urban youth, an atmosphere of friendly pride and considerate urbanity pervades this spacious city. Oddly enough, Vancouver almost didn't become one. New Westminster was originally the administrative capital of the territory, and Port Moody was initially chosen as the western terminus for the railway. But the authorities changed the Pacific destination of the trains in 1884, and with that the fate of the little community called Granville. Popularly known as ''Gastown'', the name of the railway's terminus become Vancouver in 1886.

Today the Greater Vancouver area includes the City of Vancouver, the City of North Vancouver, the District of North Vancouver, the Municipality of West Vancouver, reserves owned by the Burrard, Squamish, Musqueam, and Coquitlam Bands, the Village of Lions Bay, the University Endowment Lands, the Municipality of Burnaby, the District of Coquitlam, the City of Port Coquitlam, the City of Port Moody, the Municipality of Richmond, the City of New Westminster, the Municipality of Surrey, the Municipality of Delta, the City of White Rock, and Greater Vancouver Sub-Division A. The population of this entire area is approximately 1.2 million.

Annual precipitation in Vancouver's downtown area is 60.51 inches (1,537 mm). The further south you go in the greater Vancouver area, the more sun you'll see. The North Shore gets the least. Downtown gets 1,650 to 1,700 hours per annum; the University of British Columbia, 1,820 hrs/annum; the Airport 1,930 hours each year; and White Rock even more. Most of this sun shines in the summer, when the skies stay blue for days and days on end.

A SHORT HISTORY OF THE TOWN
by Meg Best

Vancouverites may hesitate to make a big deal of their history—a history which is as intermittent and happenstance as its weather. To view the current splendour of Vancouver, it is difficult to visualize the heavily-wooded wilderness that greeted the first Spanish and British ships in 1792. The British, led by Captain George Vancouver, were remarkably unimpressed with the area; they charted the Gulf of Georgia extensively but did not venture further inland than Point Grey on its outer tip. The coast was left untrod by Europeans for another seventy years.

It was not until the 1860s that any attempt was made to settle in the Fraser River Delta. The first hints of a town on Burrard Inlet came into being as a stop-over for transients on their way inland. The Fraser River Valley gold rush was on and people were rushing by this rugged coast where trees towered darkly over the shores.

Permanent settlers and entrepreneurs first came to the area in 1862. As one resident wrote, "Few of us came here for our health. We came to make money and to better our conditions." By other Europeans, they were looked upon as somewhat mad.

The strong entrepreneurial spirit also brought such men as John Morton, Samuel Brighouse and William Hailstone, who

Gastown, 1886

in partnership attempted to establish a brickworks. Their enterprise failed, and we still don't have much in the way of bricks in the city today.

It was the coast's most dominating feature, the forests, that gave rise to Vancouver's first industry—logging and lumber—and which endowed its future with prosperity. By 1865, shiploads of lumber from Burrard Inlet were being exported to markets as distant as Australia. A local lumber industry followed fast on the heels of this success, and naturally competition too.

One of the most notorious of those vying for timber leases was an itinerant sea captain, Edward Stamp. His Vancouver Island Spar Lumber and Sawmill Co. was to become the Inlet's most important and most lucrative mill—but under another name. Stamp, a turbulent and difficult man, ran out of money in 1868 and was forced to sell the company. The following year, Hastings Mill Enterprise, representing interests from Victoria and San Francisco, bought it from that owner. Hastings Mill had been born. The growth of the lumber market of following years ensured its success, a critical factor in the continued existence and growth of the region as a whole. Within a

decade, the shore was being cleared and logging was booming.

The early development of the lumber business established a financial base for three separate towns: Moodyville, on the North Shore where the City of North Vancouver now is; Granville, opposite on the south shore where downtown Vancouver now is; and Hastings, site of the Hastings Mill near where the Second Narrows Bridge now crosses Burrard Inlet. Although the official name of downtown Vancouver was Granville, the town was locally referred to as Gastown, after its garrulous, first hotel and saloon keeper, Captain "Gassy" Jack Deighton from New Westminster. Logging being the *raison d'être* of the area, Granville remained a very rough-hewn community for some years. It was viewed by the more respectable as "an aggregation of filth." However, just southwest of the new town, where Eaton's, The Bay and the Pacific Centre Shopping Mall now are, stood some of the best timber on the entire coast.

After much tossing about of the various possibilities for a coast terminus of the Canadian Pacific Railway, it was finally decided by a hair that Granville would be the one. Sir William Cornelius Van Horne, chairman of CPR, was primarily responsible for the decision which overnight turned a logging town into Canada's major port for the trans-shipment of prairie grain.

In 1886, John Robson, a member of the brand-new provincial legislature, suggested that Granville be incorporated as a city—in the interests of better roads, bridges, and "the preservation of law and order." No one felt that Granville was a grand enough name for a city; Sir William Van Horne, when asked, suggested Vancouver. Thus John Robson was destined to become known as the father of the city of Vancouver.

Immediately after its incorporation, on April 6, 1886, the city's first municipal election was held. The town was just settling down again, when some clearing fires in Yaletown, site of Expo 86, began to burn out of control. In less than an hour, the entire new city was reduced to ashes. Although The Great Fire, as it came to be known, finished off the original town (with the exception of the Hastings Mill Store which now houses a museum), many felt that it had brought the fledgling city welcome public notice.

During the next five years, the number of the city's residents grew from 1,000 to 13,709. In these years a significant segment of the population was made up of Asian immigrants, who had come to "Gum San" or Gold Mountain. Most stayed to work on the railway, but were denied citizenship and the right to vote. Throughout the first decades of the twentieth century, racial conflicts hang as a dark cloud over Vancouver's past. Today, the city has the second largest Chinese community in North America.

In 1893, 1913, and 1919, fortunes of the city hit depressing lows. But with the 1920s, it was back on its feet as a major port, reaping the benefits of the Panama Canal and the good harvests of the Canadian prairies in those years. Wages rose and so did profits; the city prospered. At least until the crash of 1929 and the onset of the Great Depression.

Another dark time intrudes with the Second World War, even though the city was far from the front and never itself under threat of attack. Malcolm Lowry at Dollarton on the North Shore worked on his final version of *Under the Volcano*.

With the 60s came the artists, the flower children, murals, stained glass, and a houseboat community in Deep Cove. And a new nickname for Vancouver—"Lotus Land." Its mild winters, waters, and skiing appealed particularly to easterners tired

Hastings Sawmill, Burrard Inlet

of ice, salt and slush.

Although most of the buildings that document Vancouver's earlier past have gone, the original trees of Stanley Park remain. A few years before the city, on the San Juan islands, a pigocide (or porkocide) had led to testy relations between garrisons of the U.S. Army and of the Royal British Navy, both comfortably stationed on the island. Reminded of the distant possibility of an outbreak of hostilities, the British set aside the 1,000-acre peninsula on Burrard Inlet as a military reserve. At the first meeting of City Council in 1886, it was decided that Vancouver would take this over from the army. Within six months, it was officially opened as a public park, named in honour of the province's Governor-General, Lord Stanley. Stanley Park has therefore always been one of the city's treasured assets, and is a tribute to the trees which gave it life.

In the 1930s when the Guinness family (of beer fame) proposed building a bridge across the stretch of water known as First Narrows, there was vigorous public opposition to it because it would necessitate cutting a road through the forests of Stanley Park. The bridge, however, had its claim to fame; it was at the time to be the longest suspension bridge in the British Empire. The public bowed to the future, the bridge was opened on November 12, 1938, giving access to West Vancouver's Marine Drive and the "British Properties" on the north shore.

Vancouver had come of age, and the world was about to discover it.

2 *Coming, going & getting around*

BY PLANE

Vancouver International Airport

Local legend has it that Charles Lindbergh excluded Vancouver from his triumphal tour in 1928 for lack of a suitable landing strip. Today, everything is up-to-date.

The airport's post office is open 9 am to 4 pm weekdays; foreign exchange, 6:15 am to 10:30 pm daily; and Jet Set Sam, where you can buy local salmon and have it packed for shipment with your luggage, 6 am to 11:30 pm every day of the week.

There are direct phones to a large number of hotels, car rental desks, and two information centres—**Tourism British Columbia** on Level 2 (open 7:30 am to 11 pm) and **Transport Canada Information Counter** on Level 3.

Parking lot shuttle buses travel continuously between the terminal and stations in the acres of parking lot, at all hours of the airport's operation.

Budget, Tilden, Avis, Hertz and Dollar all have car rental offices at the airport itself. If you are leaving town and need repairs done on your own car, Airport Service Centre (273–4744) offers a Fix 'n Fly service. They will deliver you to the

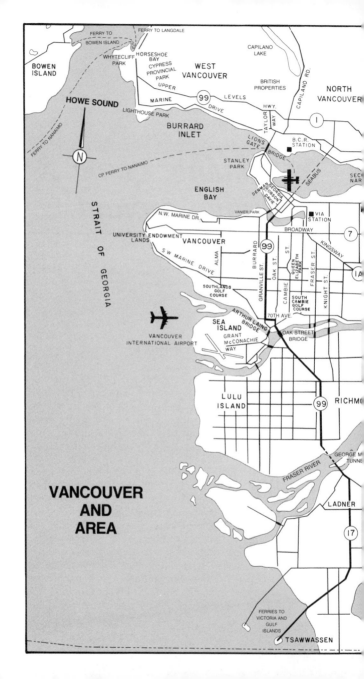

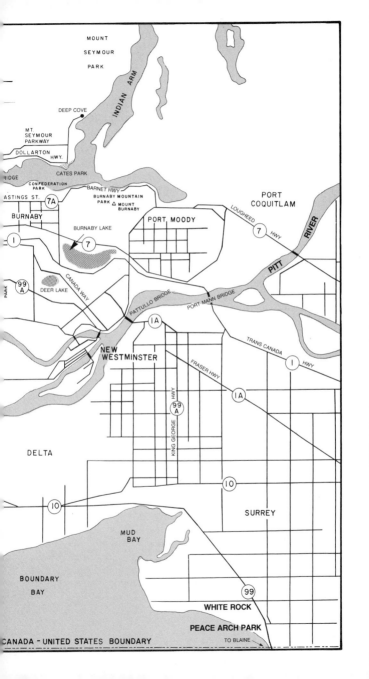

airport, fix your car while you are gone, park it (for free), and pick you up on your return.

Airport hotels that have transport bus stations at the airport are the Delta Hotel (1–800–268–1133) and the Richmond Inn (273–7878).

Taxis. There are always plenty of taxis at the airport in which the fare to downtown Vancouver will run about $10. The **Hustle Bus** (Perimeter Transportation, 273–0071), departing from Level 2, will take you downtown for $5.75 (children 4 to 12 years $4.25). Between 6 am and 12:30 midnight, this bus leaves on the hour and the half hour for the **Hotel Vancouver,** the **Westin Bayshore,** the **Sheraton-Landmark Hotel,** and the **Holiday Inn-City Centre.** At a quarter to and after the hour, it leaves for the **Downtown Holiday Inn,** the **Hotel Vancouver,** and **Georgia Hotel,** and the inter-city **Bus Depot** on Dunsmuir Street. A connecting shuttle bus will take you from Granville Street at Broadway Avenue to the **Holiday Inn on Broadway.** If you want to get off at other points along Granville Street, or anywhere along the route, just ask the driver. The staff at the information counters at the airport will help you choose a disembarkation point. If you are on the way to the airport, the bus can be flagged down from the corner of Granville and 41st, or at Broadway.

City Buses. From the Level 3 (Departures) door of the airport, the downtown trip costs $1. For the city centre, catch the #100-Midway Connector to 71st Avenue and Granville. Get a transfer. At this corner, wait for a #21-Victoria which will take you right down Granville Street to the heart of town.

South Terminal

From this airfield, next door to the International Airport, **Burrard Air** (278–7178), **Air B.C.** (685–3211), **Wilderness Airline** (689–2588), **Harbour Air** (1–800–972–0212), and **Skylink Airlines** (946–1416) make scheduled flights to Vancouver Island and the northern parts of the province. When driving to the South Terminal, watch for the small sign indicating a left turn for this terminal as you near the International Airport. A free shuttlebus runs between the two airports every half hour.

Coal Harbour

Some float planes take off from the Fraser River behind the South Terminal. The majority, however, leave from Coal Harbour downtown. **Air B.C.** (685–3211) will fly you to the Victoria or Nanaimo waterfronts. **Harbour Air** (688–1277), at the north foot of Jervis Street, flies harbour tours, and to Vancouver Island. **Tyee Air** (689–8651) flies to the Sunshine Coast, Powell River, and to some locations on Vancouver Island. **Coval Air** (Zenith 2896) flies regularly to Campbell River. **Air Caledonia** (278–6266) offers charter service to unscheduled points in B.C.

The harbour terminals can be reached from the foot of Cardero or Jervis Streets, and planes take off right in front of downtown offices.

Customs

For information on coming into Canada in your own plane, contact **Transport Canada,** SLPP, Ottawa, Ontario, Canada K1A 0N8. If bad weather or an emergency forces you to land unexpectedly, report your arrival to the nearest Regional Customs Office or the local R.C.M.P.

BY TRAIN

VIA Rail

Since the first CPR passenger train, decked in flowers, pulled into the harbour in 1887, there have been a lot of changes in the railways. Trains these days are rarely festooned with flowers, and all passenger service is now run by **VIA Rail**. Their new automated ticket service is RESERVIA (1–800–665–8630). The Victorian CPR station on the waterfront at Granville Square serves only the SeaBus.

VIA trains come into the CNR station at the foot of False Creek (1150 Station Street, at Main and Terminal Streets). Full service trains run daily between Winnipeg and Vancouver (via Saskatoon and Edmonton). For information on the transcontinental train, the "Canadian," call RESERVIA (1–800–665–8630).

VIA Rail also takes **Amtrak** reservations for destinations in the United States. Check with Make Trax Travel, 301 W. Cordova (685–6546) or RESERVIA (1–800–665–8630). A daily train between Seattle and Vancouver may be running again in 1986. At present, connecting buses run between the two cities.

In Vancouver, a taxi or a bus will take you from the station to the downtown area. City buses stop outside the station on Main Street. Board a #5-Robson or a #8-Davie for Denman Street and the West End. The #15-Cambie goes to the corners of Granville and Robson Streets in the downtown centre. To get to the station, take a #3-Main from the corner of Davie and Denman, a #19-Kingsway from the Stanley Park Bus Loop, or the #16-Fraser from the corner of Burrard and Robson.

VIA Rail offers discounted fares for round-trip tickets, groups of 3 or more persons, and children. Ambassador Fares, at one-third off, apply for seniors. For information on any of these reduced rates, call RESERVIA 1–800–665–8630 from anywhere in British Columbia, or contact your travel agent.

If you have the time and the inclination to explore the Rockies, VIA Rail offers a number of package tours of various lengths with accommodation and coach tours in some of the famous CN hotels of those mountains. For more information, call RESERVIA (1–800–665–8630).

BCR

For the pure pleasure of it, BCR's passenger service from North Vancouver to **Lillooet** and **Prince George** offers some of the most scenic rail miles (or rather, kilometres) anywhere in Canada. Originally incorporated as Pacific Great Eastern railway (PGE) and known variously as the "Province's Greatest Expense," "Past God's Endurance," and "Prince George Eventually," the PGE became British Columbia Rail in 1972. Heading into the province's interior, the passenger train runs through Cheakamus Canyon and Garibaldi Park, past the huge Mount Currie Indian Reserve, and over the Cascade Range to the gold rush town of Lillooet.

Passenger service has been discontinued beyond Prince George, but if you want to go to Dawson Creek, or even further north, there's bus service.

In Lillooet, you can visit the site of an early Hudson's Bay trading post, the museum, Heritage House, a mock-up of the

Royal Hudson, Howe Sound

gold rush days, St. Mary's Church, the salmon spawning grounds, and the start of the original Cariboo Trail.

The mountain-bound train leaves **BCR's North Vancouver station,** 1311 West First Street (984–5246, the passenger number, or 986–2012) daily at 7:30 am. It arrives in Lillooet at 12:45 noon, and a southbound train departs at 3:30 pm. Sundays, Wednesdays and Fridays; the train continues from Lillooet north to Prince George, arriving there about 9 pm. It leaves for the return trip at 7:30 the next morning (Mondays, Thursdays and Saturdays). Seats can be reserved only on trains going all the way to Prince George, and those tickets include meals.

Train reservations for June, July and August, and during the Christmas season, should be made well in advance. A one-way ticket to Lillooet costs $18.15 (a reserved seat $34.15); to Prince George, it is $53.25 (a reserved seat $76.25). From October 1 to May 31, reduced family rates apply, and Canadian senior citizens are entitled to a 25% discount year-round. On request, the railway will arrange your accommodation in any of the modern hotels in Prince George.

To get to the BCR terminal by car, cross the Lions Gate Bridge to the North Shore and follow the signs for North Vancouver. This exit will take you onto Marine Drive going east. Turn right at Pemberton for about six blocks to the station. Parking space is limited. Special buses to the North Vancouver terminal leave the downtown bus terminal (150 Dunsmuir St.) at 6:40 am. These buses also stop along Georgia Street at the regular North Vancouver-bound stops. A bus also meets the arriving evening train and will return you to downtown Vancouver.

For **skiers,** BCR (984–5246) offers a combination train and ski-lift ticket for **Whistler and Blackcomb Mountains.** The train leaves the BCR North Vancouver station at 6:30 am, serves a continental breakfast, and returns from the Whistler station for Vancouver at 5:40 pm. Bus service is available between the train and Whistler Village. Fare for travel and skiing is approximately $36. Regular return fare on this daily train is $16.

BY BUS

City Transit

Despite serpentine-looking routes, Vancouver city buses are quite easy to use and **BC Transit,** which runs the buses, offers a Transit Guide for 54¢. It's available at The Bay, Eaton's, Woodward's, most book stores, and any of the Vancouver Convention and Visitors Bureaus. A copy of the guide is posted on bus-stop shelters, and a card at each stop lets you know which buses pass that way and how frequently.

Buses in Vancouver cover miles and miles of territory. **Fares** vary according to time and day of the week. For $1 (children 50¢), except at rush hour, you can travel, if you wish, from White Rock to Horseshoe Bay. Rush hour happens between first bus and 9:30 am and between 3 and 6:30 pm, except on weekends and holidays. At rush hour times, two- and three-zone fares apply: $1 (children 50¢) within one zone, $1.35 (children 70¢) over two zones, $1.75 (children 90¢) over three zones. These fares also apply to the SeaBus (on which transfers from city buses are valid). **EXACT FARES** are required at all times, but FareSaver tickets and FareCards can be purchased at Eaton's, Woodward's, The Bay, Infocentres, 7-Eleven stores, VTC/CBO outlets. At any time a transfer will allow you to get on and off the bus for up to 90 minutes from time of boarding, as long as there is no doubling back when you reboard the bus.

Basically, buses are numbered according to the area they service. Numbers under 100 travel within the city centre; buses numbered from 100 to 200 go to Coquitlam; 200 and over go to the North Shore; 300 is Surrey; 400 Richmond; 500 - there aren't any; 600s go to the Ladner Exchange and South Delta.

If you have difficulty planning a route, call **BC Transit** at **324–3211** - open daily between 6:30 am. and 11:30 pm. Their phones are usually busy, so try Tourism B.C. (660–2300) or the Visitors Bureau (682–2222) if you can't get through.

On **Sundays and holidays, a special bus pass** allows unlimited access to city buses (including Stanley Park) and to the SeaBus (adults $2, children and seniors $1). These passes can be purchased when you board the bus.

Stanley Park. On Sundays and holidays (10 am to 7 pm) during the summer months, you can circumbus the park, getting

SeaBus, Burrard Inlet

18

on and off at stops at the various points of interest. A Sundays and Holidays pass buys you this tour for the whole day and includes (with a transfer) the city, or within 90 minutes of boarding a regular city bus, you can transfer to the Stanley Park bus. It leaves the Stanley Park Bus Loop at the foot of Alberni Street by Lost Lagoon and makes a number of stops along Stanley Park Drive.

Granville Island Express. This direct connection between downtown and the heart of Granville Island runs between the Howe Street side of Vancouver Art Gallery and the Arts Club beside Granville Market on the Island. It leaves VAG quarter after and quarter to the hour, leaves Granville Market on the hour and half hour. It costs $1, one way.

The other way to get to Granville Island is by catching the #51 Granville Island connection at Broadway and Granville.

Airport. To take a city bus to the airport, get a #20 going south on Granville Street and a transfer. Stay on until 70th Avenue. At this stop, board a #100 Mid-Way Connector, which will take you right to the airport doors. The whole ride costs one fare, except in rush hour on weekdays.

SeaBus. The SeaBus, an alternative to the congested bridges which cross the Burrard Inlet from downtown Vancouver to North Van, is perfect for those who don't need to take their cars across the water.

The design of the bus is a first in the world. It looks like a catamaran, has two front ends, so it doesn't have to turn around, is made from aluminum, and is easy on fuel. The two ferries in service, *Burrard Beaver* and *Burrard Otter,* were built in Victoria and began shuttling across the Inlet in June 1977.

The SeaBus leaves from the **CPR Station by Granville Square** on the downtown waterfront, and from the **Lonsdale Quay** at the foot of Lonsdale Avenue in North Vancouver, 6:30 am to 12:45 am (fares as on city buses, transfers accepted). Large baby carriages can't manage the long access escalators, but wheelchairs can be accommodated. Contact SeaBus at 986–1501 for arrangements. Bicycles ($1) are allowed only on weekends and on statutory holidays.

If you leave something on a bus, contact Lost and Found, 611 West Hastings (682–7887).

ALRT. Early in 1986, Vancouver's new light, rapid transit trains will be running between the downtown waterfront and New Westminster, on 22 km of track which constitute Phase One of this component of the Vancouver Regional Rapid Transit system. By 1988, the line will be extended as far as Whalley in Surrey, crossing the Fraser River by cable-stayed bridge near the Pattullo Bridge. Downtown on the waterfront, the ALRT station will connect with the SeaBus, and with Granville Square and Canada Place. The Main Street station is just outside Expo's eastern gate.

The whole system will be integrated with the existing city-bus system, and trains are expected to run between 5 am and 1 am daily at cruising speeds of 75 to 80 km/h (47 to 50 mph). The entire trip from Waterfront Station to New Westminster will take approximately half an hour.

For information on the ALRT, drop into their office at 1012 West Georgia Street or call Vancouver Regional Rapid Transit (683–8401).

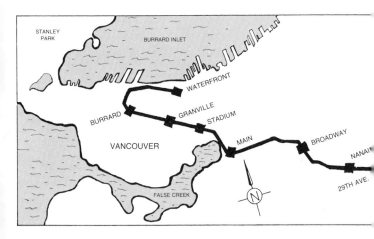

Inter-City Transit

The Vancouver inter-city **Greyhound Bus Depot** (662–3222), 150 Dunsmuir Street at Cambie, is about five blocks east of Granville Street.

From here, **Pacific Coach Lines, Maverick Coach Lines,** and **Cascade Coach Lines** service points in British Columbia. The familiar Greyhound buses leave for points all over Canada.

For information on inter-city bus services, call the depot at 662–3222. It is open from 7 am to 11:30 pm daily.

Maverick Coach Lines (255–1171) also runs a bus for **skiers** during the winter. One-way fare is regularly $10; round-trip bus fare plus combination ticket to Whistler and Blackcomb Mountains, $38. The bus leaves the downtown depot in Vancouver at 6:30 am; buses leave Whistler Village at 8:30 am, 4 pm and 6:30 pm for Vancouver, and will also pick you up at the Husky gas station opposite the gondola. No advance booking is required for this bus.

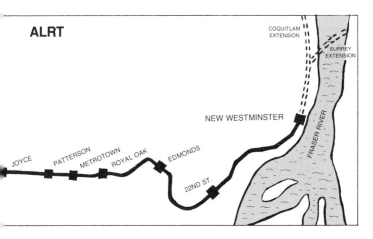

For **Victoria,** you can sail by bus from downtown Vancouver (total time 3¼ hours). Buses leave the Vancouver depot at Dunsmuir and Cambie nearly every hour from 6 am to 8 pm. Adult fare, $14.25 one way. This bus goes right on the ferry with you in it and delivers you to downtown Victoria. If you want to be picked up along Cambie Street by the bus going to Victoria, call in advance to reserve a seat.

If you want to get out of the city for a few days, **Gray Line** (872–8311) offers tours of Victoria, the Olympic Peninsula in Washington, the Canadian Rockies, and Alaska by cruise ship. Call their toll-free number 1–800–663–6446 in Canada, or 872–8311 in Vancouver.

You can also contact the **British Columbia Automobile Association**, 999 West Broadway (732–3911). They offer tours to the Okanagan, the Sunshine Coast and Vancouver Island, Williams Lake and Prince George, and the Rockies. You can also call Gray Line (872–8311) for reservations on these tours.

BY FERRY

Along British Columbia's indented shoreline, the missing link isn't the Sasquatch—it's the B.C. ferry system. And it leads to places as unusual and exciting as those of Sasquatch speculation—mountainous fjords, rock-bound passageways, and the uninhabited scenery of B.C.'s splendid coastal rain forests.

Landside travellers going along the coast will ultimately—if not sooner—require the services of this integral part of the province's transportation network. Sailings are frequent and pleasant, the scenery beautiful, the boats huge and comfortable, and, in summer or on holiday weekends, the line-ups long! Since there are no reservations, space on ferries is on a first come, first served basis. But each ship can take an unbelievable number of vehicles. Campers, recreational vehicles, motorcycles, almost any size of car or truck, and foot passengers are all accommodated on most boats for varying prices. In fair weather, any cruise across the Gulf of Georgia is a scenic experience.

BC Ferry Corporation (669–1211) carries cars and passengers between Vancouver (at Tsawwassen and at Horseshoe Bay) and Bowen Island, the Sechelt Coast, the Gulf Islands, and Van-

B.C. Ferries, Horseshoe Bay

couver Island (at Swartz Bay, near Victoria, and at Nanaimo). Ferries service points on the Sechelt Coast and islands in the Georgia Strait.

Tsawwassen.

From **Tsawwassen,** 32 km (20 mi) south of Vancouver, ferries leave for **Swartz Bay** (a 1 hour and 40 minute trip) near Victoria, and for the Gulf Islands. For the Victoria trip, foot passengers can book a seat on the Victoria-bound bus once on board. If you take this bus from the depot at Dunsmuir and Cambie in downtown Vancouver, it goes right on the ferry with you in it, and your fare ($14.25) includes the ferry crossing.

Fares are subject to change, but between Tsawwassen and Swartz Bay, run in the neighbourhood of $4 for a foot passenger, $6 for bicycle and rider, $11.50 for motorcycle and rider, $19 for car and driver, $23.50 for camper of 6'8'' (2m) and driver. Additional passengers are each $4.

During the summer, from 7 am to 10 pm, sailings leave Tsawwassen for Swartz Bay usually every hour on the hour. On holidays and weekends, extra runs are added. For fall and winter schedules, check with B.C. Ferries (669–1211). Sailing times are also broadcast on TV, Channel 10 all night after regular programming ends.

To get to Tsawwassen, take Granville Street to 70th Avenue, turn left to Oak Street, right on Oak, and carry on out, straight onto Highway 99 across the Oak Street Bridge. The turn for Tsawwassen at Highway 17, shortly after passing under the Fraser River, is well-marked. One bottleneck to watch for: at rush-hour, the traffic through the George Massey Tunnel under the Fraser River is notoriously slow.

From Swartz Bay, smaller ferries connect with the Gulf Islands. From Victoria itself, you can ferry to Seattle or Anacortes in the United States. Near Butchart Gardens, you can hop across the Saanich Inlet from Brentwood Bay, if heading up the coast of Vancouver Island. But in this case you would miss Victoria and the beautiful Malahat Mountain drive.

From Tsawwassen, ferries also leave for the Gulf Islands — Galiano, Mayne (from where another ferry connects with Saturna Island), Pender, and Saltspring. Spaces for cars or campers on these ferries can be reserved in advance (call BC Ferries at 669–1211). If booking more than 5 days ahead, pre-payment of the ticket is required. Check-in time for reservations that have not been pre-paid is 30 minutes before sailing from Tsawwassen or 20 minutes before departure time on the islands.

Fares between the mainland and the Gulf Islands are $3 for a foot passenger, $5 for bicycle and rider, $9 for motorcycle and rider, $15 for car and driver, $18.50 for a camper under 6'8" (2m) and driver, $34 over 6'8". Returning from the islands, the fare is less expensive.

Horseshoe Bay.

From West Vancouver, ferries leave Horseshoe Bay for **Nanaimo,** the **Sunshine Coast,** and **Bowen Island.** Bowen is the big island you can see from Horseshoe Bay. The ride is only ten minutes, and there's just enough time to make it up to the observation deck before docking. This mountainous island is the pleasant summer home for many from the city who maintain camps or cottages on its shores and in its forests. **Apodaca Provincial Park** is also on the island.

Ferries leave Horseshoe Bay for the 20-minute crossing to Bowen Island nearly every hour between 6:50 am and 8:55 pm. The last return sailing is at 8:25 pm. Fares are $2.50 for foot passengers, $3.50 for bicycle and rider, $7 for motorcycle and rider, $11.50 for car and driver, $14 to $25.50 for campers and trailers. Additional riders or passengers are $2.50 each.

Ferries going to **Nanaimo** on Vancouver Island leave Horseshoe Bay at relatively short intervals (during the summer months) between 6:30 am and 10:30 pm, and the 30-mile (48 km) crossing takes about two hours.

Fares on this run and on sailings to the Sechelt Peninsula are $4 for foot passengers, $6 for bicycle and rider, $11.50 for motorcycle and rider, $19 for car and driver, $23.50 to $43 for campers and trailers. Additional riders or passengers are $4 each.

To explore the **Sechelt** (pronounced Sea-shelt), or the **Sunshine Coast** (as it's known), you have to take the ferry from Horseshoe Bay to Langdale. The crossing takes 45 minutes, the drive on the other side is gorgeous. Ten ferries a day leave Horseshoe Bay beginning at 7:40 am.

Further up the Sechelt coast, another ferry crosses **Jervis Inlet** between Earls Cove and Saltery Bay. Boats leave for this 50-minute crossing every two hours. When you purchase a ticket at either Horseshoe Bay or at Saltery Bay, it is good for two crossings; you can either cross Howe Sound and return, or continue up the coast and cross Jervis Inlet on the same ticket. In the latter case, a return ticket would have to be purchased — or you could then cross the Georgia Strait at Powell River on the ferry that runs from there.

To get to Horseshoe Bay, cross the Lions Gate Bridge to the North Shore, and follow the exit for West Vancouver and Horseshoe Bay. The road loops around under the bridge. The first stop-light is at Taylor Way, turn right here. A short distance up the hill and just under a bridge, there is a poorly-marked left turn for the Upper Levels Highway. Once on it, you can't get lost. The highway takes you right to the ferry docks in Horseshoe Bay.

Going by bus? At the corner of Granville and Georgia Streets, by The Bay department store, catch a West Vancouver bus marked "Horseshoe Bay." It will take you to the docks.

Other Ferries

B.C. Ferries now operate all the saltwater ferry routes in the province. They connect Powell River and Comox, Powell River and Texada Island, Vancouver Island and Denman and Hornby Islands, Campbell River with Quadra and Cortes Islands, Nanaimo with Gabriola Island.

For scheduled sailings and fares, call B.C. Ferries (669–1211).

The province's Department of Highways operates the freshwater ferries such as the one which crosses the Fraser River at Albion in Langley.

For information on any of the Department's ferries, call 660–8200 in Vancouver or their Marine Division at 387–3045 in Victoria.

Cruising the Coastal Waters

Between **Port Hardy** on the northern tip of Vancouver Island and **Prince Rupert,** the B.C. Ferry Corporation operates a car and passenger service. The *Queen of the North* leaves Port Hardy every two days at 7:30 am during the summer months, June through September, arriving in Prince Rupert at 10:30 pm the same night. The route follows the coastline and the "Inside Passage," a protected passageway among the coastal mountains and fjords. The fare for cars on this ship is $105; passengers $50 each.

For information and reservations on this ferry, call B.C. Ferry Corporation at 669–1211, or write them at 1045 Howe Street, Vancouver, B.C. V6Z 2A9. In winters, the *Queen of the North* makes an overnight trip once a week.

Two ships, the *Sun Princess* and the *Island Princess,* cruise from Vancouver to Alaska. On the *Sun Princess,* you can sail north, tour Alaska by bus, and fly back 12 days later. The week-long tour on the *Island Princess* is entirely by boat. Both ships run from June until early September. For information on these cruise-tours of the northern coast and Alaska, call Princess Cruises, 409 Granville Street (681–1311) or Gray Line Package Tours (872–8311 in Vancouver; 1–800–663–6446 from other points in Canada or the United States).

BY CAR

Coming In

If you are coming to Vancouver by car, the long and the short of it is, there's no simple route. The **TransCanada Highway** (Hwy #1) comes right in to Hastings Street just by the Second Narrows Bridge. If you turn west, you'll reach downtown after a lot of blocks. Better routes to major arteries and the downtown are **Grandview Highway** (12th Avenue) and **1st Avenue** north of this as you come towards the city.

Don't come in by Highway 7 if you can avoid it. It's littered with stop-lights which make the extensive suburbs slow going.

From Tsawwassen it's fairly easy most of the way. Highway 17 takes you to Highway 99 which goes north through the George Massey Tunnel (at a snail's pace in rush hour). Cross over the Oak Street Bridge and follow the green signs to City Centre, or continue along Oak to Broadway. Here a left will take you to Granville or Burrard for a bridge across False Creek; a right will take you to the Cambie Street Bridge.

From Horseshoe Bay, simply follow the Upper Levels Highway (TransCanada Highway) to the well-marked exit for Taylor Way. A short drive down towards the water, then left onto Marine Drive for the Lions Gate Bridge. Get over into the two right-hand lanes as soon as possible. Across the bridge and through Stanley Park takes you right onto Georgia Street and into downtown. The adventurous could and should take the scenic Marine Drive all the way from Horseshoe Bay, but this isn't much fun at night or if you are in a hurry.

From the United States, you'll come in along Highway 99, which is the Canadian continuation of Interstate 5, south of the border. It becomes Oak Street after the Oak Street Bridge. Since Oak doesn't cross False Creek, you will have to lateral to Cambie, Granville, or Burrard to reach the downtown core.

In Canada, U.S. driver's licences are valid, but if you're from any other country, you should have an International Driving Permit. And you **must** have insurance.

Lions Gate Bridge, Stanley Park

Arrange this with your own agent before you arrive, or as soon as you get here. Always carry your driver's licence, proof of insurance of the vehicle and its registration, rental contract or (if borrowed) a letter of authorization for its use. Camper trucks or trailers more than nine feet wide are not allowed in Canada for ordinary tourist purposes.

The **British Columbia Automobile Association** offices are at 999 West Broadway (732–3911), and are open from 9 am to 5 pm, Monday to Friday, 9 am to 5 pm Saturdays. Their emergency road service telephone number is **736–5971.**

For reports on highway or traffic conditions, call 277–0112 in Vancouver.

Driving in the City

THINK METRIC! A speed-limit of 80 means kilometres **not** miles and equals 50 of the latter (1.6 km per mi or 8 km: 5 mi). 100 means that many kilometres or 62½ miles.

You can take the number of kilometres, divide it in half, and add a quarter of the half (e.g. 80 km = 40 + 10 for 50 miles), for a quick mileage equivalent.

Distances are announced in kilometres, overhead clearances at bridges in metres (1 metre = 3.3 feet), and gasoline is pumped in litres (1 litre = .22 Imperial gallons, or 3.8 litres per gallon).

If you have any metric problems, call the **Central Library** Science Division (665–3585).

Driving in the city, you'll have to deal with the warren of one-way downtown streets, and the notoriously casual driving—or "laid back" abandon—of some motorists.

Stanley Park is a peninsula, attached to a larger West End/Downtown peninsula between Burrard Inlet and False Creek, attached to the very large Point Grey peninsula between English Bay and the Fraser River estuary. So, there are always bridges to cross.

The **Lions Gate Bridge** may present the only traffic jam outside of rush-hour you'll encounter, but the spectacular view from the bridge naturally takes the edge off the annoyance. Depending on the time you cross, you will have one or two lanes open to you. The centre lane changes direction with the flow of traffic, so watch the overhead signals.

Second Narrows Bridge crosses the Burrard Inlet further east, beside the Pacific National Exhibition (PNE) Grounds at East Hastings and Cassiar. This is the TransCanada Highway route and a good way to get to Lynn Canyon, Mount Seymour Provincial Park, or the Dollarton Highway to Deep Cove.

Three bridges cross False Creek south of the downtown section—the **Burrard Street Bridge** (for Kitsilano, Point Grey and UBC), the **Granville Street Bridge** (for the Airport, Tsawwassen, and the United States border), and the **Cambie Street Bridge** (for City Hall at Cambie and 12th or Queen Elizabeth Park).

There are a few quirks in Vancouver's traffic system it might be useful to know about. Amber lights are, for instance, unbelievably short. If you see orange and try to run it, you'll get caught on the red. A separate orange hand warns pedestrians of impending amber, and this can warn drivers that the light is soon going to change.

At all **unmarked intersections,** as well as at marked crosswalks, pedestrians have the right of way. The flashing green light of some intersections means that the traffic signal is pedestrian-controlled. It is **not** a left-hand turn signal.

When driving in residential districts, don't assume that the absence of a stop sign assures you the right of way. It ain't necessarily so. Drivers on quiet streets approach intersections with some caution and even trepidation. Technically, if there are no stop signs at the intersection, the driver to your right has the right of way—but don't count on only looking in one direction.

Outside the city, highways seem designed to minimize risk and strain. Flashing amber signals about 100 metres in advance of a traffic light will warn you in time to brake for a red light or in case the intersection itself is hidden by a bend in the road. This can be a big help in the mountains.

There are also frequent reminders that Canadian speed limits are metric. Funny metal bumps along the centre of a highway (most glow phosphorescent at night) mark the highway's dividing line. They'll alert you if you inattentively cross the centre demarcation.

It takes a little while to get used to the one-way streets and no-left-turns in any city. Vancouver is no harder than most, but for finding your way around, a couple of hints might help.

Most of the city is basically on a grid pattern, running east-west and north-south. The downtown section itself is turned around a bit, and runs northwest and southeast. All east-west roads south of False Creek are called Avenues, and from False Creek south to the Fraser River most are numbered from 1st Avenue to 78th Avenue consecutively. All north-south roads are called Streets.

Ontario Street, just west of Main Street, divides the Vancouver Avenues into East and West. In North Vancouver Lonsdale Avenue divides the Streets into East and West. And in West Vancouver, Streets from the Lions Gate Bridge to Horseshoe Bay, running north and south, are consecutively numbered.

Broadway is the name for 9th Avenue.

Everywhere, blocks progress by 100s, so you can determine with some accuracy in blocks how far you'll have to go from one point to another on any road. This numbering begins at Ontario Street for Avenues, and at Burrard Inlet for Streets. Sixteen blocks south of Burrard Inlet is 1st Avenue. Therefore, for those adept at quick calculations, subtracting 1600 from a Street number will give you the number of the Avenue which crosses the Street. For example, 3600 Granville Street would be at 20th Avenue.

Parking... and Overparking

There are lots of surface **parking** lots in the **downtown** core (marked P), where you'll need lots of change.

There's indoor parking, at a higher hourly rate, under the **Pacific Centre** (enter off Howe Street going south—this one is huge), at **The Bay Parkade** (off Richards going south or Seymour Street going north), under the **Royal Centre Mall** and the **Hyatt Regency Hotel** (off Burrard Street), and at the **Hotel Vancouver** (off Burrard going south or Hornby Street going north).

Without a special permit, **parking is not allowed in the lanes** that run behind buildings in the downtown area. Also, unless posted, there's no parking between 8 am and 5 pm beside schools in session. Some schools hold classes in the summer, so "No Parking" signs are posted.

In rush-hour, don't, whatever you do, park illegally on a main street. Between 7 and 9 am and 4 and 6 pm, you won't get a ticket—you'll lose your car! It's not posted, but that's the way it is. During these busy hours, offending parked cars are considered to be obstructing traffic and are simply (and quickly) towed away. If you can't find yours, call **Unitow Services,** 1717 Vernon Drive, Vancouver (251–1255) or the **Police Department** (665–3535), and be prepared to pay the impoundment price of at least $17 in addition to a parking ticket.

Metered parking lots usually post the name and telephone number of the company that has snatched your "violating vehicle," and you'll have to call them.

Unitow Services (251–1255) is open all year for service calls, and will start your battery or change a tire at the regular rate anytime. During July and August, they give stalled or stranded tourists a 10% break.

Car Rentals

To save your fingers the walking through the Yellow Pages, we've summarized the price ranges of major car rental companies for comparison shopping. Figures are quoted for the smallest and largest type of car offered. By the time you're here, prices are bound to have increased.

The following companies have services at the Vancouver International Airport as well as downtown offices.

Avis Rent-a-Car, 757 Hornby (682–1621). Airport (273–4577). Daily $29.95 to $35.95. 100 free km/day, then 12¢/km. Weekend $26.95 to $32.95, 200 free km/day.

Budget Rent-a-Car, 450 West Georgia (685–0536). Toll-free Airport number (1–800–268–8900). Daily, $26.95 to $33.95: 200 km/day free; 12¢/km. Weekly $159 to $209: 1,000 km/week free. Discount coupon book given with each rental.

Dollar Rent-a-Car, 497 Robson Street (688–2233). Airport (278–2528). Daily $27.95 to $34.95: 100 km/day free; 12¢/km. Weekend $25.95 to $31.95: 200 km free. Weekly $159 to $209: 1,000 km free. Rates vary summer and winter.

Dominion U-Drive, 901 Seymour (684–6113). Airport (278–7196). Daily $25 to $29: 150 km/day free; 12¢/km. Weekly, $143 to $197: 1,000 km/week free. Rates vary summer and winter.

Hertz Rent-a-Car, 666 Seymour (688–2411). Airport (278–4001). At the Bayshore Hotel (682–7117). Toll-free number 1–800–268–1311. Daily $29.95 to $35.95: 100 km/day free; 12¢/km. Weekend $26.95 to $32.95. Weekly $154 to $210: 1,400 km/week free. They can arrange for hotel pick-up. Automobile club members get a 20% discount or unlimited kilometrage.

Tilden Rent-a-Car, 1140 Alberni (685–6111). Airport (273–3121). Daily $29.95 to $35.95: 100 km/day free; 12¢/km. Weekend $26.95 to $32.95: 200 km/day free. Weekly $159 to $209: 1,000 km/week free. Will contribute up to $3 for your taxi fare to their offices.

Other rental companies are listed in the yellow pages of the telephone book; the following offers bargain rates.

Rent-a-Wreck, 350 Robson (688–0001). Daily on used cars $8.95 to $18.95: 9¢/km. Weekly on used cars $62 to $99. For new cars daily $24.95 to $29.95: 11¢/km. Weekly on new cars $149 to $189: 1,000 km/week free. For 99¢/day, you can take out Physical Accident insurance to cover injuries to anyone in the car. Phone in advance to find out what cars this company has available.

The following companies, specializing in renting fully-equipped recreational vehicles or truck-campers, are listed with the Vancouver Convention and Visitors Bureau.

Go West Campers, 1577 Lloyd Ave, North Vancouver (987–8587). Van conversions and various sizes of motorhomes from $29/day: 13¢/km to $68/day: 18¢/km. They will help you plan your trip and supply information on campgrounds and routes in four European languages. Downtown Vancouver pick-up can be arranged.

5 Star Motorhome and Camper Rentals, 11351A Bridgeport Rd, Richmond (270–1100). Weekly $275 to $825: 16¢ to 20¢/km. Unlimited mileage rates apply to rentals of two weeks or more. 75 km/day free in off-season, Sept to mid-June. One-way rentals (with drop-off charge) available between Calgary/Edmonton and Vancouver. Convenience package ($30) available.

Pennys Rents a Car, 2300 Cambie (684–1241). Campers and trucks, van conversions and motorhomes. $270 to $450/

week: 100 km/day free; 12¢/km. Summer rates are about 15% higher.

Westcoast Mountain Campers, 1500 Alberni Street (687–4311). Volkswagen campers available at a downtown location. Daily $60. Weekly, $420. A convenience package available ($35).

If you really want to impress or celebrate in style, you could rent a red Ferrari 308 GTS, a steel blue Mercedes Benz 380 SL or a cream and white Porsche SC 911 from **Exotic Car Rentals,** 2567 York Ave (733–9194). It worked on the owner's girlfriend; they're now married.

At **Ambassador Leasing,** 1600 West 6th (736–8434), you can rent a Rolls, a Jaguar, a Cadillac or a Lincoln, with or without chauffeur.

Classic Limousine Service, 320 Industrial (669–5466) has the Superstretch version of the Cadillac as well as your basic Cadillac, Lincoln or Mercedes-Benz.

Huff Hall Chauffeur Services, 1362 Venables (254–4912) rents chauffeurs in a Fleetwood or Seville Cadillac or a Rolls-Royce.

Taxis

Yellow Cabs (681–3311) are the most common in the city. They do go everywhere, whereas some other companies do not. Their motto is "The Thinking Fellow calls a Yellow."

Black Top (681–2181) and **McClure's** (683–6666 or 731–9211) are also large companies.

Check the Yellow Pages of the telephone book for complete listings of taxi-cab companies.

A local innovation is the fleet of modified Checker Cabs run by **Vancouver Taxi** (255–7322), 1717 Vernon. The roofs of these now-grey taxis have been raised so that each vehicle can accommodate a wheelchair. The conversions were all done in North Vancouver, and the company owns 30 of them. The company also has a TDD (Telecommunication Device for the Deaf) on their office telephone. Fares are the same as those for regular taxis.

Vancouver Pedicabs that you see peddling passengers about the streets of the downtown or Granville Island are to be bargained for. That is, you hail one, tell the driver your destination, and then haggle on the price.

CUSTOMS INFORMATION

Although visas are seldom required for entry into Canada, a passport is essential for all visitors except citizens of the United States. U.S. visitors should, however, bring some formal identification, such as a birth or baptismal certificate. If you are not sure whether or not you need a visa, check with the nearest Canadian embassy or consulate.

Coming into Canada, you may bring small gifts for friends or relatives and articles for your own use: cameras, fishing tackle, your boat, motor, or trailer, and a two-day supply of food.

Burrard Street Bridge, False Creek

Because of the risk of spreading disease, you may *not* carry certain fruits into B.C. You *can* bring an American plant, provided it has the required "phytosanitary certificate."

The family dog or cat can come with you from the U.S. as long as you have a veterinarian's certificate indicating that the animal has been vaccinated against rabies within the last three years.

Hand, sawed-off, silenced, and automatic guns are prohibited in Canada and cannot even be carried through the country. To do so is a serious criminal offence. They must be shipped from a point outside Canada for, say, Alaska.

Guns for hunting can be brought in but must be declared at the border. If you are planning to hunt or fish, write to the Ministry of Environment, **Fish and Wildlife Branch,** Regional Office, 10334–152A Street, Surrey V3R 7P8 (584–8822) for a non-resident card and hunting number. You need these in order to get a hunting licence — which you also need and can then get at Woolco or Woodward's.

For further information on customs regulations, contact Canada Customs, 1001 West Pender Street, Vancouver, B.C. V6E 2M8 (666–1545).

It is also a good idea to check with your own customs authorities about what you can or cannot take home, either before leaving or at your consulate in Vancouver. Residents of the United States, returning after a stay of 48 hours, may take with them — every 30 days — merchandise for personal or household use to the value of $400 duty free. The next $1,000 worth are subject to a 10% duty. After a visit of less than 48 hours, you are only allowed $25 worth of duty free goods. For more specific information, contact the **U.S. Customs Office** at the Vancouver International Airport (278–1825) or the **U.S. Consulate** (685–4311).

3 Pressed for time and cash

No matter how short your stay in Vancouver, you will probably want to catch some of the natural beauty of the city's location, pick up some anthropology and history, and check out Vancouver's special attractions. If the weather is clear, head up some nearby height to get a look at the city as a whole. The elevator on the outside of the **Harbour Centre Tower,** on Hastings Street between Richards and Seymour, gives you a southward view on the way up or down and an all-round viewing deck on top. Adults $2, children and seniors $1.50. For the price of a drink, you can comfortably orient yourself on top of the Blue Horizon Hotel (1225 Robson Street), the **Sheraton-Landmark Hotel** (1400 Robson Street), or the **Denman Hotel** (Comox and Denman Streets—after 5:30 pm). The cafeteria at the **Planetarium Restaurant** in Vanier Park has a good ocean view. Fine views can be had for free at the **Bloedel Conservatory** in Queen Elizabeth Park (33rd and Cambie) or along any of the city's beaches. From the **SeaBus,** which crosses Burrard Inlet, you can see Vancouver's harbour for the price of a city-bus ticket.

Or you can get above the city on any one of a number of neighbourhood mountains. **Simon Fraser University** sits on top of **Burnaby Mountain,** which has a real mountain air just above Burnaby and magnificent views of Indian Arm, the North Shore mountains and Vancouver to its west. In North Vancouver, you can drive up **Mount Seymour;** in West Van, up the **Cypress Park Highway** to the bowl formed by Hollyburn, Strachan, and Black Mountains. Also in North Vancouver, sparkling over the city, is **Grouse Mountain.** The **Skyride** up to the mountain top, from the top of Capilano Road, is open until 10 pm. Adults $7, children (7 to 12) $3.50, under 6 free, families $18. City-buses will take you up Capilano Canyon road (with a transfer) to the **Capilano Suspension Bridge** (adults $3.50, children—under 12—$1), the **Salmon Hatcheries,** the **Cleveland Dam,** and the foot of **Grouse Mountain.** From the SeaBus terminal in North Van, a §229-West Lynn bus takes you up **Lynn Valley** (the number of the bus on Sundays is 228) to the free **suspension bridge** there and the **Lynn Valley Ecology Centre.**

If the clouds are hanging low on the heights, you might visit **Chinatown** or **Gastown** for history, shopping, or food. See Chapters 9 and 10 for guided walking tours. **Stanley Park** is

Simon Fraser University, Burnaby

always a noteable urban excursion. The walk around its seawall takes under two hours and gives a good indication of Vancouver's unusual location. For a quicker trip, you can rent a bicycle at Stanley Park Rentals (681–5581), 676 Chilco Street for about $4 an hour and peddle around in 40 minutes or so. In parts of the interior of the park, where well-kept and frequented paths traverse the woods, there are trees that were here before the city was. The Zoo is free as are the nearby gardens; the Aquarium charges admission for the whale shows. On Sundays, buy a special pass on the Stanley Park bus and get on and off in the park where you want.

At the **Museum of Anthropology** (228–3825), on the UBC campus, and at the **Vancouver Art Gallery** (682–5621), on Robson Street, admission is free on Tuesdays. At other times, it's reasonable. At the **Vancouver Museums and Planetarium** (736–7736), in Vanier Park, Tuesdays are also free for seniors. Adjacent to the Vancouver Art Gallery is the **Robson Square Media Centre,** which puts on open-air concerts, has an art gallery and hosts films, poetry readings, and special events. In winter, there's skating on its artificial ice. **BC Tourism** (660–2300) has its offices here. If it's not actually raining, you might walk the **UBC campus,** taking in the Nitobe Gardens, the Rose Garden, the Botanical Gardens, the Cyclotron, and a cinnamon bun at S.U.B.

One of the most popular spots in town is **Granville Island,** a modern harbour/marina, public market (closed Mondays) and shopping/restaurant area built among the sturdy structures of this once-industrial park. Emily Carr College of Art lives here beside a small community of residential houseboats. Several theatres, a Kids' Market, a water park, and the Granville Island ferries for access from Vanier Park or the Aquatic Centre by sea, make Granville Island a favourite—except in terms of parking the car. Take the Granville Island Express bus from the Art Gallery or the §51-Granville Island from Broadway and Granville Streets.

For eating, there are muffins, salads, fish and chips, and more at stands in the **market** itself. Elsewhere, in Vanier Park, the **Planetarium Restaurant** prices are modest. At UBC, try **S.U.B.,** the Student Union Building's well-known cafeteria. **Food Fare** in Robson Square offers concession-style eating from around the world.

If culture is on your mind, many of the theatres have much-reduced rates for show previews and dress rehearsals. Call playhouses about upcoming dates. Or, on the day of a performance itself, you might be able to buy a half-priced ticket from **Front Row Centre** (683–2017), 1025 Robson Street. They are open Monday to Saturday, from noon to 7 pm, and carry tickets, when available, to the Arts Club theatres, Theatre Sports, and other major playhouses.

For $3 at the **Hollywood Theatre** (738–3211), 3123 West Broadway or for $4.50 (seniors $2) at the **Vancouver East Cinema** (253–5455), 2290 Commercial Drive at 7th Avenue, you can always see a double bill. Call the theatres for programme information. At the **Ridge Theatre** (738–6311), 3131 Arbutus Street, admission per film on Tuesdays is $2.

On Granville Island, there are open air concerts in the park beside the Granville Island Hotel, 1253 Johnston Street, Saturday and Sunday afternoons, evenings Thursday through Sunday.

If you've read this far in the chapter, you might like the idea of checking local or community newspapers for events and local bargains. Public happenings are always very hospitable.

Kitsilano Beach

4 *Accommodation*

Vancouver is a city that caters to its visitors. Within a three-mile radius of Georgia and Burrard Streets, in the heart of downtown, there is accommodation to match every style and budget. For the economically minded, there is the **Vancouver Youth Hostel** overlooking English Bay on Jericho Beach. At the other end of the spectrum, there's the gigantic Japanese-built **Pan Pacific Vancouver Hotel.** The latest in luxury, the Pan Pacific towers over Canada Place, site of the new Trade and Convention Centre, on the harbour at the foot of Burrard Street.

The strands of motels you would expect in any town are dotted about the North Shore, and spread along the urban length of the Kingsway Highway to the southeast of the city.

Most of the larger establishments and hotel chains are located in the city centre, close to just about everything you might want. The **Hotel Vancouver** with its green copper chateau-styled roof is one of the city's landmarks. The **Sylvia,** site of Vancouver's first lounge and the first highrise to be built in the West End, is an old favourite. Always in demand, even in winter, you must book well in advance.

The **Four Seasons** and the **Hyatt Regency** hotels, with their comfortable lounges, respected dining rooms and conference

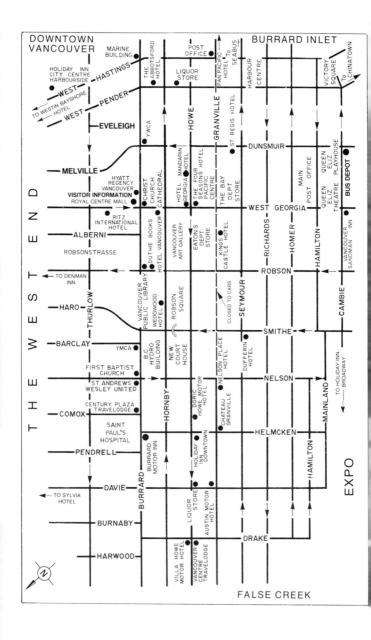

facilities, are convenient for both business traveller and tourist alike. The **Westin Bayshore** and its tower sit on the shore of Coal Harbour where you can get a room with a view of Stanley Park and the North Shore mountains.

The new **Wedgewood Hotel,** with its popular luncheon bistro and night-time disco, is in full swing. Here you might get a room that overlooks and overhears the fountains of the law courts. At the **Mandarin,** hints of oriental elegance in the decor enhance a feeling of quiet luxury. Afternoon tea, ironically in the English tradition, is served daily between 2 and 4:30 p.m.

Vancouver's booming **Bed and Breakfast** industry offers a delightful alternative to the hotel or motel. Ranging from modest to luxurious, styles of accommodation come in anything from a simple, but clean, comfortable bed and hearty breakfast, to a suite, to a penthouse overlooking English Bay. Some are in old mansions. One comes with a butler, maid and gourmet cook (!!for $50/night). Others have pools, saunas, hot tubs or jacuzzis. One at Crescent Beach has acres of flowers and greenery, like those of Butchart Gardens, and a small house to put you in (also for $50/night). The range is varied and worth looking into.

In the following listings, the phone numbers given all have the **area code 604.** Prices quoted are based on double occupancy and are included for comparison shopping purposes. In winter (the off-season), rates are usually lower; prices will undoubtedly go up for Expo. Some hotels drop their rates on weekends or offer special weekend packages. Many include children in the same room as their parents at no extra charge, and some provide airport pick-up and drop-off services. All rates are subject to the B.C. provincial tax.

Bookings can be made directly or through the Province of B.C.'s new centralized reservation service **ResWest** (662–3300), Box 1138, Station A, Vancouver, B.C. V6C 2T1. For a small fee of $5 and any major credit card, ResWest will book you into a hotel, motel, bed and breakfast, trailer park or campsite. ResWest is also the official reservation service for Expo 86.

For those who prefer some of the comforts of home without the household headaches, there's **Executive Accommodations** (669–1950), Division of West Coast Executive Accommodation and Services Ltd., 1431 Howe Street, Vancouver, B.C. V6Z 1R9. They specialize in short term apartment rentals. Get your own coffee in the morning, but let the maid clean up.

If an early morning flight has you nervous, the **Delta Airport Inn** (278–9611) and the **Delta River Inn** (278–1241) are situated right beside the airport.

HOTELS AND MOTELS

Downtown

Anywhere you stay in the area from Burrard Street north of Nelson Street and east as far as Beatty Street, puts you right in the heart of Vancouver's financial district, and close to all the major services and facilities of the city. More than likely, it also puts you in one of the city's larger hotels.

With Stanley Park and the West End to the west, Chinatown and Gastown to the east, Burrard Inlet to the north and False Creek and the new Expo site to the south, you are at the hub of Vancouver.

As well as a large number of tourists, banks and financial institutions, the area also accommodates Eaton's and The Bay department stores, Pacific Centre and Granville Mall, shopping on Robson, St. Paul's Hospital, Robson Square and Media Centre, the Central Public Library, the Law Courts, the world-class Vancouver Art Gallery, B.C. Place Stadium and the city's new Trade and Convention Centre.

Here you will find the **Hotel Vancouver** where Queen Elizabeth resides when visiting the coast. Across the street is the refurbished **Hotel Georgia.** Known as "the Grand Old Lady of Georgia Street," the Hotel Georgia has occupied the corner of Howe and West Georgia since 1927.

Abbotsford Hotel, 921 West Pender (681–4335). $55. Restaurant, lounge, pub, parking in nearby lots.

Coast Georgian Court Hotel, 773 Beatty (682–5555). $110. Restaurant, dining-room, bar, lounge, gym, whirlpool, sauna, parking $5/day.

Dufferin Hotel, 900 Seymour (683–4251). $35. Restaurant, bar, cabaret/dance club, free parking.

Four Seasons Hotel, 791 West Georgia (689–9333). $150 to

$190. Dining-rooms, garden court cafe, disco, exercise facilities, lounges, pool, adjacent to shopping centre, parking at a price.

Holiday Inn-Harbourside, 1133 West Hastings (689–9211). $109 weekdays; $82 weekends. Revolving dining-room, restaurant, lounge, bar, pool, sauna, exercise area, free parking.

Hotel Georgia, 801 West Georgia (682–5566). $108 to $127.

Hotel Vancouver

Dining-rooms, lounge with dancing, pub, live entertainment, parking at a price.

Hotel Vancouver, 900 West Georgia (684–3131). Off-season prices start at $58, are $97 for the "Silver" floor and $120 for deluxe accommodation. Dining-rooms, restaurants, coffee shop, lounges, live entertainment, parking at a price. Special rooms for the handicapped and special floors for non-smokers.

Hyatt Regency, 655 Burrard (687–6543). $120. Dining-rooms, restaurants, lounges, bar, live entertainment, pool, sauna, adjacent to shopping mall, free parking.

King's Castle Hotel, 750 Granville (682–2661). $32. Restaurant, pub, reduced parking rate at nearby lot.

L'Hôtel Méridien, 845 Burrard (682–5511). $75 to $95. Dining-rooms, lounges, exercise facilities and pool shared with La Résidence, beauty salons, parking at a price.

La Résidence Travel Apartments, 855 Burrard (689–7666). One bedroom—$65/night for a stay of at least three nights (there is a surcharge for stays of less than three nights). Two bedroom—$90/night. Health club, beauty centre, jacuzzi, pool, parking $4/day.

Mandarin Hotel, 645 Howe (687–1122). $185 weekdays; $125 weekends. Dining-rooms, English-style afternoon tea, exercise rooms, squash and racquetball, pool table, parking $8/day.

Nelson Place Hotel, 1006 Granville (681–6341). $40. Restaurant, beer parlour, free parking.

Pan Pacific Vancouver Hotel, 999 Canada Place (662–8111). $150 to $200. Dining-rooms, restaurants, lounge, fitness and racquet club, squash and racquetball, steam room, sauna, aerobics classes, heated outdoor pool, whirlpool, paddle tennis, parking in city lot under the hotel.

St. Regis Hotel, 602 Dunsmuir (681–1135). $41. Restaurant, lounge, pub, parking nearby.

Wedgewood Hotel, 845 Hornby (689–7777). $95 to $148. Dining-room, bistro/lounge, disco, valet parking $7/day.

Uptown

"Uptown" refers to the area around False Creek and the new Expo site, both north and south. Besides proximity to Expo, hotels here are also close to the new B.C. Place Stadium,

Chinatown, Granville Island and the downtown. Those on Broadway and Cambie, south of the Granville Street Bridge, are slightly removed from the downtown, but in the company of Gerry McGeer's City Hall at 12th and Cambie.

Basma's Motor Hotel, 1060 Howe (682–3171). $52. Restaurant, pool, lounge, free parking.

Burrard Motor Inn, 1100 Burrard (681–2331). $49. Restaurant, dining-lounge, free parking.

Centennial Motor Hotel, 898 West Broadway (872–8661). $57. Some kitchen suites, dining-lounge, pub, free parking.

Century Plaza Travelodge, 1015 Burrard (687–0575). $86. Kitchen suites, dining-room, coffee shop, pool, sauna, parking at a price.

Chateau Granville, 1100 Granville (669–7070). $90. All one bedroom suites (two of them fully equipped for the handicapped), restaurant, lounge, free parking.

City Centre Motor Hotel, 2111 Main at 6th Avenue (876–7166). $34. Restaurant, lounge, pub, pool, free parking.

Granville Island Hotel, 1253 Johnston on Granville Island (683–7373). $110. Dining-room, bistro with outdoor cafe, lounge, dance floor, live entertainment, marina, boat charters, limousine service, free parking.

Holiday Inn-Broadway, 711 West Broadway (879–0511). $82. Restaurant, lounge, pool, sauna, exercise room, theatres in complex, free parking.

Sandman Inn-Howe, 1110 Howe (684–2151). $83. Dining-room, coffee shop, lounge, live entertainment, pool, free parking.

Sandman Inn-Georgia, 180 West Georgia (681–2211). $77. Dining-room, coffee shop, lounge, saunas, pool, whirlpool, free parking.

Sheraton Plaza 500 Hotel, 500 West 12th at Cambie (873–1811). $66 to $96. Kitchenettes available if staying three days or more, restaurant, lounge, pub, free parking.

Vancouver Centre Travelodge, 1304 Howe (682–2767). $61. Restaurant, pool, one family suite with kitchen, free parking.

West End

In this densely populated area, west of Burrard over to Stanley Park, between English Bay and Coal Harbour, you will find

Four Seasons Hotel, Vancouver

more apartment-style accommodation. Full of activity, the area sports many fine restaurants, a number of bars, lounges and night spots, the beach at English Bay and shopping on Robson Street. You are also within walking distance—sometimes a healthy one—of Stanley Park.

The historic **Sylvia** and large **Denman Hotel** sit close to English Bay. Movie stars seem to favour the **Palisades,** and it is alleged that Pierre Trudeau and Howard Hughes chose the **Westin Bayshore** when in town.

Best Western Sands, 1755 Davie (682–1831). $72. Kitchenettes, dining-room, lounge, live entertainment, free parking.

Blue Horizon Hotel, 1225 Robson (688–1411). $74 to $80. Kitchens, restaurant, lounge, pool, free parking.

Buchan Hotel, 1906 Haro (685–5354). $40. A residential, quiet hotel, with dining-room.

Centennial Lodge Apartment Hotel, 1111 Burnaby (684–8763 or 688–2474). $58. Housekeeping suites, laundromat, weekly rates in winter months, parking at a price.

Denman Hotel, 1733 Comox at Denman (688–7711). $110 to $150. Kitchens available, dining-room, restaurant, lounges, live entertainment and dancing, pool, sauna, squash and racquetball, Universal gym, aerobic classes, shopping mall, downtown limousine service, free parking. Cannot guarantee view suites.

Greenbrier Apartment Hotel, 1393 Robson (683–4558). $40. One-bedroom apartments, free parking.

Ming Court Hotel, 1160 Davie (685–1311). $80 for a studio suite. Price is reduced on third night and again on fourth. Some kitchenettes, dining-room, lounge, live entertainment, outdoor heated pool, valet parking.

Oceanside Apartment Hotel, 1847 Pendrell (682–5641). $50 for one-bedroom suite with kitchen. $300/week.

Palisades Hotel, 1277 Robson (688–0461). $80 weekends; $87 to $94 weekdays. Some kitchen facilities, dining-room, lounge, coffee shop with sidewalk cafe, heated outdoor pool, exercise room, saunas, free parking.

Riviera Motor Inn, 1431 Robson (685–1301). $34. Some kitchens, free parking.

Shato Inn Apartment Hotel, 1825 Comox (681–8920). $60 to $65 for a studio; $75 for a suite. Free parking.

Sheraton Landmark Hotel, 1400 Robson (687–0511). $78 to $88. Revolving dining-room and lounge, sauna, Roman baths, free parking.

Sylvia Hotel, 1154 Gilford (681–9321). $41 to $56. Some housekeeping suites, restaurant, lounge. Reserve well in advance.

Westin Bayshore, 1601 West Georgia (682–3377). Dining-room, restaurants, lounges, indoor pool, saunas, whirlpool, exercise room, complimentary downtown bus service, marina, free parking.

North Shore

Across the Burrard Inlet at the foot of the North Shore mountains, you'll find a number of motels and several hotels—all just a bridge or SeaBus-ride away from downtown. Here you are close to Grouse Mountain, Cypress and Mount Seymour ski areas, the B.C. Ferry Terminal at Horseshoe Bay, Capilano Canyon, Park Royal Mall, the beaches and boutiques of West

Vancouver and Lonsdale Quay in North Vancouver.

The **Park Royal Hotel** is right beside the Capilano River at the end of the Lions Gate Bridge.

Avalon Motor Hotel, 1025 Marine Drive, North Vancouver (985–4181). $47. Kitchen suites, restaurant, coffee shop, lounge, pub, free parking.

Canyon Court Motel, 1748 Capilano Road, North Vancouver (988–3181). $55. Some kitchenettes, heated outdoor pool, laundromat, free parking.

Capilano Motel, 1634 Capilano Road, North Vancouver (987–8185). $42 weekdays; $45 weekends. Housekeeping units, pool, sauna, laundromat, free parking.

Coach House Inn, 700 Lillooet, North Vancouver (985–3111). $54 on parking lot side; $60 on pool side. Restaurant, lounge, pub, pool, free parking.

Maples Motor Lodge, 1800 Capilano Road, North Vancouver (987–4461). $55. Some kitchens, pool, children's playground, laundromat, free parking, off-season rates.

Park Royal Hotel, 440 Clyde, West Vancouver (926–5511). $58 to $66. Dining-room, pub, live entertainment, pool, free parking.

Ranch Motel, 1633 Capilano Road, North Vancouver (988–7101). $55. Kitchens available, restaurant, pool, laundromat, free parking.

Vancouver Lions Gate Travelodge, 2060 Marine Drive, North Vancouver (985–5311). $60. Accommodation for the handicapped, pool, off-season rates, free parking.

Kingsway, Vancouver

A veritable motel row. **Highway 99a/1a** from the United States border becomes the Kingsway as you get into town. We've listed only motels that are within Vancouver's city limits, and have not by any means included all that are along this route. There is tremendous variation in value for dollar, so it is best to ask to see the room before checking in. As rates are due to change, phone for prices.

Best Western Motor Inn, 3075 Kingsway, one block east of Rupert (430–3441). $51 to $60. Some kitchenettes and suites, whirlpool, sauna, free parking.

Biltmore Motor Hotel, 395 Kingsway at 12th Avenue (872–5252). $43 traffic side; $47 away from traffic. Restaurant, coffee shop, live entertainment, pool, free parking.

Cariboo Motel and Trailer Park, 2555 Kingsway (435–2251). $40. Kitchen options. $14 for trailer hook-up. Central washrooms and showers, on city bus route, laundromat across the street.

Eldorado Motor Hotel, 2300 Kingsway at Nanaimo (434–1341). $44. Restaurant, pub, live entertainment, free parking.

London Guard Motel, 2227 Kingsway one kilometre east of Knight Road (430–4646). $32 to $40. Some family suites and kitchens, adjacent to restaurant, free parking.

Mr. Sport Hotel, 3484 Kingsway (433–8255). $42 including breakfast. Waterbed suites available, restaurant, lounge, cabaret, pub, heated outdoor pool, free parking.

2400 Motel, 2400 Kingsway (434–2464). $27. Some housekeeping units, free parking.

Pan Pacific Hotel and Vancouver Trade and Convention Centre, Burrard Inlet

Burnaby and Surrey

South and east of the city, the following hotels and motels are located outside the Vancouver city limits.

Astor Motor Hotel, 4561 Kingsway (Highway 99a) close to Boundary Road (433–0551). $29 to $34. Dining-room, coffee shop, free parking.

King George Highway Motel, 13245 King George Highway (Highway 99a), Surrey (588–0181). With kitchen, $36; family suite, $42 plus; weekly rates, $200 to $225.

Lake City Motor Inn, 5415 Lougheed Highway, Burnaby (294–5331). $48. Some kitchenettes, some family suites, heated pool, coffee shop, close to Brentwood Shopping Centre, free parking.

Lougheed Hotel, 4343 Lougheed Highway, Burnaby (299–6202). Restaurant, lounge, live entertainment, close to Second Narrows Bridge, free parking.

Sheraton-Villa Inn, 4331 Dominion, Burnaby (430–2828). Phone for rates. Dining-room, coffee shop, lounge, indoor and outdoor pool, free parking.

BARGAINS, HOSTELS, BED AND BREAKFASTS

You won't find a telephone in every room, and you may have to share a bathroom—you may even have to share a room—but accommodation at the **YWCA** or **YMCA** is clean, comfortable and right in the heart of town. A little further from downtown, set in the magnificent University Endowment Lands, you can get a one-bedroom suite through the **UBC Conference Centre** for a reasonable price.

Check into a bedroom-plus-sitting-room combination at the **Kingston Hotel,** Vancouver's first Bed and Breakfast hotel. There are no elevators and you'll have to be your own porter, but the rooms are pleasant and cozy. Or enjoy the Victorian flavour and congenial atmosphere of **Katie's Bed 'N' Breakfast** in North Vancouver. Here you can sleep in the butler's anteroom, now converted to a charming double, complete with bath and brass fireplace. Their bridal suite has an antique brass bed and adjoining sunroom.

Some Bed and Breakfast accommodation is less elaborate,

some more, and some does not have private bath; but all offer genuine hospitality. As types of accommodation in this category are too numerous to list individually, we have included the agencies who can book you into the B & B of your choice. There is no agency fee for the person making the booking.

A good reference book is **Town and Country Bed and Breakfast in B.C. Canada.** It is the only guide book of its kind and covers most areas in B.C., including Vancouver, the west coast of Vancouver Island, farms and ranches throughout the province. Available by mail (allow up to four weeks for delivery), the book costs $9.95 Canadian, plus $1 postage (book rate) and handling. Phone the publisher (731–5942), or write Town and Country Bed and Breakfast in B.C. in Canada, P.O. Box 46544, Station G, Vancouver, B.C. V6R 4G6.

Bed and Breakfast Agencies

The area code for all numbers listed below is 604.

AAA Bed and Breakfast (464–6488). $30 to $60. Hundreds of homes in the Lower Mainland, ranging from modest to luxurious. Lots in Vancouver, even downtown. Some are in old mansions in Kerrisdale; some, like the penthouses at Beach and Bidwell Streets, are apartments vacated by their owners. Get a butler, maid and gourmet cook, or stay in a garden setting at Crescent Beach.

Bairich Bed and Breakfast Registry, 7241 Cambie Street, Apt. 805, Vancouver, B.C. V6P 4H3 (324–5159). $35 to $70 for a double; $30 to $65 for a single. Homes in Vancouver and outlying areas, some with pools.

Born Free Bed and Breakfast Agency, 4390 Frances Street, Burnaby, B.C. V5C 2R3 (298–8815). $30 to $50 for a double; suites, more. Homes, rooms and suites with special accommodation available for long stays or special requirements. Tours and car rentals can also be arranged.

Continental Bed and Breakfast, 104 Edinburgh Drive, Port Moody, B.C. V3H 2T6 (461–7066 or 461–4868). $15 to $55 for single and couples. Homes in the Greater Vancouver area, all adjacent or close to public transportation. Can arrange car rental and airport pick-up.

Dorle International Bed and Breakfast Registry, 4022 Mountain Highway, North Vancouver, B.C. V7K 2J6 (988–

7936). $20 for a single to $35 for a double. Rooms, suites and homes. Also offer sightseeing tours, trail tours, skiing, boat and fishing charters, baby sitting and car rentals.

Old English Bed and Breakfast Registry, 363 East 8th Street, North Vancouver, B.C. V7L 1Z2 (986–5069). $35 to $55 for a double. Modest to luxurious, including mountain hideaways, one with pool. Owner designed her business on the basis of a two month look at English Bed and Breakfasts.

Vancouver Bed and Breakfast Ltd., 1685 Ingleton Avenue, Burnaby, B.C. V5C 4L8 (291–6147).

Western Comfort Bed and Breakfast, 180 Carisbrooke Road, North Vancouver, B.C. V7N 1M9 (985–2674). $35 to $65 for a double.

The Kingston Hotel Bed and Breakfast, 757 Richards Street, Vancouver, B.C. V6B 3A6 (684–9024). $20 to $35 for a single; $25 to $45 for a double. This is not an agency, but a charming Bed and Breakfast hotel in downtown Vancouver. Sauna, laundry facilities.

Vancouver Hostel

1515 Discovery Street, Vancouver, B.C. V6R 4K5 (224–3208).

Right on Jericho Beach, the Vancouver Hostel provides clean, low-cost overnight accommodation. Members $7.50; non-members $9.80; meals and linen extra. Group and family accommodation is also available.

The large white building can sleep 278 and is expecting to open further sections in the near future. Reservations during the summer and ski season are advised. A deposit of one night's fee is required with advanced bookings, and cancellations must be made no later than the day prior to the date of reservation. If the hostel is full, the maximum stay allowed is three consecutive nights.

CHA members under 14 years of age must be accompanied by an adult of the same sex over 18. Non-members must be 16 to stay unaccompanied.

Facilities include linen rental, showers, laundry, recreational room, parking and tourist information. The cafeteria is open for breakfast and dinner, and kitchen facilities are available if you want to get your own meals. Packed lunches for groups must be booked in advance.

From downtown Vancouver, take a 4th Avenue bus from Granville Street to N.W. Marine Drive. Proceed down the hill on foot to the first right at Discovery Street.

Besides full-fledged hostel operations in **Victoria** and at Alta Lake in **Whistler,** there are also a number of mini-hostels throughout the province whose owner-operators offer similar services to those of the Vancouver Hostel. These are usually situated in private homes or small commercial hotels. Reservations must be made directly with mini-hostels. For a complete list of mini-hostels, call the **Canadian Hostelling Association,** B.C. Region (736–3116), or write to their office at **Vancouver Pack & Boot Shop,** 3425 West Broadway, Vancouver, B.C. V6R 2B4.

UBC Conference Centre

5959 Student Union Mall, University of British Columbia, Vancouver, B.C. V6T 1K2 (228–5441).

In the middle of the UBC peninsula, single and twin-bed rooms in two campus residences are available from early May through August. One-bedroom suites with kitchenettes can be had on a year-round basis. $35 for a single; $45 for a double. Bathrooms are shared, campus cafeterias are handy, cooking utensils are not supplied.

YMCA/YWCA

YMCA, 955 Burrard Street, Vancouver (681–0221). Men, women or couples can stay here. $23 for a single; $39 for a double. Shared washrooms and showers; $4 key fee. Mastercard, Visa accepted.

YWCA, 580 Burrard Street, Vancouver (683–2531). Single, double and triple rooms available for women, couples and families. $32 for a private room for a single, $29 for single with semi-private washroom, $25 without washroom, $15 for just a bed (one night only). Accommodation other than just a bed for the night can be reserved in advance. A free pass to the YWCA fitness facilities and pool comes with your accommodation. Stays can be booked for a month at a time; $350 per month with semi-private washroom.

CAMPSITES AND TRAILER PARKS

Right in the middle of town, you will find the **Capilano Trailer Park** under the Lions Gate Bridge in North Vancouver. Other campsites and trailer parks, while more removed, are still surprisingly close. During Expo, a special bylaw allows homeowners to have recreational vehicles parked on their lawns. So, some in the Burnaby area will be hanging out a shingle. Look for this possibility if stuck with an RV and no place to park it.

Prices quoted are for two people, with the charge for each additional person given in brackets.

North Vancouver

Capilano Trailer Park, 295 Tomahawk Avenue, North Vancouver, B.C. V7P 1C5 (987–4722). Trailers $12.50 with full hook-up (extras $2). 200 trailer sites, electricity, sewer, water. Complete hook-ups, laundromat, propane, sani-station, washrooms. No reservations June to August.

Squamish

Famous for its pulp plant and fumes, Squamish is located at the head of the Howe Sound, 65 km (41 mi) north of Vancouver and half-way to Whistler via the Squamish Highway (99).

Klahanie Recreational Campground, Box 1396, Squamish, B.C. V0N 3G0 (892–3435). Campsites $8; trailer sites $8, electrical and water hook-up $1, sewer $1 (extras $1). 35 campsites, 35 trailer sites. 45 km (28 mi) north of Horseshoe Bay opposite Shannon Falls. Showers, laundromat, water and electrical hook-ups, sani-station, restaurant.

Kingsway, Vancouver

Southeast of the city along motel row.

Cariboo Motel and Trailer Park, 2555 Kingsway, Vancouver, B.C. V5R 5H3 (435–2251). Motel units $40; trailer hook-ups $14 (extras $1). 33 motel units, 34 trailer sites. Kitchen option, central washrooms and showers, on city bus lines, laundromat across street, no pets.

Burnaby

To the east of the City of Vancouver is the Municipality of Burnaby. It is bounded on its west by Boundary Road and on the east by North Road. To the south is New Westminster, to the north, the Burrard Inlet. The Lougheed Highway, the Trans-Canada Highway, Canada Way and Kingsway all pass through this major urban community. Hastings Street and the Barnet Highway also pass through this area following the south shore of the Burrard Inlet.

Blue Haven Motel and Trailer Park, 7026 Kingsway, Burnaby, B.C. V5E 1E7 (524–8501 or 524–8502). Motel units $35 to $40; trailer hook-ups $14 (extras $1). 34 motel units, 10 trailer sites. Housekeeping units, hook-ups, showers, laundromat, pets extra.

Buena Motel, 4575 Kingsway, Burnaby, B.C. V5H 2B3 (434–4545). Motel units $20; trailer sites $12/day or $65/week. 14 motel units, 38 trailer sites. Housekeeping units, complete hook-ups, no pets, no TV.

Rainbow Auto Lodge, 5958 East Hastings Street, Burnaby, B.C. V5B 1R6 (298–1828 or 299–9436). Motel units $27; trailer hook-ups $8.50, sewer $1 (extras 50 cents). 24 motel units, 9 trailer sites. Housekeeping and sleeping units, laundromat, complete hook-ups, washrooms, showers.

Coquitlam

The District of Coquitlam lies to the east of Burnaby on the north shore of the Fraser River between North Road and the Coquitlam River. On the other side of the Coquitlam River, where the Pitt River flows into the Fraser River, is Port Coquitlam. To reach these areas, follow Highway 7 (a continuation of East Broadway) and the Lougheed Highway. A slightly slower route leads along East Hastings and the Barnet Highway to Port Moody. From here you reach the Lougheed Highway and the districts of Coquitlam and Port Coquitlam.

Cedar Acres Trailer Court, 3015 Lougheed Highway (7), Coquitlam, B.C. V3B 1C6 (464–6929). Campsites $10; trailer sites $11 (extras 50 cents). 20 campsites, 29 trailer sites. Open all year round for self-contained vehicles. Hook-ups, washrooms, hot showers, maximum stay seven days. No reservations.

Four Acres Trailer Court, 675 Lougheed Highway (7), Coquitlam, B.C. V3K 3S5 (936–3273). Campsites $8; trailer sites $10. 10 campsites, 5 trailer sites. Washrooms, hot showers, sani-station.

Port Moody

This city sits on the shore at the tip of the Burrard Inlet. Highway 1, the Barnet Highway (7a) and the Lougheed Highway all go into this area.

Cedar Brook Mobile Estates, 3315 Dewdney Trunk Road, Port Moody, B.C. (461–7421). Campsites and trailer sites $8, electricity $1.50 (extras in both cases $1). No full hook-ups, groceries, showers, picnic tables.

Ioco

A small community located beyond Port Moody on the north shore of the inner end of Burrard Inlet, Ioco is a beautiful area about 20 miles from the downtown Vancouver centre.

Anmore Campground, Sunnyside Road, Anmore, R.R. 1, Ioco, B.C. (461–1939). Campsites $10; trailer sites $14 (extras $2). Hookups, hot showers, laundry facilities, sani-station, ice, grocery store, recreation room. Horseback riding next door. Fishing, swimming and boating close by.

Surrey

The rural communities of the Municipality of Surrey lie to the southeast of Vancouver across the Fraser River. To get there in a hurry, take the TransCanada Highway (1) which crosses the river via the Port Mann Bridge. An alternate route crosses the river over the Pattullo Bridge from New Westminster. To get to New Westminster, take either Canada Way or Kingsway (99a).

Dogwood Campgrounds, 15151 112th Avenue, Surrey, B.C. V3R 6G8 (588–1412). Campsites $10; trailer site with full hook-up $14 (extras $1.50). Hot showers, laundromat, grocery store, pool, jacuzzi, children's playground, dumping station, ice and propane, trailer supplies, gift shop, and in July and August, bus tours to Vancouver and Victoria. 20 miles east of Vancouver, east of the TransCanada Highway.

Hazelmere Riverside Campgrounds, 18843 8th Avenue, Surrey, B.C. V3S 5J9 (531–2167). Campsites $9; trailer with full hook-up $12 (extras $1). 120 campsites, 120 trailer sites. Laundry facilities, groceries, L.P. gas refill, sani-station, picnic tables, playground, accommodation for camping groups available. From the U.S. border, take the Cloverdale exit 2.4 km (1.5 mi) east on Highway 15.

Plaza Mobile and Tourist Park, 8266 King George Highway (99a), Surrey, B.C. V3W 5C2 (594–9030). Campsites $12; trailer sites $15, including hook-up. (extras $2). Campsites on adjoining campground, 32 trailer sites. Complete hook-ups, laundromat, showers, cablevision. 16 km (10 mi) north of American border.

Timberland Campsites, 3418 King George Highway (99a), Surrey, B.C. V4A 5B5 (531–1033). Campsites $7; trailer sites $14. 9 campsites, 9 trailer sites. Sani-station, showers, laundromat, power and water hook-ups, 30 minutes from Vancouver.

Delta

Delta is exactly that. Located at the mouth of the Fraser River, the large rural Municipality of Delta is about 22 km (14 mi) south of Vancouver via the George Massey Tunnel.

ParkCanada Recreational Vehicles Inns, Box 1022, 4799 Highway 17 (via 52nd Street), Delta, B.C. V4M 3T2 (943–5811). Campsites $11; trailers with full hook-up $15.50, water and electricity only $13.50, electricity only $13. Campsites 75, trailer sites 75. Partial and 3-way hook-ups, washrooms, showers, laundromat, lodge, groceries, propane refills, playground, pool, recreation lounge, sani-station. From Highway 17, turn north on 52nd Street then immediately left onto service road. Next to Splashdown Park waterslide and close to the B.C. Ferry Terminal for Victoria.

White Rock and Crescent Beach

On the water, this area is about 2 km (just over a mile) north of the American border and approximately 45 km (30 mi) south of downtown Vancouver.

Parklander Motor and Trailer Court, 16311 8th Avenue, White Rock (531–3711). Campsites $8; trailer sites $10 (extras $1). 20 campsites, 25 trailer sites. Travel trailer spaces, some complete hook-ups, shady campsites, hot showers.

Sea Crest Motel and Trailer Park, 864 Stayte Road, White
Rock, B.C. V4A 4W4 (531–4720). Campsites $8; trailer
hook-up $10. 4 campsites, 18 trailer sites. Blacktop, wash-
rooms, showers, laundry, cablevision.

PROVINCIAL PARKS

Of the major Provincial Parks within a three-hour drive from
Vancouver, only Alice Lake, Brandywine Falls, Golden Ears,
Cultus Lake and Manning Parks have developed campground
accommodation. Both tents and recreational vehicles are welcome; prices are minimal. Reduced rates apply for seniors.
There are no hook-up facilities, and trailers over 20 feet in
length usually won't fit into the parking spurs. Grounds close
between 11 pm and 7 am. There is no advance reservation
system and, in many cases, occupancy is limited to fourteen
days.

Alice Lake and Brandywine Falls to the north and Golden
Ears to the east are within an hour and a half drive of the city.
Cultus Lake is a little further east and Manning Park, a good
three-hour drive from Vancouver.

Wilderness camping is allowed at Garibaldi, Mount
Seymour in North Vancouver, Golden Ears and Manning
Parks, but you *must* contact the District Office of the park in
which you'll be, before setting out. Cypress Park has no camping facilities. Mount Seymour, minutes from downtown Vancouver, allows overnight parking for self-contained recreational vehicles only in Parking Lot 3 at the base of the chairlift.

For more information, contact **The South Coast Region
Office,** 1610 Indian River Drive, North Vancouver (929–1291).

Alice Lake Provincial Park, 23 km (14 mi) north of Squamish
near Brackendale. The turn for the access road is 12 km (7½
mi) north of Squamish. Swimming, change-house, picnic tables, piped drinking water, flush toilets, sani-station near entrance, campsites and parking spurs.

Brandywine Falls Provincial Park, 20 km (12½ mi) north of
Squamish or 8 km (5 mi) south of Whistler on Daisy Lake. 15
sites, swimming, fishing, boat launch, picnic tables, sani-
station.

Cultus Lake Provincial Park, on Cultus Lake, 11 km (7 mi) southeast of Chilliwack. 4 camping areas. Swimming, picnic tables, boat launch, trails, sani-station, campsites and parking spurs. Chilliwack Lake Provincial Park is also in the area and Kilby Historical Park, with 38 sites, is near Harrison Mills.

Golden Ears Provincial Park, 11 km (7 mi) north of Maple Ridge. Alouette Lake and Gold Creek Campgrounds. Swimming, change-house, picnic tables, boat launch, hiking and riding trails, wilderness area, sani-station, campsites and parking spurs. Rolley Lake Provincial Park is just beyond Golden Ears and Sasquatch Provincial Park near Harrison Hot Springs is situated on three lakes and has two campgrounds.

Manning Provincial Park, on Highway 3, 225 km (140 mi) east of Vancouver. 4 campgrounds—Coldspring, Lightning Lake, Mule Deer, Hampton. Fishing, conducted nature walks (July to August), Nature House (July to August), Manning Park Lodge, restaurant, sani-station, hiking, Gibson Pass Ski Resort, campsites and parking spurs.

Service

Vancouver Motor Camping, 10700 Cambie Road (at Highway 99 next to the Airport Inn), Richmond (273-4454). Service to all makes of recreational vehicle, accessories, tent trailers and travel trailers. Rents and sells them too.

English Bay Cafe, English Bay

5 *Eating Out*

VIEWPOINTS

In the last ten years or so, there has been a population explosion in Vancouver's restaurants. And everybody seems to be enjoying it. Entrepreneurs have made names for themselves, architects have been inspired, and interior designers have created a West Coast flavour. While some restaurants have come and gone, what hasn't changed is Vancouver's magnificent setting.

For a Vancouver view, nothing tops **The Grouse Nest,** 6400 Nancy Greene Way (984–0661), on the heights of Grouse Mountain any clear day or night. With reservations at the restaurant, the ride up the Superskyride is free.

From a little closer, you can see the city at **Humphrey's Restaurant** (688–7711) on top of the Denman Inn, at **Cloud 9** (687–0511) which revolves on the Sheraton-Landmark Hotel, and at the **Harbour House Revolving Restaurant** (669–2220), Harbour Centre Tower.

On top of Queen Elizabeth Park (33rd and Cambie Streets), the **Quarry House** (873–3644) also has a good view of the city, even though from a much lower altitude. It is open for lunch and dinner every day as well as for brunch on Sundays.

Down on the ground, **The Teahouse** (669–3281) at Ferguson

Point in Stanley Park looks out over the waters of English Bay. Known for its glassed-in conservatory dining-room, chocolate pecan pie, and a winter specialty called ''The Polar Bear,'' The Teahouse is an elegant restaurant for a special occasion. Lunch here will make you feel you are really treating yourself. If driving to The Teahouse, you have to take the roadway around Stanley Park all the way to its south side. Watch carefully for the entrance at Ferguson Point; once past it, you can't turn around on the one-way street. If you are walking around the seawall, you'll find stairs leading up to The Teahouse lawns. Here you can stop to replace all those calories lost on the walk.

Seaside, by the entrance to Stanley Park at Denman and Davie Streets, are the distinctive, viridian-green awnings of the **English Bay Cafe,** 1795 Beach Avenue (669–2225). Upstairs, the dining-room overlooks the waters of English Bay and, on a clear day, the setting sun. A personal favourite, this restaurant never disappoints and always has a fine house wine on the menu. The bistro on the ground floor serves lighter meals. The Cafe opens at 11:30 am (Sundays, 10 am), and takes orders for dinner until 11:45 pm. There's free valet parking to save you from those West End what-am-I-going-to-do-with-the-car blues.

For aeons, **Salmon House on the Hill,** 2229 Folkestone Way (926–3212), has been serving westcoast-style barbecued salmon. The restaurant is high enough up on the North Shore to command a superb view of English Bay, and is open every day for lunch and dinner as well as for brunch on Sundays. To get there, take the 21st Street exit off the Upper Levels Highway in West Vancouver.

If you continue along the Upper Levels Highway and take the turn for Squamish-Whistler at Horseshoe Bay, you'll find **Sundowner's** on Sunset Beach in Lion's Bay about 5 km (3 mi) up the road. This fine restaurant overlooks Howe Sound where the summer sun sets late into the evening.

In North Vancouver at the foot of Lonsdale Avenue beside the SeaBus terminal, the ship of the **Seven Seas Seafood Restaurant** (987–3344) floats on the waters of Burrard Inlet. Their seafood buffet is immense and well-frequented; reservations are recommended. From here, you'll see the skyline or lights of Vancouver's downtown.

On the south shore of Burrard Inlet, amidst the real workings of the harbour, is **The Cannery,** 2205 Commissioner Road (254–9606). This restaurant prides itself on purchasing the pick of the catch from local fishermen who bring their boats into the nearby fishdocks. The decor of huge beams, hanging fishnets and gear, and heavy wooden furniture was conceived by Vancouver's restaurant designer, Dave Vance. A table near the windows will give you a view of the harbour's activity set against a backdrop of the North Shore mountains.

FISH

It is said by the native peoples of the coast that the salmon in Burrard Inlet were once so plentiful that you could cross the water on their backs. There aren't quite so many today, but you'll find salmon in plentiful supply in the restaurants as well as other dishes fished year-round from local waters.

The Only Cafe, 20 East Hastings Street (681–6546), is almost an institution. This counter-style, modest restaurant has been around as long as anyone can remember, serving fresh fish, boiled or fried. Customers line up along the walls to wait for a vacant seat or one of the two booths. Prices are modest, and the clam chowder (a specialty) is Manhattan style. It is open Mondays to Saturdays, 11 am to 10 pm; Sundays, noon to 8 pm.

Down on the docks where the fishing boats come in, you can eat fresh seafood at another favourite haunt of fishermen and fish-lovers—**The Marine View Coffee Shop,** Campbell Avenue Fish Docks (253–0616). This establishment is open only during fishing hours—6 am to 3:30 pm, Mondays to Fridays.

On False Creek across from the Expo site, a new restaurant is currently making a big splash with fish. At **Snapper's,** 656 Leg-in-Boot Square (872–1242), you have to book two weeks ahead for a Saturday night at present.

On Granville Island, two restaurants specialise in fish. **Jonathan's Seafood House,** Pier 32, 1333 Johnston Street (688–8081), sits on the waterfront between the Granville Island Hotel and Emily Carr College of Art. The food is very fresh, not cheap, and comes with a great view of False Creek and the Expo site. **Bridge's Seafood Restaurant,** 1696 Duranleau Street (687–4400), is at the other end of the island, beside the

Burrard Street Bridge and with the downtown skyline forming a backdrop for the view. All the fish here is excellent.

Across False Creek at the junction of Hornby Street, is **A Kettle of Fish,** 900 Pacific Avenue (682–6661). Dishes depend on the catch of the day, plants festoon the large rooms, and a downstairs lounge affords a look at some of the Expo scene. Diagonally across the corner, **La Cantina,** 1376 Hornby Street (687–6621), gets high praise for its fish Italian-style.

In West Vancouver, **La Belle Sole,** 235 15th Street (926–6861), specialises in westcoast seafood but at the same time offers other temptations to gourmandise.

The only native-style restaurant in the city for such dishes as pan-fried oolichans, is **Quilicum Restaurant,** 1724 Davie Street (684–7044). The barbecued salmon here would be the most authentic in town.

Of course, fish and chips are around. **Bud's Halibut and Chips,** 1007 Denman Street (683–0661), are particularly good, and Bud's is licensed. Those you buy at the stalls of Stanley Park are also recommended. And out at Horseshoe Bay on the western end of West Vancouver, **Troll's,** 6408 Bay Street (921–7755), has been serving fish since 1945. There are no reservations, but customers are used to lining up next door to the big ferries' dock for the excellent oyster-burgers, fish and chips, and other seafood dishes.

DOWNTOWN LUNCH

During the day, downtown establishments cater to a wide range of tastes and pocketbooks. Those in the downtown core have styles ranging from the elegantly continental to pub and sandwich. On Robson Street and in its West End vicinity, you'll find the chic and the unusual. Both north and south of False Creek, you'll come across some fine restaurants with a downtown tone.

Granville Island, with its numerous restaurants and the whole Public Market to munch from, is one of the most popular spots for being out to lunch in particularly during the warm weather. Its restaurants are detailed elsewhere in this chapter and noted in the chapter on Granville Island (Chapter 9). Gastown's eating spots range from modest to fancy and appear in Chapter 10.

In the downtown core of Vancouver and close to the business districts, good continental lunches are served at **Chardonnay's,** 808 West Hastings (684–1511); at **Da Carlo Ristorante Italiano,** 695 Hornby Street, in the Georgia Medical Building (683–1931); at **Alfredo's Ristorante Italiano,** 815 Burrard Street at Robson (669–2946); and at **La Perla Italian Restaurant,** 1339 Richards Street (669–7688).

Jean Pierre's Restaurant at 1055 Dunsmuir Street in the Bentall Centre Tower Four (669–0360), not only elegantly caters to the business crowd at noon but also opens at 7 am for breakfast (both North American and continental).

Charlie Brown's, on the sixth floor at 595 Hornby Street (681–9561), has excellent roast beef, and **Hy's Encore,** 637 Hornby (683–7671), is renowned for its steak. **Ten-Sixty-Six,** 1066 West Hastings Street (689–1066), serves a pub lunch in English pub comfort and convivial style.

At the **Four Seasons Hotel** (Georgia and Howe Streets), on the mezzanine level, open-face sandwiches are served among the plants and fountains of the indoor Garden Court Lounge (689–9333). In summer, lunch by the indoor-outdoor pool on the third floor of this hotel is very pleasant.

At the **Mandarin Hotel,** 645 Howe Street, (687–1122), the Clipper Lounge offers oriental elegance. Mid-afternoon, between 2 and 4:30 pm, "afternoon tea" is served.

The up-tempo crowd frequents the Bacchus Lounge at the **Wedgewood Hotel,** 845 Hornby Street (689–7777). A fireplace makes this also a busy cocktail-hour spot.

For excellent English pub fare, try the George V in the lower level of the **Georgia Hotel** (682–5566). From the main floor Rodeo Lounge, you can see the Vancouver Art Gallery and its fountains with lunch.

The Peacock Lounge of the **Hyatt Regency Hotel,** 655 Burrard Street (687–6543), on the mezzanine level, is a cut above your standard hotel bill of fare.

Closer to B.C. Stadium at the eastern end of Robson Street, at Rigney's in the **Georgian Court Hotel,** 765 Beatty Street (682–5555), you can eat your fill of luncheon salads for $6.50.

For lunching a bit lighter, there's **Scanwich,** 551 Howe Street (687–2412), where you place your order before being shown to your seat. The flavour is Scandinavian. **Benedict's,**

1177 West Pender Street (684–4505), has great sandwiches too (take out or eat in) and a patio out back for sunny weather. **Pastel's Pantry** (also eat in or take out), 1055 Dunsmuir Street (685–8148), sells delectables and wicked cakes.

In the vicinity of the Vancouver Art Gallery and the shopping on Robson Street, there are a number of restaurants that appeal to both the working crowd and shopping throngs alike. At **Melville's,** 1171 Melville Street (687–6615), or **Le Bistro,** 747 Thurlow Street (681–3818), you will never be disappointed. **Le Crocodile,** 818 Thurlow Street (669–4298), and **Kamei Sushi,** 811 Thurlow Street (684–4823) are thriving. Le Crocodile features fine French cuisine in an intimate atmosphere. Kamei places its sushi chef right in the middle of the action.

Café de Medici, 1025 Robson Street (689–9322), is a little gem tucked into the Robson Galleria. **Café de Paris,** 715 Denman Street (687–1418), serves an excellent *repas* in a very French ambience. **Le Bistro La Palette,** across the street at 774 Denman (681–6844), is receiving rave revues.

In Robson Square, there are several lunching sites as well as a large cafeteria serving noon-time bargains. **The Barrister** (named for the Law Courts south of the square) has a pub-style lunch; **Mozart Konditorei** (688–6869) makes fancy sandwiches. In summers, both establishments serve at outdoor tables on the square.

At Robson and Thurlow, another outlet of Pastel's Pantry is open all day and until quite late at night for take out or eat in sweets and delicatessen fare. **Monte Cristo,** 1098 Robson Street (682–4940), is a cafe/patisserie/chocolateria. New York flavoured **Binky's Oyster Bar,** 784 Thurlow Street (681–7073), is appropriately housed in the Manhattan Apartments. Here you can read one of the restaurant's newspapers with your lunch.

Bananas, 1044 Robson Street (682–2411) offers "California" fare and an array of banana dishes. **Earl's on Top,** 1085 Robson Street (669–0020) has what you might expect of Earl's fare anywhere—burgers and beer—in this case among chrome palm-trees. On Coal Harbour, beside the Westin Bayshore, are two Keg restaurants appealing to 'beefy' appetites—the **Keg Boathouse** (669–8851) and the **Keg Prime Rib** (682–5608)— both at 566 Cardero Street.

McGuiggan's Inn, 1119 Robson Street (682–2868), is a family-style restaurant in an old family house. At **Pots, Stews and Fondues,** 1221 Thurlow Street (681–9862), the stews and fondues come in pots.

On the north side of False Creek, a block from the Burrard Street Bridge, **Eight One Nine Pacific,** 819 Pacific (689–4819), offers continental cuisine and is run by one of the former co-owners who made The Chef and The Carpenter a success.

On the south side of False Creek, **Papillote Restaurant Provencal,** 195 West Broadway (876–9256) and **Fado Restaurante,** 881 West Broadway (874–6531) are also comfortably continental. **Chez Béat,** 1127 West Broadway (734–2735), is Swiss and breezy in style.

STEPPING OUT

A number of restaurants in the hotels of Vancouver have earned their high ratings for comfort, quiet elegance and fine dining. The plush **Le Pavillon,** at the Four Seasons Hotel, 791 West Georgia Street (689–9333); the elegant **William Tell,** now at the Georgian Court Hotel, 765 Beatty Street (688–3504); and the stalwart **Timber Club** at the Hotel Vancouver, 900 West Georgia Street (684–3131), all fall within this category. As do their prices.

Two newcomers are also in the running: The **Wedgewood Room** at the Wedgewood Hotel, 845 Hornby Street (689–7777) and the **Cristal Restaurant,** in the Mandarin Hotel, 645 Howe Street (687–1122), where the service is definitely "white glove" and the atmosphere formal.

Besides the delightful view and pleasant decor, **Bridge's** upstairs dining room, 1696 Duranleau on Granville Island (687–4400), serves some of the best fish in town. The sauces are never overpowering, desserts are decadent, and when available, the swordfish is a treat.

Le Napoleon, 869 Hamilton Street (688–7436 or 687–3254) is intimate dining. Private salons for private dinner parties are available, and the enclosed Garden Terrace caters to a luncheon crowd.

One of Vancouver's more prolific restauranteurs has recently put his recipes in print. Umberto Menghi (of **The Umberto**

Menghi Cookbook) has four restaurants in town, one in Whistler, two in Seattle and another in San Francisco. His style originates in Vancouver. Reminiscent of a farmhouse in Tuscany, **Il Giardino,** 1382 Hornby (669–2422), specializes in game and fowl. **La Cantina,** next door at 1376 Hornby Street (687–6621) emphasizes fish. At **Umberto's,** 1280 Hornby (687–6316), the cooking comes from northern Italy. In Gastown, **Umberto's Al Porto,** 321 Water Street (683–8376), is a little more informal but displays the flare for quality Umberto is famous for.

For some of the city's history, you could dine in style at **Hy's Mansion,** 1523 Davie Street (689–1111), originally the home of Benjamin Tingley Rogers. "B.T.", B.C.'s biggest sugar baron, established the B.C. Sugar Refinery in 1890, and his name still appears on all the refinery's products.

At **La Brochette,** 52 Alexander Street in Gastown (684–0631), you can enjoy a drink before dinner in front of their hearth and watch the rotisserie chef cook your dinner to a turn.

La Gavroche, 1616 Alberni Street (685–3924), and **Le Côte d'Azur,** 1216 Robson Street (685–2629) are both long-time residents of the West End serving traditional French cuisine. **The Chef and the Carpenter,** 1745 Robson Street (687–2700), obviously like cooking. The more recently arrived **Le Crocodile,** 818 Thurlow Street (669–4298), is both very popular and very good.

In Kitsilano, **Mark James Restaurant,** 2486 Bayswater (734–1325), above and behind the men's clothing store of the same name, specialises in the local fish of the season. **The Frog and the Peach,** 4473 West 10th Avenue (228–8815), calls itself "a rather unique restaurant," and is trying to keep its prices reasonably affordable.

Over on the north shore, **The Tudor Room** at the Park Royal Hotel, 440 Clyde Avenue (926–5511), has an elegant setting on the Capilano River. On a sunny day, this dining room opens onto the riverside patio. At the **Ambleside Inn,** 1495 Marine Drive (922–0101), the fare is continental and comes with a view of the city.

WESTCOAST CASUAL

In Kitsilano and on Granville Island, you can catch the action

The Teahouse, Stanley Park

at some of Vancouver's most sociable restaurants—usually to music and often with dancing. **Mama Gold's,** 1516 Yew Street (726–8828), is currently "hot." The music doesn't start until about 9 pm, but once it does the crowd usually stays put. Meeting at **Orestes,** 3116 West Broadway (732–1461), over a Greek salad and a bottle of wine is another current Vancouver trend. The restaurant has lots of room for dining in more or less peace and quiet.

At the **9th Avenue Bar and Grill,** 3204 West Broadway (736–8481), there's live music Friday and Saturday nights, some of the best ice cream in town, a dining-room, bar, and congenial 1950s atmosphere. At **Greer's,** 2204 York Avenue at Yew (732–6111), dining is quiet, the music usually piano or unamplified guitar, and the menu varied enough to suit a wide variety of tastes and wallets.

For real variety in beer, try **Fogg on Fourth,** A Fogg n' Suds at 3292 West 4th Avenue (732–3377). They carry 73 different brands of ales and have an easy-to-recall telephone listing— 73B–EERS.

On Granville Island **Bridges Bistro,** 1696 Duranleau Street

(687–2861), stays open quite late. In summers, it serves on the wharf. **Mulvaney's,** 1535 Johnston Street (685–6571), under the Granville Street Bridge between the Arts Club Theatre and the cement plant, has been a popular restaurant and evening congregating spot since it opened in 1975.

P. J. Burger, at 2966 West 4th (734–8616), serves what you think it does—and has a great selection of old juke box tunes. Closer to Burrard Street on 4th, **The Greenhaus,** 2059 West 4th (734–4124), and **The Grapevine** (with music), 2042 West 4th (736–8346) are neighbourhood restaurants. Try **Mr. Munchie's,** 2043 West 4th (732–8884), for fun or a 99¢ breakfast until 10 am.

On the other side (north) of the Burrard Street Bridge, **Dem Bones,** 801 Pacific (669–7336), gives you a big plate of pork or beef ribs and a big bucket for the bones. For music most nights of the week, you might try **Carlo's and Bud's** (Frank Zappa did), 555 Pacific Avenue at Seymour (684–5335), serving TexMex food and rockabilly blues in a converted garage.

One establishment is currently making headway on the section of Pender Street devoted to second-hand bookstores and dance studios. **The Montgomery Cafe,** 433 West Pender (685–5524), is a new-wave restaurant cum art gallery, which prides itself on serving fresh, wholesome diner fare in an atmosphere to match. Not to be outdone by the creations of the Vancouver artists who show their work there, the Cafe recently placed third in the Vancouver Sun's city-wide hamburger survey (after first-place O'Doul's and second-place 9th Avenue Bar and Grill). Shows change every two weeks, and the restaurant is open until 11 pm weekdays, Friday and Saturday nights till 1. It is closed Sundays and holidays. **O'Doul's Restaurant,** 1300 Robson Street (684–8461), is another popular meeting spot.

At 777 Thurlow and Robson, opening November 1985, will be a restaurant named after a particular Vancouver hero. Seraphim Forte was a Jamaican who was shipwrecked in Vancouver in 1888. He later became Vancouver's first bartender, but then quit that job to lifeguard as a volunteer at English Bay Beach. Everybody, children in particular, loved him, and everybody called him Joe. **Joe Forte's Seafood and Chop Restaurant** plans to be as popular and sociable. It has been granted Vancouver's first "extended hours" license and will stay open until 3 am.

Other late night spots to stop for a light bite are **Monte Cristo,** 1098 Robson Street (open until midnight), **Binky's Oyster Bar,** 784 Thurlow in the courtyard (681–7073, open until 2 am), and **Fresgo Inn,** 1138 Davie Street (open all night). On 4th Avenue, **Las Tapas,** 760 Cambie Street (669–1624), near the Queen Elizabeth Theatre, stays open late enough for you to catch a bite after the show.

Gladys', north side between Arbutus and Maple, a sandwich and coffee shop and a Kitsilano landmark, stays open as long as there is someone there.

The younger crowd currently enjoys itself in shades of pink and grey at Earl's various "fun" locations. Concept burgers, fried zucchini, and margaritas are staples at them all: **Earl's on Top,** 1185 Robson Street (669–0020), **Earl's Tin Palace,** 303 Marine Drive in West Vancouver (984–4341), **Broadway Earl's,** 901 West Broadway (734–5995), and **Earl's Place,** 4397 West 10th (222–1341), where the decor is green.

The Keg on Granville Island (685–4735) is usually crowded, and **The Keg Coal Harbour,** 566 Cardero Street beside the Westin Bayshore Hotel, has dancing to top-40 tunes, Tuesdays to Saturdays with either seafood (at **The Boathouse**) or beef (at **The Keg Prime Rib**). Also popular with a younger crowd is the **King's Head Inn,** 1618 Yew Street (733–3933), serving North American food in an English pub setting.

For non-smoking vegetarians, the favourites are **The Naam,** 2724 West 4th Avenue (738–7151); **Sweet Cherubim,** 3629 West Broadway (731–3022), 4242 Main (875–1082), and 1105 Commercial (253–0969); and **Woodland's,** 2582 West Broadway (733–5411), 1632 Robson Street (687–4855), and 1813 West 4th Avenue (733–5528). The selections are varied at them all. Some nights, there's music at The Naam.

BRUNCHING

A lot of restaurants in Vancouver that are usually only open for lunch and dinner, open their doors at an earlier Sunday hour to serve brunch. The Vancouver Hotel dining room in the **Panorama Roof** (684–3131) has a long-standing reputation for its lavish spread. This, in fact, is one of the few times during the week that the Panorama Roof is open. It's open from 10 am to 2 pm, costs $15.50 per person, and reservations are recommended. **The Harvester Cafe,** in the Four Seasons Hotel (689–9333), is also open for Sunday brunch, from 10 am to 2:30 pm (cost is $18), as is the mezzanine dining room at **The Mandarin Hotel** (687–1122), where there is a menu.

On a fine day, you might consider brunch at **Salmon House on the Hill,** 2229 Folkestone Way in North Vancouver (925–3212). Along with the great view and traditional brunch-type items, you can have steak, salmon, and salad. **The Tudor Room** at the Park Royal Hotel on the Capilano River, 440 Clyde Avenue in West Vancouver (926–5511) is open for breakfast every day of the week.

The Quarry House Restaurant in Queen Elizabeth Park (873–3644) would offer a fine prospect on a sunny Sunday. It's open for brunch that day from 11 am to 2:30 pm. Afterwards (or before), you could tour the Bloedel Conservatory and the Quarry Gardens.

In any kind of weather, **The Teahouse,** Ferguson Point in Stanley Park (669–3281), is a favourite for brunch. It is open both Saturday, from 11:30 am to 2:30 pm, and Sunday, from 10:30 am to 2:30 pm. Their brunch specialties include smoked salmon and seafood. Reservations are a good idea. **English Bay Cafe,** 1795 Beach Avenue (669–2225) also serves brunch, Saturdays from 11 am to 3 pm and Sundays from 10 am to 3 pm.

On Granville Island, you can have a Sunday buffet brunch at **Jonathan's** on Johnston Street (688–8081) from 10:30 am to 2 pm. If you don't mind the lack of a booze option and table-cloths, you can pick up fruit salad, muffins, and cappuchino in the Public Market, and eat in the sun on the wharf. There will usually be entertainment by magicians, jugglers, and some of Vancouver's best buskers. **Isadora's Co-op Restaurant,** with a playground for the kids, 1540 Old Bridge Street (681–8816) is also open for brunch both Saturday and Sunday from 9 am to 3 pm. Light lunches are also served there at this time.

On Coal Harbour, **The Boathouse,** a Keg restaurant at 566 Cardero (669–8851) offers you all you can eat for Sunday brunch at $9.95 (kids, 50¢ per year of age). It's open Sundays from 10 am to 2 pm. On Robson Street in the Robson Galleria,

Château Beirut, l025 Robson Street (687–1105), offers a Mediterranean brunch, Sundays from 11 am to 5 pm.

In Kitsilano, on the waterfront in an elegant old Vancouver mansion, **Brock House Restaurant,** 3875 Point Grey Road (224–3317), opens for brunch Sundays from 10 am to 3 pm. (Most days the house serves as a very active senior citizens' centre, but it is open for dinner from 5:30 every night.) **Jacques Spratte's,** 1812 West Broadway (734–0414) has a calorie-wise, light cuisine version.)

If brunch Italian-style is your fancy, there's **Tommy O's Off Broadway,** 2590 Commercial Drive (874–3445). He's open Saturday and Sunday, 10 am to 3 pm, and soon will be on one of the new ALRT stops.

NATIONAL NOSHING

The only truly westcoast native peoples restaurant in town is the recently re-opened **Quilicum,** 1724 Davie Street (681–7044). Its decor imitates that of the interior of a traditional longhouse, replete with the sweet smell of cooking-wood smoke and taped traditional westcoast music. The music fascinated Healey Willan, who came out here in the 1920's with an early version of a recording machine to tape examples of it. The food is prepared in traditional style and includes such dishes as barbecued oysters, panfried oolichans, roast cariboo, and whipped soapalillie berries. Authentically, the floor would be covered in stones, but the owners of the restaurant found that such a flooring was too hard on ladies in high-heeled shoes. That's why they've put the planking in. The entrance to the restaurant, beside and beneath a late-night grocery store, is unprepossessing; inside you'll be caught up in alder smoke and chants.

Other Vancouver restaurants are grouped below according to nationality of their cooking.

Chinese

Our favourite restaurants in this category are not all that easy to get to and are generally very busy. Expect a wait. **The Shanghai Palace,** 2068 Commercial (254–5214), is a fairly small restaurant, serving specialties such as juicey buns and beggar's chicken (the latter you have to order in advance). Last orders of the day are taken about 8 pm. **Yang's** has been at 4186 Main Street at 26th (873–2116), for ten years. Some claim this is the best Chinese food in town. Whether or not that is true, it is a fact that the noodles are made fresh daily right on the premises, in fact right in the dining room during the day.

The Grandview Restaurant, 60 West Broadway (879–8885), is a little larger than these two. Still it is full at dinner time most nights of the week. Their hot and sour soup is becoming a city-wide favourite. And at Burrard and 3rd, where you least might expect to find something like it, is **King Restaurant,** 1945 Burrard (733–6831). This kitchen has a large menu, daily specials, and does about an equal amount of eat-in and pick-up-to-take-out business.

Downtown, some of the recommended restaurants are the **Regent,** across from the Law Courts, 888 Nelson Street (687–8898), for dim sum and Cantonese seafood; **Snow Garden Restaurants,** 513 West Pender Street (682–8424) and 6692 Main Street (327–2013), for spicey Mandarin cooking; **Park Lock,** 545 Main Street at Keefer (688–1581), for dim sum between 10 am and 3 pm, the only hours they are open; and **Kingsland,** 984 Granville Street (687–6674), for dim sum.

In not-so-downtown Chinese restaurants, **Rickshaw Chinese Food,** 820 West Broadway (879–6208) has lots of variety and home delivery; **Miramar,** 2046 West 41st Avenue (266–1001) is recommended for dim sum; and **Flamingo House Chinese Restaurant,** 7510 Cambie at 59th Avenue (325–4511 or 325–4618), may have the best dim sum in the city. It also has a huge selection.

In North Vancouver, **Marco Polo,** 83 Chesterfield Avenue just west of Lonsdale (986–1155) serves Chinese food smorgasbord-style at very reasonable prices. It not only has such treats as fried or barbecued oysters and pork or duck appetisers but also exquisite gardens and a pleasant atmosphere. At the foot of Grouse Mountain is the **Capilano Chinese Restaurant,** 5020 Capilano Road (987–9511). This company has other branches in West Vancouver at 2396 Marine Drive (922–2922) and in Kitsilano at 3135 West Broadway (738–6252). The restaurant at the foot of Grouse overlooks a garden, and is rated as excellent by our North Shore gourmand informant. And then, in a little mall on Delbrook Avenue just off Westview between Lonsdale and Capilano, is a really good take-out stop—**Woon Lee Inn,** 3751 Delbrook (986–3388).

Japanese

The most exciting sushi bar in town must be **Ichibankan,** 770 Thurlow (682–6262). Here the chef performs the traditional wizardry of sushi-making and sends off his creations on a very modern conveyor belt. Patrons select what they wish from what is going by, and pay according to the colour of the dish of their selection.

Quieter but equally special is **Kibune Sushi,** 1508 Yew Street (734–5216). Here not only the cooking but the carpentry is traditionally Japanese. On weekends, there are usually line-ups at peak hours—customers usually do not have to wait long. Upstairs at 811 Thurlow, south of Robson Street, is **Kamei Sushi** (684–4823), another popular spot. They also have a restaurant in Richmond, 8300 Granville Avenue (273–7874).

Maiko Gardens, 1077 Richards Street (683–8812), can serve various sizes of groups in its individual rooms. This elegant restaurant has been here a long time.

A restaurant with a view, more western-style seating, and both sushi and sashimi is **Koji,** 601 West Broadway (876–9267). On a good day, you can see the Lions (in the North Shore mountains) from here. Also on West Broadway is **Emily Kato Restaurant,** 2281 West Broadway (734–7820), open Friday and Saturday from 5:30 pm to 11 pm. This is becoming a popular place for moderate-priced sunomono, salads, and pasta dishes.

Vietnamese/Korean

The **Saigon Restaurants** of Vancouver are of varying sizes (for instance, the West Broadway location is fairly small), but all are licensed. They have been serving this deservedly admired blend of French and Chinese cooking for quite a few years now. Their six locations are 2394 West 4th Avenue (731–1217); 1043 West Broadway (732–7608); 1500 Robson Street (682–8020); 140 Lonsdale Avenue in North Vancouver (980–5778); 4600 No. 3 Road in Richmond (276–2921); and 403 North Road in Coquitlam (939–2288). Steadily they are turning their customers on to the lightness and delicacy of their style.

More recently **Vina Vietnamese Cuisine,** at 851 Denman

Street in the West End (688–3581 or 688–3232), 1905 Cornwall in Kitsilano (738–3138 or 732–9113), and at 2508 Marine Drive in West Vancouver (926–6001) all are garnering praise both for the cooking and the quality of their service. Not only that, they all stay open quite late, except on Sundays when they close around midnight.

At the **New Seoul Restaurant,** 1682 East Broadway (872–1922), you barbecue your own on a fire in the centre of your table. It's open seven days a week, and also has a location at 845 East Hastings Street (255–8625 or 255–5022).

Mexican

The oldest Mexican restaurant in town and the one fans of Mexican food swear by is **Topanga Cafe,** 2904 West 4th Avenue (733–3713). It's more a cafe-style or family restaurant than one for an evening out. **Cisco's,** 1885 York Street (733–1166), on the other hand, does everything with a nightclub flair. The restaurant occupies two open indoor storeys within an office complex at the corner of Cornwall and Cypress at the south end of the Burrard Street bridge. Here the California-style tostadas and burritos come standing up tall in their shells. The meal is a show in itself.

Pepitas, 1170 Robson Street (669–4736), is currently crowded; **Las Margaritas,** 1999 West 4th Avenue (734–7117) and 754 Thurlow Street (669–5877), are California style. The 4th Avenue restaurant has an outdoor patio for sunning with a margarita, if you like.

Italian

In addition to Umberto's fine Italian restaurants—Umberto Al Porto, 321 Water Street (683–8376), Umberto's, 1280 Hornby Street (687–6316); La Cantina (for fish), 1376 Hornby Street (687–6621); and Il Giardino (for game and fowl), 1382 Hornby Street (669–2422)—a few others stand out.

Tommy O's Off Broadway, 2590 Commercial Drive at 10th (874–3445), is an elegantly old-fashioned longtime city resident. Here, the Italian decor has a distinctly westcoast flavour. Tommy O himself is Irish—an O'Doul. The restaurant is a popular and relaxed spot, open from 11:30 am Monday to Friday, and from 5 pm Saturday and Sunday.

Da Carlo Ristorante, 695 Hornby Street (683–1931), invites you to "spend an evening in Italy with the Finucci family," a great many of whom help out at the restaurant. The pasta is made fresh on the premises. They close daily from 3 pm. to 5:30 pm and on Sundays.

Rave notices are given by our North Shore gourmet friend to **Corsi Trattoria,** 1 Lonsdale Avenue in North Vancouver (987–9910). That's high praise, and you'll have to try this one for yourself, where, natch, the pasta is made fresh daily.

Piccolo Mondo, 850 Thurlow Street (688–1633), got a couple of honourable mentions, for 5-star service and good food. No need to be put off by its unprepossessing exterior.

La Perla d'Italia, 1339 Richards Street near Pacific (669–7688), has also been recommended, and will be in a good position for West Gate Expo business come 1986.

Greek

Our favourite for roast lamb has always been **Yianni's,** 1642 Robson Street (681–8141), in the West End. Another contender is **Athene's,** 3618 West Broadway (731–4135). A half lamb or more is roasted daily on the spit right out in the restaurant. Lamb is also good at **Romio's Greek Taverna,** 2272 West 4th Avenue (736–2118 or 736–9442), as is their squid. **Aretousa,** 1967 West Broadway (734–4212), **Vassili's Greek Taverna,** 2884 West Broadway (733–3231), and **Acropol,** 2946 West Broadway (733–2412), all in Kitsilano.

Orestes', 3116 West Broadway (732–1461), is a favourite Kitsilano meeting place and watering-hole. The restaurant is large but broken up into more intimate areas on several levels. With dinner, there is often a belly dancer. Right next door, the restaurant has opened a take-out facility—**O to Go** (736–6388).

Spanish

Las Tapas, serving those light appetisers of the name, has two popular locations—760 Cambie Street (669–1624), handy to the Queen Elizabeth Theatre, and 131 West Esplanade in North Vancouver (986–1181).

La Bodega, 1277 Howe Street (684–8815), serves tapas as well, and has a relaxed atmosphere; **Chateau Madrid,** 1277 Howe Street (684–8814), is only open for dinner, from 6 pm.

Indian

Deserving of mention is **Raga,** 1177 West Broadway (733–1127), where the accomplished chef is trained in fine Indian cuisine and has cooked for some very famous people in his career. Behind a glass panel looking into the kitchen, you can see the tandooris being made in a deep, round clay oven. From there they come hot and fresh directly to your table.

FAMILY FARE

White Spot restaurants are a local chain and a Vancouver, family-style, hamburger institution. They serve 'em fresh-fried rather than charcoal-broiled. Their famous burger comes smothered in mushrooms. At twenty-two locations throughout the city, the restaurants at Georgia and Burrard, at Burrard and Robson, and at Broadway and Larch are licensed.

One of the nicest and oldest and still great spots for the family is **The Butler's Foodsmith,** 3566 West 4th Avenue (734–2929). The dinner menu changes daily, is very affordable, and will suit the whole family. It is open for dinner, Tuesday to Sunday from 5:30 pm, but, because the restaurant is small, it would be a good idea to phone ahead.

Other restaurants for the whole family include **The Naam,** 2724 West 4th Avenue (738–7151), a no-smoking, vegetarian restaurant; **Mother Tucker's Food Experience,** 1630 Alberni (683–5701), for good-sized portions; and **Isadora's Co-op Restaurant,** 1540 Old Bridge Street on Granville Island (681–8816). Isadora's was put together by 1700 shareholders who each bought a share in it. It serves nut burgers, fish dishes, and steaks. A playground for the kids is located next door.

The Old Spaghetti Factory, 53 Water Street (684–1288), has sauces a bit too bland for the lover of Italian food, but is just right for those little ones with less sophisticated tastes. The decor is intriguingly antique, and there's an old British Columbia Electric trolley car for the kids to play in while you finish your dinner. It's fully licensed and open from 11:30 am.

In Kitsilano, **The Eatery,** 3431 West Broadway (738–5298), has an entertaining menu, affordable food, and a large non-smoking section. The kids get treats with their meals. It's also fully licensed.

For birthdays, parties, and special celebrations, nothing

beats **Chuck & Cheese's,** 9898 Government Place in Burnaby just off the Lougheed Highway. It's a pizza, games, and entertainment emporium, said to be as much fun for the grown-ups as for the kids who are totally occupied and well looked after. It is noisey. Phone for directions on how to find it.

In North Vancouver, the **Burger King,** 1493 Marine Drive (980–2272), is worth seeing. It has a merry-go-round and a space ship slide. Next door at the **Daily Scoop Ice Cream Parlour,** 1461 Marine Drive ((986–9870), their fine ice cream is served in old-fashioned, home-made cones. **Charley Potatoes Oyster Bar and Grill,** 60 Semisch Way at Esplanade (984–0274), just a five-minute walk away from the SeaBus terminal, has a menu to suit all ages of your family. Portions are large, and a favourite of ours is the unusual onion rings pie ("Onion Loaf" on the menu). Call for reservations if your party is of six or more.

The Hobbit House, 3560 Capilano Road up near the foot of Grouse Mountain and right across from the Capilano Suspension Bridge (981–3388), is always fun. Here, hobbits serve hot and cold sandwiches in a cosy log-cabin setting. It seems the hobbit has now an offspring—in the West End, at 1025 Nelson Street (688–1084)—**The Hobbit House Restaurant and Coffee House.** Back in West Vancouver, **Canyon Gardens,** 3381 Capilano Road (988–6101), was recommended to us by a father of two.

Apparently the **MacDonald's** in West Vancouver, at 1219 Marine Drive (985–5133 or 985–8513), gives you more than a burger and a shake. There's a theatre which shows cartoons to keep the kids entertained while they munch.

For fish and chips, most people like the stands in Stanley Park. There's one behind the Aquarium on the north side of the park, and others (which may not be open in winter) at the beaches on the park's south side. Two other spots deserve honourable mention: **Bud's Halibut and Chips,** 1007 Denman (683–0661), where parking can be a bit of a problem but you can get a beer if you wish, and **The Bounty Inn,** 3219 Oak Street at 16th (733–5312), open seven days a week.

We like the fish and chips at **Greer's,** 2204 York Street (732–1611). This is the sort of restaurant where the young ones can order a burger, those in between the huge fish and chips or lasagna, and old appetites something like chicken teriyaki or a veal dish with a glass of wine. Most nights, there's also music.

For pizza, we've been ordering in from **Olympia Pizza,** 2599 West Broadway (732–5334, 732–5622, or 732–3626), for years. They also have locations in the West End at 1156 Denman (688–6775), and in the East End at 1613 Nanaimo (253–5126).

John's Party Pizza, 1108 Davie Street (685–0551 or 685–4412), has been around forever. You can eat in the restaurant and listen to their jukebox, or pick your order up to take out. They stay open late and sleep-in in the mornings. The restaurant is open from 4 pm to 1 am, Monday to Thursday, and from 4 pm to 4 am, Friday to Sunday.

Chicago Pizza Works, 996 Homer at Nelson (688–0477), is a new kid on the block, with intentions of setting the town on its ear with the excitement of their pizza.

At **Pizza Rico's,** aka. Pizzarico Pizza Bar, 1106 Robson Street (669–2900), there's also art. Pizza Rico features local artists in his tiny shop. The shows change often and are conversation pieces.

For the health-conscious pizza-eater, there's **Simpatico,** 2222 West 4th Avenue (733–6824), where the crust is made of whole wheat flour. Toppings here are ordered and charged for individually.

TAKE OUT, ORDER IN

If you don't want to go to all the bother of going out, you can eat in—in style. **The Lazy Gourmet,** 2380 West 4th Avenue (734–2507), has a wide selection of main dishes and desserts, or can custom-make your meal.

To order in a boxed lunch, call the **Galloping Gourmet,** 660 Leg-in-Boot Square, False Creek (872–4012). They offer two specials a day, including dessert, for $3.75 delivered to your door. For a twelve o'clock lunch, you have to order before 10 am. They put out a menu bi-weekly, so you can see what's coming up.

Another gourmet home delivery outfit is **E.A.T.** (Eat At Home Tonight) (324–6047). For $12 a head, they will deliver the whole dinner "ready to heat" for anywhere from 2 to 30 people. Some of their offerings include leek and Stilton cheese salad, beef Wellington, cajun prawns, and they change their menu every week. The chefs here are the creators of the original Decadence chocolate cake, served at Bridges on Granville Island.

Pastel's Pantries, in the Bentall Centre, 1055 Dunsmuir, and at 1101 Robson Street (corner of Robson and Thurlow), at 2274 West 4th Avenue and in the Oakridge Shopping Centre, are popular for their yuppie yummie cakes, quiches, salads and pasta. The Robson street store is open til 9 pm., most nights except Sunday, until 10 pm. Thursday, Friday, and Saturday.

Orestes has opened a take-out outlet beside the restaurant on West Broadway—**O to Go** (736–6388)—which has souvlaki, spinach pie, calamari, and fish and chips. If you want to take-out Italian, there's **Umbertino's,** 1232 Robson Street (669–3232), an offspring of Umberto Menghi's restaurants which lets you take home his good Italian cooking. Other Umbertino outlets are soon to open at Oak Street and 49th Avenue, and at 501 North Road in Coquitlam.

At **Salvador Deli,** 1626 West Broadway (736–7951), you can have your sandwich custom-made. **Chateau Deli,** 2805 West Broadway (734–2026), also makes good sandwiches to eat in or to go. Their carrot cake is a favourite.

Max's Delicatessen and Bakery, 3105 Oak Street (733–4838), makes excellent sandwiches and at lunch-time is understandably busy. And **Szasz,** 2881 Granville Street (738–7922), a Hungarian delicatessen and restaurant, is Vancouver's answer to Zabar's of New York.

ALRT, Main Street

6 Sites, Sights & Attractions

TOURING IN THE CITY

By Bus

The **Gray Line** bus company (872–8311) offers tours of the city in several varieties. From downtown, the Kingsway, North Vancouver and points in Richmond, you can "Discover Vancouver" from the top of a British double-decker bus. These buses also do a short city tour ($14.50) with Expo option ($20). The tour goes from your hotel and ends at the Expo gates, from where you can either spend the day at the fair or be returned to your hotel. At the end of your day at Expo, the buses will return you to your hotel. The company also offers, by touring coach, a Deluxe Grand City tour, a tour of the North Shore (including a ride on the SeaBus and the mountain scenery of the Cleveland Dam), a tour of the shores of West Vancouver and the mountains of Cypress Bowl, and a tour of the city's evening highlights. Their reservation desk—872–8311—is open 24 hours a day.

Intercom Inc., 213-1744 Robson Street, takes you on Gray Line's "Discover Vancouver" tour in several languages—European and oriental. Call 687–2622 about arrangements for these Culture and English tours, and about the other pub, shopping, and westcoast culture tours they can arrange to your specifications.

Pacific Coach Lines (662–7575) also offers city tours, with downtown hotel pick-up, of Vancouver highlights, the mountains of the North Shore, and the evening scene from the top of Grouse Mountain. These tours are by coach and have a guide.

Other companies provide tours in smaller vehicles, the city's highlights including Granville Island, Queen Elizabeth Park, Gastown and Chinatown. **City and Nature Sightseeing** (254–5015) specialises in "friendly, personalized tours," particularly of the mountain scene. For rainy weather, they have a tour of museums, ethnic communities, and the Oakridge Shopping Centre. The guides speak English, French, Dutch and German. **Mini-Bus Tours of Vancouver** (879–0288) offers similar tours, and also has a dinner-and-entertainment-on-Grouse-Mountain evennng tour. They can also provide guides in several languages. Call either of these companies to arrange for pick-up at your hotel or the University of British Columbia (in the case of Mini-Bus Tours) or anywhere downtown (for City and Nature Sightseeing).

Town Tours (733–4711) leaves from the Ming Court Hotel for a tour of the city by mini-bus, and will arrange to pick you up at your downtown hotel to join the tour. Both this company and **Landsea Tours** (687–5640) include some of the residential highlights in their city tour. Landsea Tours also has a dinner and show evening. **Vance Tours** (733–2513) can pick you up at any downtown location for city tours by 12-passenger bus which allow for detours of personal interest. They also have a dinner tour.

Horizon Coach Lines (669–3866) has three types of vehicles (40 in all) and will arrange the tour that suits yourself or group in a highway coach, mini-bus or limousine. You decide where you want to go, and they will take you there.

Touring by Boat and Train

The city from the water presents another face altogether. **Harbour Ferries** (687–9558) is currently running several sternwheelers on tours of Burrard Inlet, English Bay and False Creek. The boats are all recently-built, and come with fully-stocked bar, lounges and snack facilities. In False Creek, the boats are currently, and will be during Expo, travelling between the East Gate beside the Expo Centre and the three "marine gates" of the fair. When not in active service, they can be chartered for evening parties in the harbour.

False Creek Ferries operated by Granville Island Ferries (684–7781) are the little blue and white boats that you'll see crossing the water from the West End (at the Aquatic Centre) to Granville Island's shopping and restaurants. Departures from the Aquatic Centre and from Granville Island are constant between 7:30 am and 7:00 pm weekdays, from 10 am to 5 pm on weekends. At present, they are offering a tour of the Expo site from the water, but won't be ferrying across to the fair when Expo is in progress.

One of the most popular tours going is the **Royal Hudson/ MV Britannia** circuit, a day's outing in Howe Sound by steam train, cruise ship or both. The train is a 1930s steam engine pulling nine coaches refurbished with items from the train which carried King George VI and Queen Elizabeth across Canada in 1939. It travels between the BCR Rail Terminal at

SeaBus, Burrard Inlet

the foot of Pemberton Street in North Vancouver to Squamish on a section of track completed as recently as 1956 and considered ''an engineering feat.'' The scenery is spectacular. The cruise ship MV Britannia sails between Vancouver, at the foot of Denman Street next to the Bayshore Hotel, and Britannia Beach just south of Squamish. You can sail both ways, take the train both ways, or do one of each. Optional tours of local glaciers are available from Alpine Adventures (985–8988), which you can take during the stopover in Squamish. In Vancouver, a shuttle bus will return you to your point of origin. To get to North Vancouver to make the train, you can catch a bus marked ''Train Connection'' at the Dunsmuir Street bus depot at 9:30 am or along its route at Georgia and Granville Streets, Georgia and Denman, on Marine Drive at the north end of the Lions Gate Bridge, at Capilano Road and at Pemberton. In the evening, a bus will return you to your original boarding point. Food service is available on both boat and train.

For information on the Royal Hudson/MV Britannia tours, fares, departure times, and reservations (which are advisable), call Harbour Ferries (687–9558), B.C. Rail (987–5211) or Tourism B.C. (660–2501).

Touring in the Air

Flying from their terminal on Coal Harbour 3 blocks east of the Bayshore Hotel, **Harbour Air** can show you the city and English Bay from the air. The tour is just under 30 minutes long (20 minutes of flight time), leaves regularly during the summer months (at your convenience in groups of 3 or more), and costs $49 per person. They offer other tours of the B.C. coast, the Gulf Islands, the Sunshine Coast, Princess Louisa Inlet (with picnic stop), Garibaldi Lake set among the coastal mountains (with stop at the lake), or to Butchart Gardens direct. With advance notice, they can arrange your fishing holiday, flying you from Coal Harbour to a chartered fishing yacht 30 minutes away. Call Harbour Air (688–1277) for further information on these tours.

For a little bit of the air, the city, the mountains and the coastal forests by helicopter, **Vancouver Helicopters Inc.** (525–1484, twenty-four hours a day) operates seven days a week, weather permitting. They fly from the Gastown Heliport just east of the SeaBus Terminal at the foot of Columbia Street and from the Vancouver International Airport Northside Heliport.

On top of **Grouse Mountain,** you can catch a helicopter for a short look at the coastal mountain scenery from up in the blue. The Mini-Tour ($15 per person) gives you a panoramic idea of the city's setting; the Wilderness Tour ($30 per person) takes you over the interior mountains; and the City Scenic Tour ($50 per person) shows you both the snow-capped mountains and the city's grandeur. Helicopter picnics are also available. These flights take off from the heli-pad next to the mountaintop terminal of the Grouse Mountain Skyride gondola, between 11 am and sunset seven days a week—weather permitting, naturally.

With **Harbour Air** (753–9833), **Burrard Air** (278–7178), **Tyee Air** (689–8651), and **Staron** (278–8484), you can arrange charters .

If something really different is your fancy, you might go up in a balloon. **Pegasus Ballooning Ltd.** (946–2278) flies hot-air balloons from their launch pad (?) in Ladner for sightseeing and just plain excitement. Their balloons are also available for rental. Call the company for lift-off times and fares, or write them at 6045 Brodie, Ladner, B.C.

On Your Own Steam

Naturally, one of the most pleasant ways of spending a clear day is to wander about or around the Seawall of Stanley Park, looking in on the zoo, at the totem poles, meeting the geese, the older trees, seeing the city from the number of prospects in the island-like park. If walking isn't your style, you can take the **Stanley Park Bus,** Sundays and holidays (adults $2, children and senior $1), and with a Sundays and Holidays Pass, get on and off wherever you wish along its circuit.

For a view of the downtown from the water, nothing beats the **SeaBus** (adults $1, children 50¢). Catch this ship either at the old CPR Station on Coal Harbour or at Lonsdale Quay in North Vancouver.

If you have a car and would like a guide, **CanTrav West** sells a taped guided tour (with map) for $19.95. The tour of the sights and sounds of Vancouver is two hours, non-stop, and can be purchased at the offices of the Greater Vancouver Convention and Visitors Bureau, on B.C. Ferries, in gift shops in

Stanley Park and at the Cara Newstand at the airport. Or call 669–0900, 24 hours a day.

If bicycling is your thing, tour maps, bikes, helmets and pant clips are available through **Robson Cycles,** 1463 Robson Street (687–2777). Special guided tours of the trails and seawall of Stanley Park, including an "early morning ride," are also available. Departure times vary with the season, so call them to book your ride.

A two-hour walk through downtown Vancouver, Gastown and Chinatown, led by **Vancouver Walking Tours** (324–6470), leaves from the Art Gallery fountain on Georgia Street daily at 2 pm. The cost is $6 per person, and the guide will fill you in on history and current happenings.

Both universities in town also offer guided walking tours of their spectacular campuses. Tours of the **University of British Columbia's** extensive, treed and garden-like setting leave twice a day during the summer months. Call 228–3131 to book for them, and bring your walking shoes—the campus is huge.

Simon Fraser University, at the other end of town in Burnaby, occupies a more modest area but is no less prepossessing. Designed by Arthur Erickson, this university sits on top of Burnaby Mountain overlooking Burrard Inlet and the mountains of the North Shore. Tours of its intriguing campus leave from the Administration Building every day on the half hour between 10:30 am and 3:30 pm. In winters, tours leave Sundays only at 12:30, 1:30, 2:30 and 3:30 pm. For information on these tours or to arrange special tours, call 291–4323.

Museums

Vancouver itself may not be very old, but the original inhabitants of this area of the Pacific Northwest coast go much further back in time. The gentle cultures of the coast Indians specialised in domestic arts, trading, carving (masks, household articles, totem poles, canoes, some of which were even used for whaling), and settled, communal living in a structure known as the "long house." Records of their civilizations and of their continuing vitality are gathered at the University of British Columbia **Museum of Anthropology;** of their age, at the Simon Fraser University **Museum of Archaeology and Ethnology;** and of their crafts, at the **Vancouver Museum** in

Vanier Park. The totem poles of Stanley Park and in the Museum of Anthropology's Thunderbird Park are authentic.

Other municipal museums have their own collections of westcoast artefacts as well as relics of the days of European settlement. At the **Vancouver Art Gallery** resides Emily Carr's testament, paintings of the coastal landscape and its people.

A number of museums notably specialise in more recent history: **Cap's** in cycles, **Deeley Classic** in motorcycles, and the **Canadian Museum of Flight and Transportation** in vintage aircraft. One interesting piece of fairly recent history isn't in a museum at all. On the west end of Spanish Banks beach is a searchlight tower below the gun emplacements on the cliffs at the site of the old **Point Grey Fort** (where the Museum of Anthropology is now). In June of 1942, an unidentified ship entered Vancouver's waters. An alert was sounded and the guns of Point Grey fired a warning shot across the front of the ship. But the shell, touching the water, careened off course and into a freighter nearby. The freighter sank. The unidentified vessel turned out to have been a local fishing boat with a forgetful captain.

The following is an alphabetical listing of museums, large and small, that you'll find in the Lower Mainland area in and close to Vancouver.

B.C. Museum of Mining, Britannia Beach (896–2233, or, in Vancouver, 688–8735). Open May to September; adults $4.50, seniors and children under 12 $2.50, students $3, preschoolers free, families $18, group rates are available. A guided tour of the huge, Anaconda mine by underground railway, live demonstrations of diamond drilling and copper mining at this gravity fed mill, "History House," slide show, gift shop, and cook tent. You can also pan for gold—and find some.

B.C. Sports Hall of Fame, B.C. Pavilion, P.N.E. Grounds (253–2311). Open all year, Monday to Friday, 9:30 am to 4:15 pm, closed on weekends; no admission charge. History of sports in British Columbia, of the Olympics and B.C.'s participation in them and of Terry Fox as well as exhibitions dealing with over 50 sports, professional teams, and medals. After Expo, this museum may be moving to the B.C. Pavilion on the Expo grounds.

B.C. Sugar Museum, foot of Rogers Street off Powell Street, one block west of Clark Drive (253–1131). Open Monday to Friday during office hours (9 am to 4:30 pm), or in the evenings for groups by appointment; no admission charge. History of sugar-making in British Columbia and of Rogers Sugar Company which has been making sugar here since 1890, film about the process, and tour of the refinery.

B.C. Transportation Museum, 2971 Viking Way, Richmond (278–6821). Open year round, 9 am to 3 pm, Mondays to Fridays; no admission charge. A provincially-owned collection of 65 heavy-duty transport vehicles, restored to original and running condition. The museum is at Viking Way and Bridgeport Road, not far from the Richmond end of the Knight Street Bridge.

Burnaby Village Museum, Deer Lake Avenue, Burnaby (294–1233). Open March to December, Tuesdays to Sundays, 11 am to 4:30 pm; adults $3, children, senior and students $1.50, under 6 free, families $7. A re-creation of a turn-of-the-century town, created in 1971 for B.C.'s centennial celebrations, where you can visit a blacksmith, a sawmill, a printer, an

Museum of Anthropology, University of British Columbia

ice-cream parlour, an herbalist, a barber, a photographer, a tinsmith, a pioneer log cabin, the church, or the dentist.

Beside the town is the **Burnaby Central Railway,** operated by the B.C. Society of Model Engineers and featuring child-size, model steam engines, built locally. The trains run Tuesdays through Sundays in July and August, on weekends and public holidays from Easter to Thanksgiving.

Canadian Museum of Flight and Transportation, 13527 Crescent Road, Surrey (531–3744 or 531–2465). Open March 15 to September 30, seven days a week, 11 am to 4 pm; no admission charge. A guided walking tour of this outdoor display of vintage aircraft and a few military machines is provided for those who come from all over the world to look at the collection. To get to the museum fields, take Highway #99 south to the White Rock/Crescent Beach exit, go 1½ miles (2.4 km) towards Crescent Beach to the museum which will be on your right.

Cap's Cycle Museum, 420 East Columbia Street, New Westminster (524–3611). Open during store hours, Tuesday to Saturday, 9 am to 5:30 pm, Thursday and Friday nights until 9 pm; no admission charge. Phone first to see if Cap will be there to show you around (he's usually pretty busy on weekends, so weekdays are a better time to visit). This collection is Cap's personal hobby and is enormous; it even includes a bicycle-built-for-six.

Deeley Classic and Antique Museum, 12260 Vulcan Way, Richmond (273–5421). Open 8 am to 4:30 pm weekdays; no admission charge. More than 50 impeccably restored motorcycles from around the world, some very rare Harley-Davidsons. Take the Oak Street Bridge, exiting for Richmond at the south end of the bridge via Bridgeport Road and continue on this road to #5 Road where you turn left; the first road on your right is Vulcan Way, and the museum is right there.

Delta Museum and Archives, 4858 Delta Street, Ladner (946–9322). Open Tuesdays to Saturdays, 10 am to 3:30 pm, Sundays, 2 to 4 pm; adults 50¢, children 25¢. Coast Salish artefacts of the area, a maritime display, turn-of-the-century scenes and furnishings from Delta.

Grocery Hall of Fame Museum, 1241 Homer Street, Vancouver (669–2214). Open Saturdays, 9 am to noon; no admission charge. Cans, pictures, posters of food, from the 1800s to today.

Irving House and Museum, 302 Royal Avenue, New Westminster (521–7656). Open May through August, Tuesdays through Sundays, 11 am to 5 pm, in the winter months on weekends from 2 to 4 pm; donations. Group tours can be arranged. The house, now restored, was built in 1864 and purchased from descendants of the original owners by the City of New Westminster in 1950. The Museum's collection includes the coach originally built to carry Lord and Lady Dufferin on their visit to the Fraser River gold fields in 1876, cameras and household objects, maps and photos belonging to the Royal Society of Engineers, and a 1928 Mack fire truck.

Langley Centennial Museum and Exhibition Centre, 9135 King Street, Fort Langley (888–3922). Open Tuesdays to Saturdays, 10 am to 5 pm, Sundays, 10 am to 4 pm; no admission charge. Changing exhibitions of local Indian artefacts and memorabilia of the early pioneers. Diagonally across from here is Fort Langley (888–4424) itself, open seven days a week, 10 am to 4:30 pm. Originally a Hudson Bay fort, it was here that the document proclaiming British Columbia a colony was signed.

Murchie's Tea and Coffee Museum, 1200 Homer Street, Vancouver (662–3776). Open Mondays to Fridays, 9 am to 4:45 pm; no admission charge. Teapots, coffee pots, maps and pictures sponsored by this Vancouver coffee-and-tea merchant company, which is today owned by the grandson of its founder.

Posthouse, the Canada Post Exhibit Centre, 1010 Howe Street, Vancouver (662–1349). Open Mondays to Fridays, 9 am to 4 pm; no admission charge. An inside look at current postal technology, stamp collecting exhibits.

Old Hastings Mill Store Museum, 1575 Alma Street, Vancouver (228–1213). Open mid-May to mid-September, daily, 10 am to 4 pm, in winter weekends only, 1 to 4 pm; donations. Indian artefacts, old photographs, and period household items and furniture (including a very big, early knitting machine, a bizarre-looking 1910 vacuum-cleaner, and a wooden washing machine). Built c. 1865, the building originally sat on Burrard Inlet at the foot of Dunlevy Street where it functioned as the town of Granville's store, post office, library and community centre. It was one of very few buildings to survive the Great Fire of 1886 in the city, and was moved to its present location in 1930 and dedicated as a museum in 1932. If its old door sticks, give it a good shove.

North Shore Museum and Archives, 209 West 4th Street, North Vancouver (987–5618). Open Wednesdays to Sundays, 1 to 4 pm; no admission charge. A collection of local household pioneering memories as well as travelling exhibits. The museum and archives are in the Presentation House complex.

Royal Westminster Regiment Museum, New Westminster (526–5116). Artefacts from the first militia unit of the Colony of British Columbia.

Simon Fraser University Museum of Archaeology and Ethnology, Burnaby Mountain (291–3325). Open Mondays to Fridays, 10 am to 4 pm, Saturdays and Sundays, noon to 3 pm;

Old Hastings Mill Store Museum

no admission charge. A collection of artefacts of British Columbia's coastal tribes, many of which have been purchased from collectors in other countries, and a collection of artefacts of anthropological interest from around the world.

Station Museum, Mahon Park, 16th Street and Jones Avenue, North Vancouver (987–5618). Open Sundays (except in the month of September), 1:30 to 4:30 pm, or for groups by arrangement; no admission charge. In the old Pacific Great Eastern Railway Station, a collection of items relating to the history of transportation on the North Shore and to the ferry system. Mr. Baker, the curator, offers guided tours for school groups, by arrangement, during the week.

Surrey Museum, 17679-60th Avenue, Surrey (574–5744). Open seven days a week, noon to 4:30 pm; donations. Pioneer farm implements, hand-made furniture, household items, early Indian crafts, and an antique toy train collection, in Surrey's original Municipal Hall built in 1881. The museum is just across the Pattullo Bridge from New Westminster, off the Fraser Highway.

University of British Columbia Entomology Museum, Biological Sciences Complex, Room 4341 (228–3379). Open weekdays; no admission charge. Check if the curator is around. This museum deals in bugs.

University of British Columbia Herbarium, Biological Sciences Complex (228–3344). Open 9 am to 4 pm, weekdays; no admission charge. Plants from both British Columbia and other parts of the world.

University of British Columbia Museum of Anthropology, 6393 N.W. Marine Drive, Vancouver (228–3825, for times and shows; 228–5087 for the office). Open Wednesdays through Sundays, 11 am to 5 pm; adults $2.50, students, seniors, and children $1, under 6 free. Open Tuesdays, 11 am to 9 pm; no admission charge. In existence since 1947, the Museum got striking new quarters in 1971 to celebrate the centennial of B.C.'s joining Confederation. The building, designed by Arthur Erickson, has 45-foot-high windows facing north from the top of the Point Grey cliffs, and affording a full prospect on the tall totem poles that stand in Thunderbird Park in front of the museum. Inside is a dramatic collection of northwest coast art carvings.

The museum also houses a multi-media theatre gallery, research collections, and an archaeology laboratory. A large collection of Pacific and Asian artefacts includes pottery from Peru, textiles from China, primitive art from New Guinea, and robes from Tibet. The museum prides itself on having ninety-five per cent of its material in visible storage; those drawers under the display cases are meant to be opened. The contents of each are safely under glass.

University of British Columbia M.Y. Williams Geology Museum, Geological Sciences Centre (228–5586). Open Mondays to Fridays, 8:30 am to 4:30 pm; no admission charge. The Sutton-Thompson collection of approximately 9,000 specimens of over 1,000 mineral types as well as fossils, and an authentic skeleton of a Lambeosaurus dinosaur.

University of British Columbia Vertebrate Museum, Biological Sciences Complex, Room 4349 (228–4665). Open weekdays, check if the curator is there; no admission charge. Tours can be arranged.

Vancouver Museums and Planetarium, Vanier Park at the south end of the Burrard Street Bridge (736–4431). Open daily, 10 am to 5 pm; adults $3.50, students, seniors and children $1.25, families $7.25 for combination tickets to both the Maritime Museum and the Vancouver Centennial Museum. Tuesdays, no admission charge for seniors. A complex of museums, including the housed *St. Roch (*an RCMP ice-breaker and the first vessel to circumnavigate North America), a ship restoration site on the harbour, the H. R. MacMillan Planetarium, the three galleries of the Vancouver Museum, the **Gordon Southam Observatory** (open on clear evenings, except Sundays, from 7:30 to 10:30 pm; no admission charge), and a splendid **cafeteria** in the Planetarium building overlooking the harbour and Vanier Park (open Mondays, 9 am to 5 pm; Tuesdays through Sundays, 9 am to 8 pm).

Admission to the **Vancouver Museum** (736–7736) alone is adults $2.50, students, seniors and children $1, families $5.50. This museum concentrates on the culture of the Pacific Northwest Coast Indians, the history of exploration and settlement in British Columbia, and Vancouver's early history. It has two rooms furnished in Edwardian style, a complete CPR passenger coach, a display dealing with the lumber industry, and some particularly elaborate and intriguing Indian masks.

Upstairs in the **H. R. MacMillan Planetarium** (736–3656), space-age film equipment projects stories of the stars onto the overhead screen. Call the Planetarium for programme information. Outside the theatre is a collection of photographs of some of the nebulae out there in other sections of the universe.

The **Museum Gift Shop** (731–4158), open 10 am to 6 pm daily, specialises in Northwest Coast Indian and Eskimo carvings, gold and silver jewellery, fine weaving, and prints. It has a solid reputation among Vancouver residents, and an extensive book section.

The **Maritime Museum** (736–7736) houses both a collection of model ships, marine relics and technological displays as well as the *St. Roch*. For times of the guided tours of this two-masted schooner, restored to the period when it policed the Northwest Passage, call 732–4362. Admission to the Maritime Museum and *St. Roch* is either by your combination-ticket to the Vancouver Museums and Planetarium, or adults $1.75, students, seniors and children 50¢, families $3.75. The *St. Roch* tours take place between 9:30 am and 6 pm.

Outside the Maritime Museum, to its southwest, is a very tall

Vancouver Museum and Planetarium, Vanier Park

totem pole, a duplicate of the Centennial totem pole presented to Queen Elizabeth II for British Columbia's centenary in 1958.

Art Galleries

In wandering about Vancouver, it might strike you that the city makes no secret of its art. The crab sculpture outside the Vancouver Museum and Planetarium, the bird-like construction outside Eaton's at Georgia and Granville Street, *Spring* next to the entrance of the government offices to the south of Robson Square, and Bill Reid's leaping killer whale at the entrance to the Aquarium in Stanley Park all declare that Vancouver likes to show its work. The following are some of the indoor spots for more of the same.

The Vancouver Art Gallery, 750 Hornby Street (682–5621). The new home of the city's art gallery is a nineteenth-century, neo-classical heritage building which used to be the provincial courthouse. Its front faces Georgia Street and the fountain of the courthouse plaza, but its main entrance is off Robson Square around the back. Special galleries are dedicated to Emily Carr, who left 173 of her paintings of Vancouver Island's forests and people to the province. The gallery also owns excellent works by such American artists as Warhol, Rauschenberg, Jasper Johns, and Oldenburg.

The **Children's Gallery** there aims at a younger crowd; the **Gallery Library** is open to the public (Tuesdays to Fridays, 10 am to 4 pm) for reading and research; the **Gallery Shop** (open 10 am to 5:30 pm, Tuesdays through Saturdays, and during gallery hours until 5:30 pm, Sundays) carries a large selection of books and reproductions; and the **Gallery Restaurant** (open Mondays to Saturdays, 8 am to 6 pm, and Sundays for brunch from 10 am) is elegant. The reataurant's telephone number is 683–8956.

The Gallery hosts changing exhibitions, and tours are available at 10:30 am and 2:30 pm, Tuesday to Friday. For groups of 10 or more, tours can be booked in advance. In addition, the Gallery's Education Department offers noon-hour talks on current exhibitions, Tuesday to Friday, 12:10 to 12:30 pm. The Gallery is closed Mondays.

Admission to the Gallery is adults $2.50, students, seniors

and children $1, under 12 free. Tuesdays are FREE for all. Memberships are available. The Gallery is open Tuesdays to Saturdays from 10 am to 6 pm, Sundays from 1 to 6 pm.

One established locale for art is south Granville, south of the Granville Street Bridge. **Bau-Xi Gallery,** 3045 Granville (733–7011), specialises in the work of Canadian artists such as Jack Shadbolt, Tony Urquhart and Joe Plaskett. Its open storage allows you to view a large selection of the work of any artist of particular interest to you. The gallery, which has been in business for 20 years here, is open 9:30 am to 5:30 pm, Mondays through Saturdays.

Kenneth C. Heffel Fine Art Gallery, 2247 Granville Street (732–6505), housed in an historic building, carries Group of Seven works and those of Vancouver's Toni Onley. The gallery is open Tuesdays to Saturdays, 10 am to 6 pm.

Equinox Gallery, 1525 West 8th Avenue, on the third floor (736–2405), shows top-flight American and Canadian painters and graphic artists. It is open Tuesday to Saturday, 9:30 am to 4:30 pm, and well worth it for the serious art hound.

The Art Emporium, 2928 Granville Street (738–3510), has works by such international lights as Andrew Wyeth, Salvador Dali, Juan Miro, and B.C.'s Jack Shadbolt. Open Monday to Saturday, 9:30 am to 5:30 pm.

For westcoast native art, **Bent-Box Gallery,** 1520 West 15th Avenue, just off Granville Street (734–3133), has a longstanding reputation. Its name refers to the watertight cedar boxes made here by Pacific coast native peoples out of a single continuous piece of bent wood. Open Tuesday to Saturday, 10 am to 5:30 pm, and Mondays from May to August.

Krieger Galleries, 775 Homer Street (687–6335), carries fine native Indian prints. Open Tuesdays to Saturdays, 10 am to 5 pm.

Others specialising in native Indian art and crafts are **Arctic Loon,** 3095 Granville Street (738–9918), and the **Indian Gallery,** 456 West Cordova Street, Gastown (689–4101).

Both universities have art galleries, which host changing exhibitions. **University of British Columbia Fine Arts Gallery,** Main Library (228–2759), is open Tuesday to Saturday, 10:30 am to 5 pm, and Mondays during July and August. **Simon Fraser University Art Gallery,** South Court Mall (291–4266), has purchased one of the largest private collections of Eskimo graphics, prints and soapstone carvings in North America. It is open weekdays only.

Shows at the **Charles H. Scott Gallery,** Emily Carr College of Art and Design, 1399 Johnston Street, Granville Island (687–2345), are always exciting.

For the very contemporary in Canadian and Vancouver art, there are **Diane Farris Gallery,** third floor, 165 Water Street, Gastown (687–2629), and **Contemporary Art Gallery,** 555 Hamilton Street (687–1345). Both feature emerging Canadian artists and are closed Mondays; neither opens before 10 or 11 am. **Atelier Gallery,** 3039 Granville Street (732–3021), also specialises in Canadian art. It is closed Sundays and Mondays.

Coburg Gallery, 314 West Cordova Street (688–0866), is the city's only gallery devoted exclusively to photography. It is open Tuesdays to Saturdays, noon to 5 pm, or by appointment.

Pitt International Galleries, 36 Powell Street (681–6740), keeps up with the leading edge in the avant-garde of artists. It is an artist-run, "alternate" gallery, and open noon to 5 pm, seven days a week.

On Granville Island, the shows at **Cartwright Street Gallery,** 1411 Cartwright Street (687–8266), have featured demonstrations of unusual pottery-making techniques and glass-blowing. A non-profit organisation, this gallery exhibits the works of local B.C. crafts people.

Municipally, **Robson Square Media Centre** (683–4358), hosts changing exhibits of various sorts in its gallery below the skating rink level, and **Presentation House Gallery,** 333 Chesterfield Avenue, North Vancouver, near Lonsdale Quay (986–1351), hosts travelling exhibits.

In a more casual setting, you might pick up a bite to eat and some art at **Montgomery Cafe,** 433 West Pender Street (685–

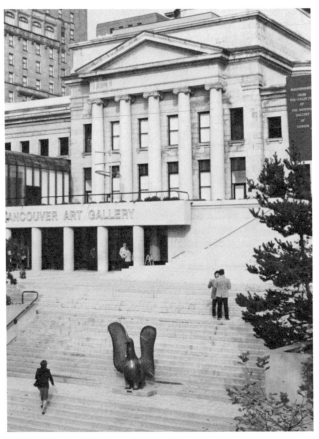

Vancouver Art Gallery, Robson Square

5524), where the excellent, light food, clientelle, and decor compete with the art on the walls for attention. Shows change every two weeks and represent artists from all over the country. The cafe is closed Sundays, open other days from 11:30 am to 11:30 pm, Friday and Saturday nights until 1 am.

102

At **Pizzaricco Pizza Bar,** 1106 Robson Street (669–2900), the owner creates a special pizza in honour of the artist currently showing in the pizzeria. You can buy single slices of this or any other pizza in the store for $1.75. Open Mondays to Thursdays until 11:30 pm, Friday and Saturday nights until 2 am, for pizza and paintings.

GARDENS AND WILDERNESS

Queen Elizabeth Park. On top of the city between Main and Cambie Streets south of 33rd Avenue, Queen Elizabeth Park has some of the most popular gardens in town, particularly for wedding photos. In addition, there are a Conservatory, under a geodesic dome, and surrounding quarry gardens decorating the city's emergency water reservoir. The architect imported a Dutch builder to construct the dome, and by the time it was finished, fourteen members of his family had come over to lend a hand. The **Bloedel Conservatory** (872–5513) is open every day from 10 am to 9:30 pm during summer, until 5:30 pm during the winter. Adults $2, students, seniors and children $1.

In addition in the Park are scores of tennis courts, a cafeteria and the Quarry House Restaurant overlooking the city. From Granville Mall, a #15-Cambie bus will take you to the Park's entrance at 33rd Avenue.

VanDusen Botanical Gardens, 37th Avenue and Oak Street (266–7194) tends and grows one of Canada's most comprehensive collections of ornamental plants. The 55 acres of what was once the Shaughnessy Golf Course are now owned jointly by the city and the province. Each section of the garden has a distinct botanical theme; the Sino-Himalayan garden of rhododendrons, for example, pays tribute to the floral bounty of China and the regions bordering the Himalayas. A three and a half acre Meadow Garden will be VanDusen's centennial project and open in 1986. Outside Sprinkler's Restaurant grow the herbs used for its cooking.

Within the Gardens is **MacMillan-Bloedel Place** (263–2688) on a quiet pond which is home to a number of ducks and geese. This award-winning display centre is a gift of the MacMillan Bloedel Company to the city. The displays deal with the forest cycle. Resource persons are on hand. Kids apparently love to have birthday parties here. Between mid-October and

Bloedel Conservatory, Queen Elizabeth Park

the end of March, the centre is closed on Saturdays.

The VanDusen Gardens are open 10 am to 8 pm in summer, 10 am to 4 pm during the winter. Admission (including MacMillan-Bloedel Place) is adults $3, students, seniors and children $1.50, families $6. Sundays at 2 pm, there are free guided tours. The Gift Shop has a horticultural theme and sells unusual seeds as well as crafts and prints.

From Granville Mall, a #17-Oak Street bus will take you right to the Gardens' entrance at 33rd Avenue.

At the **University of British Columbia,** the gardens are well worth looking up. At the south end of the campus, bordering the Thunderbird Stadium, are the **Botanical Gardens.** These tour the world botanically, continent by continent, delve deeply into the plants native to British Columbia, and show off an alpine garden, a collection of rhododendrons and Asian plants, and a herbal garden. Tours and wheelchairs can be arranged by calling the Botanical Gardens office (228-3928).

On the north side of the campus, not far from the Museum of Anthropology, are the **Rose Gardens,** a teaching and experimental garden disguised as an explosion of colour and scent. There are also lovely gardens at the **Cecil Green house,** on Cecil Green Park Road northeast of here. This beautiful stone house was given to the university by the Greens, and has a magnificent view of English Bay and the North Shore mountains.

Just up the road from the Museum of Anthropology, west of West Mall and sitting in behind the new and unmistakable Asian Studies Centre, are the exquisitely laid-out and tranquil **Nitobe Gardens** (228-3928). Every prospect from the lake to the little swamp where the waters that run through the garden disappear, declares the harmony of this Japanese art of landscaping. The Gardens are dedicated to the memory of Doctor Inazo Nitobe, an internationally-known educator and landscape architect. They are open from 10 am to dusk, closing about 3:30 pm in the winter. Adults 50¢, children 10¢, under 10 free. For a guided tour of the Gardens or wheelchair arrangements, call 228-3928.

To get to the north side of the University of British Columbia's campus, take 4th Avenue which becomes Chancellor Boulevard in the University Endowment Lands and then merges with Marine Drive just before the Museum of Anthropology. For the south side of campus, take 16th Avenue. A #10 bus from Granville Street or along Broadway will take you to the mid-campus bus loop, outside the Aquatic Centre.

At the back of the Chinese Cultural Centre, 50 East Pender Street, the **Dr. Sun Yet-Sen Gardens** are under construction. These will include a Ming dynasty garden, landscaping,

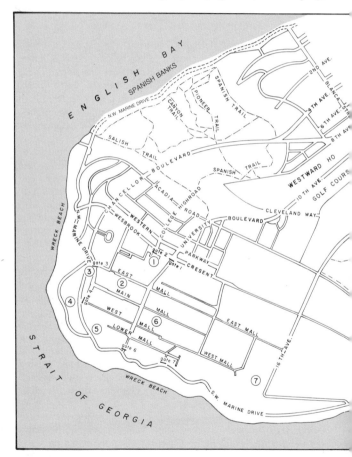

bridges and a temple. For more information on these gardens, call their office at 689–7133.

University Endowment Lands. The University of British Columbia campus on the tip of Point Grey is separated from the rest of the city by the extensive forests of the University Endowment Lands. Outside municipal boundaries, it's really a

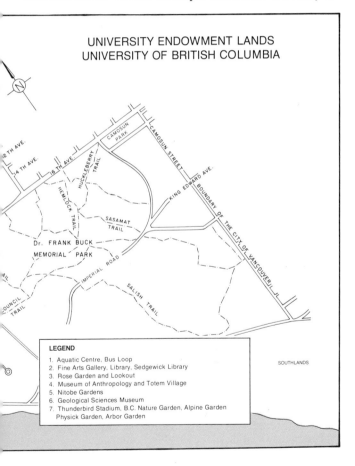

UNIVERSITY ENDOWMENT LANDS
UNIVERSITY OF BRITISH COLUMBIA

N

2TH AVE.

14 TH AVE.

16 TH AVE.

CAMOSUN PARK

CAMOSUN STREET

KING EDWARD AVE.

BOUNDARY OF THE CITY OF VANCOUVER

HUCKLEBERRY TRAIL

HEMLOCK TRAIL

SASAMAT TRAIL

Dr. FRANK BUCK MEMORIAL PARK

IMPERIAL ROAD

SALISH TRAIL

COUNCIL TRAIL

AIL

SOUTHLANDS

LEGEND

1. Aquatic Centre, Bus Loop
2. Fine Arts Gallery, Library, Sedgewick Library
3. Rose Garden and Lookout
4. Museum of Anthropology and Totem Village
5. Nitobe Gardens
6. Geological Sciences Museum
7. Thunderbird Stadium, B.C. Nature Garden, Alpine Garden Physick Garden, Arbor Garden

mini-city, and provides for its own sewers and water. In 1923, the provincial government set aside some 3,000 acres here as a source of revenue for the young university. Some of this has been ceded to the university itself, some has been developed.

But 1,700 undeveloped acres remain. As a source of income, the endowment is outmoded, but as a natural and educational resource, the University Endowment Lands are a priceless treasure.

The UBC motto, *Tuum est,* could be translated in at least two ways—"it's up to you" or "it's for you"—both of which extend to the lands with which the university is endowed. Their numerous forest trails are cleared but not sign-posted, and entrances in the bloom of summer can be missed. Also, since there is no regular maintenance staff for the lands, maintenance is up to you. Don't leave your litter.

If you have muck boots, you can walk all around the shoreline of Point Grey from Spanish Banks to the log booms on the south side of the peninsula. It's only over there that you really need your boots, as at high tide there isn't too much room for a shore. A short steep trail, marked "Old Trail to Wreck Beach", leads to this south part of the beach from S.W. Marine Drive.

On the other side of the campus, across from the main entrance (Gate 3) off Chancellor Boulevard, another trail leads to the part of Wreck Beach famous for casual undress. If you're prepared for some nude views, you can sun or walk here. Along this section, past the Second World War searchlight towers, you will see the spectacular effects of erosion that are threatening the sandy cliffs of the shoreline.

From Doggie Park by Spanish Banks, several trails into the interior of the Endowment Lands branch out through the ravines and forest. The Plains of Abraham, once the site of a dairy farm, is a pleasant picnic spot. In spring its western side bursts with cherry blossoms. The paths in the surrounding woods are well-cleared even though not named, and there is little danger of getting lost. And there's a good chance that you might sight a blue heron on the shore, a bald eagle in the tree-tops, or pheasant in the undergrowth. Here and there, you will come across huge lonely boulders deposited by the glaciers that once covered this area.

Most of these lands, except for a portion on the tip of the

peninsula, had been logged over about the time of the founding of the university and are now covered with mature second growth.

On the south side of the Endowment Lands, there are more trails which can be reached from Imperial Road or 16th Avenue. A grassy clearing, just off 16th near Trimble, offers a pleasant picnic site and, in season, good berry picking. Not far from the end of 33rd Avenue is another meadow.

To get to the Endowment Lands, take the #10 bus from Granville Street, but if you are bicycling, avoid this 10th-Avenue route. There's an easier grade on 8th Avenue, as well as a beautiful view of the bay and the mountains. S.W. Marine and N.W. Marine Drive are also easier on the cycling legs. From Blanca Avenue to the campus, paved cycle routes run alongside University and Chancellor Boulevards.

The University Endowment Lands are managed by an office separate from the University itself. The address is 5495 Chancellor Boulevard (224–3251), and you can call for further information or drop in and pick up maps of the Endowment Lands trails.

If heading up **Burnaby Mountain** to Simon Fraser University, you might consider packing your hiking shoes. To the south of the Science Complex is a series of trails, playgrounds and natural retreats in the bush created by the university's students. On the Port Moody side of the mountain are relatively easy trails leading up to the university. At Burnaby Mountain Park, there are more trails through the woods of this definitely mountain-fresh, view-offering, wooded backyard of the Simon Fraser University campus.

Capilano Canyon, North Vancouver. High above this mountain-side gorge, the **Capilano Suspension Bridge,** 3735 Capilano Road (985–7474), swings its stomach-testing 450-foot length. The first bridge across the canyon was built of wood and hemp, and called "Laughing Bridge" by the native peoples. It is open 8 am to dusk in summer, until 5 pm in winter; adults $3.50, students, seniors and children $2.50, under 12 $1. **Capilano Canyon Park** beneath is full of mountainside trails with steps built in to help in the steeper sections. You might see people fishing off the rocks by the river that comes down from Capilano Lake and which has been an access

Capilano Canyon Suspension Bridge, North Vancouver

route for salmon to their spawning grounds. You can enter this park from either Capilano Road in North Vancouver, or from Rabbit Lane in West Vancouver.

Near the top of the Canyon is the **Capilano Salmon Hatchery,** 4500 Capilano Park Road (987–1411), which can incubate two million salmon eggs annually, has a huge salmon corral out back, and features educational displays dealing with the salmon-spawning cycle. It is open daily 8 am to dusk; no admission charge.

Upstream about 3 km (2 mi) from the Suspension Bridge, the **Cleveland Dam** holds back the waters of Capilano Lake, which provide about a third of Vancouver's water supply. This is a good spot for a picnic by the uninhabited mountain lake.

Lynn Canyon, Lynn Valley, North Vancouver. Two miles up Lynn Valley Road above the Upper Levels Highway in North Vancouver is Lynn Canyon Park where the **Lynn Canyon Ecology Centre** (987–5922) resides. The 300-acre park straddles a breath-taking gorge cut by glacial boulders, and has its own short suspension bridge (no admission charge) which is even a little higher in the air than the one over Capilano Canyon. The Ecology Centre is built in the shape of the province's emblem, the dogwood flower, each wing (or petal) featuring a different aspect of ecological study. The Centre's pet racoon is always a favourite with children.

The Ecology Centre is open Monday to Friday from 10 am to 5 pm, and Sundays, noon to 5 pm, except during December and January. There is no admission charge.

From the SeaBus terminal at Lonsdale Quay, a #229–West Lynn bus will take you to the corner of Peters and Duval, just west of the Park's entrance. On Sundays, you have to take a #228–Lynn Valley bus from the same spot to the corner of Peters and Lynn Valley Roads, again just west of the Park entrance.

East Gate, Expo 86, False Creek

7 *Expo*

*Vancouver requests the pleasure of your company
at "The World in Motion—The World in Touch"
May 2, 1986 to October 13, 1986
on the shores of False Creek in the heart of the city
and on Burrard Inlet at Canada Place
for a World Exposition
coinciding with Vancouver's centennial celebrations
and the 100th anniversary of the first western run of
Canada's transcontinental trains.*

The two waterfront sites of Vancouver's 1986 transportation-theme exposition are joined by the downtown core of the city. On the 165-acre (66.6-hectare) **False Creek site** south of downtown, will be over 80 pavilions, theatres, plazas, and restaurants stretching along the shores of that inlet. To the north on 8 acres (3.4 hectares) on Burrard Inlet is **Canada Place,** its pavilion sailing into the harbour like a many-masted schooner. The complex consists of pavilion space (to become the World Trade Centre after the fair); a 505-bed, Japanese-built, luxury hotel (Pan Pacific Hotel); a five-berth facility for ocean liners (more than 200 are expected to dock during Expo); and office space. Near both the water and the train tracks, this location will allow for rail and deep sea demonstrations in conjunction with the fair.

The two sites will be joined by a "dedicated line" on the city's new ALRT (or Automated Light Rapid Transit) system, and there will be no charge for fairgoers travelling between the two locations.

ALRT stops will also service the False Creek Expo site, at East Main Station (beside Expo's East Gate) and at Stadium Station (beside the Stadium Gate to the Expo grounds).

With admission to the grounds come free rides on the 5½ km (3 mi) elevated **monorail,** which circles the grounds with stops at east, west, central, stadium, and Canada Place connecting stations. At east and west ends of the fair, you can "skyride" in a 6-passenger, **aerial gondola.** Skyrides will run between the Air Canada and the General Motors Pavilions in the west, between the Folklife Centre and the East Land Plaza on the other Expo end. These rides sponsored by Air Canada are included in the price of admission to the grounds. In addition, on the waters of False Creek, sternwheeler **steamboats** will ferry between Folklife (east), the Marine Plaza (centre) and the Pacific Bowl (west). A **ferry** from the Marine Plaza, around

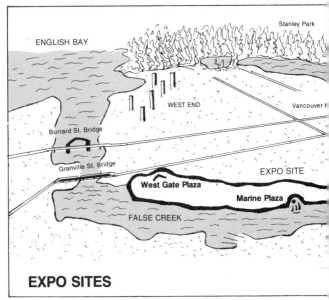

EXPO SITES

Stanley Park and under the Lion's Gate Bridge to Canada Place, is planned.

Expo's **East Gate** is on Quebec Street, one block west of Main and Terminal Streets. The **West Gate,** at the other end of the fair, is at Drake Street and Pacific Avenue, just east of the Granville Street Bridge. Expo's **Stadium Gate,** southeast of the highly visible B.C. Place sportsdome, is on Pacific Avenue. Admission at the **Canada Place Gate** will include admission to the False Creek site. Plenty of parking at East and West Gates has been promised. Look for the Impark sign and the Expo 86 logo. Free shuttle buses will travel from these lots to the Expo gates.

Expo One-Day Admission – $20
Three-Day Pass – $45
Season's Pass – $160

One-Day Admission tickets can be purchased at the Expo gates.

Season's Passes are sold at Woodward's Stores in British Columbia and Alberta, and at The Bon Stores in Washington State.

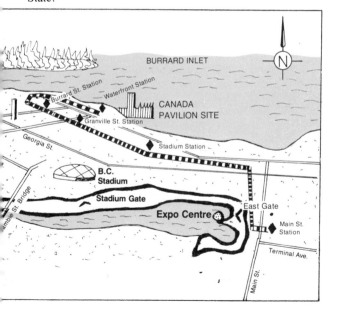

Three-Day Passes are also available at Royal Banks throughout Canada, Woodward's Stores and at SeaFirst Banks in Washington State.

All types of tickets mentioned can also be purchased by telephoning (604) 660-3976/EXPO or writing Expo 86, P.O. Box 1850, Station A, Vancouver, B.C., Canada V6C 3A9.

Substantial discounts (up to 50%) are available for senior citizens, children (6 to 12 years), the disabled, and in the case of advance purchase. For group discounts (20 people or more), phone (604) 660–3976/EXPO, or write Expo 86 Group Sales, P.O. Box 1986, Station A, Vancouver, B.C., Canada V6C 2X5. For early purchase discounts, mail orders must be post-marked on or before the last day of the discount period.

Admission to the grounds includes admission to all exhibits and regularly-scheduled entertainment and events, as well as on-site and inter-site transportation. Other rides and special events may have their own admission charges.

For general information on the fair and admissions or events, call (604) 660–3976/EXPO, or write Expo Info, P.O. Box 1800, Station A, Vancouver, B.C., Canada V6C 3A2

At all times on the grounds, there will be guides, attendants, vendors, security personnel, maintenance personnel, and medical staff. The **Service Building,** inside and to the south of the Expo East Gate, houses a first-aid, security and communications centre. At the East Gate and elsewhere around the fair are **Guest Relations Booths** to assist you.

At both East and West Gates will be **dog kennels** where a small fee and Expo's staff will take care of your dog for the duration of your visit to the fair.

More than 90 outlets will provide **food,** fast or fancy; **rides** include a parachute drop and a high-tech, new twist, thriller roller coaster.

For accommodation in the province of British Columbia, you can book with **ResWest,** the official Expo co-ordinator of credit card bookings. Their computerized listings will allow you to specify the price and type (hotel, motel, or campground, for instance) of your preference. You are charged a $5 fee for each reservation. Call ResWest at (604) 662–3300, or write them at Box 1138, Station A, Vancouver, B.C., Canada V6C 2T1, including your credit card number.

In addition to hotel accommodation (which is expected to be heavily-booked), a large number of **Bed & Breakfast** services are available. Contact the Vancouver Visitors and Convention Bureau about agencies or refer to this guide's chapter, "Places to Stay." There are also campgrounds near and even in the city. See what Tourism BC (660–2300), 800 Robson Street, in Robson Square, has on these. Inviting RVs to sojourn on the lawns and driveways of willing residents, is being considered. The new ALRT train system will be running all the way to New Westminster by then, so it will not be essential to find a downtown spot to park yourself or your car.

Greyhound Lines of USA have arranged package Expo tours to include Expo admission, accommodation in Vancouver, and sightseeing in the city and Victoria.

Holland America Westours Inc. is the official Expo cruise line. During the fair, Vancouver will be one of the ports of call for all of this company's ocean liners. Accommodation in the city can be arranged through that company if you are booking passage with them.

Participants and Pavilions

Over 80 nations, provinces, states, and corporations in British Columbia will be exhibiting their transportation and communication ideas, practises and history at the main Expo site on False Creek. For the first time, China, the U.S.S.R. and the United States will all be attending the same World Fair. The European Economic Community will be here too. Brunei is making its first North American appearance.

Norway's participation coincides with the 1000th anniversary of the Viking discovery of North America, and exhibits will focus on Norway's famous explorers as well as on the technology of offshore and subsea industrial operations. At the Hong Kong Pavilion, we will learn of this crowded country's "people-moving systems." Hong Kong not only moves a lot of people about but also operates one of the world's largest ferry services. Some of the historic transportation challenges of Canada's North will be presented at the Yukon Pavilion and will have to do with the fur trade, the Klondike Gold Rush, and construction of the Alaska Highway. The United States is planning to give us a look at the sights and sounds of a voyage into space. The highlight of the Japanese exhibit will be a 450-metre demonstration ride on their high-speed, magnetic levitation train. France is installing a mezzanine-level, inter-building transport system between their pavilion and the European Plaza. Cars will leave every 15 seconds for continuous "people-moving."

The Expo Corporation is presenting three pavilions. **Rameses II,** at the fair's west end, will deal with the historical beginnings of transportation and communication. At the east end, in the refurbished CPR **Roundhouse,** Expo in conjunction with ESSO will look at more current states of the art. And set on pilings in the east end of False Creek's waters, is **Expo Centre,** the double-layered, "neo-geodesic" dome which, you guessed it, will deal with the future. Its Omnimax Theatre's hemispherical screen is so large that its film's director had to be careful to pick up the cigarette butts littering the Appian Way during filming; on the screen they would have appeared to be the size of loaves of bread. The 240 stainless-steel panels out of which the Expo Centre is constructed are intended to reflect light in order to give a sense of the world in motion.

British Columbia's Pavilion, mid-fair and opposite the B.C. Place Stadium, is constructed out of 6,000 square metres of glass and, being the tallest structure on the grounds, will afford excellent views of the fair as a whole. Beside it is the **Plaza of Nations,** where opening ceremonies and major celebrations will take place; the steps leading down to the water will form an amphitheatre for viewing loggers' and water sports, marine displays and night-time fireworks. A Tourism Information Centre, with 150 hosts and hostesses to answer questions on any area of the province, will be a major feature of the B.C. Pavilion building.

The structures of the **Folklife** complex, adjacent to the Expo Centre in the furthest corner of the fair (where the paddle-wheelers dock), are made of giant cedars, and demonstrations here will focus on food and domestic crafts. At the **Telecom Canada Pavilion,** you will be able to take a "fibre ride," a visual tour through the insides of a telecommunications network, to a TV broadcasting station.

Some of Expo's structures are intended to remain after the fair is over: Expo Centre, CPR Roundhouse, B.C. Pavilion, Expo Theatre, the wharves and marine plazas, for instance. Those moveable buildings not slated to stay will be dismantled

Canada Pavilion, Expo, Burrard Inlet

and shipped to locations throughout British Columbia for use as community buildings.

One structure of note will be *The Rowingbridge,* a monumental sculpture by Vancouver's Geoffrey Smedley. It will be installed on Expo's West Gate Plaza and will consist of two narrow 43-foot columns, on top of which the 70-foot long "rowingbridge" will cross. Its oars will move hydraulically, and the whole will suggest the gateway that man-propelled motion is.

Special Events

Throughout Expo, periods of from five days to two weeks (detailed below) have been set aside for designated themes. During these times, related events, seminars, conferences, and special demonstrations will be taking place. And all over the grounds, throughout the fair, clowns, jugglers, minstrels, dancers, and even robots will entertain. The Royal Canadian Mounted Police will perform their Musical Ride at the Pacific Bowl, every day the fair is open.

Additionally, Expo and the Royal Bank are sponsoring a **World Festival** of music, dance, and theatre. Among those scheduled to appear are Leningrad's Kirov Ballet (May 14 to 19), Great Britain's Royal Ballet (July 8 to 13), dancers from Bali (Aug 15 to 17), the Philadelphia Orchestra (May 25 and 26), and Dame Kiri Te Kanawa (May 4 and 5) and Dame Janet Baker (May 10, 12, and 13) with the Vancouver Symphony Orchestra. The Vancouver Opera Association and the Vancouver Playhouse Theatre will also be staging special performances.

Tickets are already on sale for World Festival events through Vancouver Ticket Centres or Expo at (604) 660–3976/EXPO, Expo Info, P.o. Box 1800, Station A, Vancouver, B.C., Canada V6C 3A2

An Expo Calendar

May 2	Opening ceremonies, Plaza of Nations, including a 1,986-voice choir
May 5	Commencement of UBC Research Forest Expo '86 Tour Programme, taking parties from the Expo site to the UBC Research Forest in Maple

Ridge for tours and demonstrations. Call (604) 463–8148 or write UBC Research Forest, R.R. #2, Maple Ridge, B.C., Canada V2X 7E7, for informa tion.

May 5–11	Polar Transportation and Communications
May 12–18	Search and Rescue Operations
May 23–June 1	Steam Expo, a gathering and consorting of steam trains and enthusiasts
June 7	Parade of the DC-3 Airmada in the skies, including more than 50 DC-3's
June 9–15	Trucks and Inter-City Buses
June 16–30	Urban Transit
July 6–19	Automobiles
July 7–9	Vintage International Antique and Auto Tour Convention, with over 700 classic automobiles from North America and Europe participating
July 11–19	Innovative Vehicle Design Competition, the 8 university-student winners will display their 2-man, futuristic creations
July 20–25	Transport and Mobility for the Elderly and the Disabled
July 21	Passenger Rail Heritage Day. The VIA Rail Station at Main and Terminal Streets outside the Expo East Gate, now under renovation, will showcase rail history and display vintage trains from the 1920s
July 21–31	Marine Commerce
July 25–31	Tall Ships Assembly, having sailed from Hawaii to Vancouver Ceremonial arrival of a 16-metre Haida war canoe. This canoe is being carved from the trunk of a huge Queen Charlotte Islands cedar, under the direction of Haida artist Bill Reid, who has been instrumen-

B.C. Pavilion, under construction

	tal in reviving this traditional Haida art.
Aug 1–10	Aviation
Aug 4–7	Air Fair '86
Aug 8–10	A special celebration of the world-renowned Abbottsford International Air Show
Aug 8–17	Alternative Fuel and Power Systems for Transportation
Aug 12–14	Dance in Canada
Aug 14–16	Ballet Gala, Queen Elizabeth Theatre
Aug 18–24	Human-Powered Transportation
Aug 25–31	Transportation for Recreation
Sept 7–13	Communications
Sept 13–21	Underwater and Offshore Resources
Sept 29–Oct 5	Modern Rail

Looking Ahead from Here

Vancouver is getting ready to invite the world to Expo; 13.8 million visitors are expected. The city is preparing to handle the estimated 93 daily tons of garbage to be disposed of. A fully-automated traffic light system (such as is apparently saving commuters in Toronto 40% in travelling time) will be in place. Taxis in the downtown core will have information on events of the day at the Expo site. By that time the new Cambie Street Bridge across False Creek will be completed.

For information on Expo 86, call (604) 660–3976/EXPO, or write:

Expo Info
Box 1800, Station A
Vancouver, B.C. Canada
V6C 3A2

Brockton Point, Stanley Park Seawall

8 *Stanley Park*

Where in the world could 1,000 acres of ancient forest reside in the heart of a major city? Vancouver—naturally. Literally within minutes of downtown, the huge expanse of Stanley Park, floating in the sea like an island of green, harks back to the hospitable virgin wood that once sheltered the coast's native people.

Opened in 1889 on land originally set aside as a military reserve, the park is dedicated "to the use and enjoyment of people of all colours, creeds and customs of all time." The military reserve, now HMCS Discovery, has been confined to the small corner called Deadman's Island.

The name of this island derives from an Indian legend in which 200 men exchanged their lives for those of their wives and children who were being held by an enemy tribe. The Squamish Indians called the site of the slaughter, "The Island of the Dead Men". The commemorative aspect of the modern name is typical of Stanley Park, where some of Vancouver's favourite memorials stand.

The road that encircles the Park passes Deadman's Island (on your right) just after the main entrance to the Park's Zoo and Aquarium. Just beyond here is a good collection of **totem poles** on your left near **Hallelujah Point,** so-named for the Salvation Army meetings which used to be held there. The totem poles

ENTRANCE TO VANCOUVER HARBOUR
PROSPECT POINT
PROSPECT POINT RESTAURANT
SS BEAVER CAIRN

SEAWALL PROMENADE

SIWASH TRAIL

AVISON TRAIL

ELDON TR.

games area
PICNIC AREA

RESERVOIR TRAIL

HOLLOW TREE

99
1A

HANSON TRAIL

MERILEES TRAIL

SIWASH ROCK

THOMSON TRAIL

LAKE TRAIL

CYCLE PATH

BEAVER LAKE

THIRD BEACH

PAULINE JOHNSON MONUMENT

FERGUSON POINT

TEA HOUSE
LOVERS WALK

TATLOW WALK

LAKE

LEES TRAIL

CYCLE PATH

CATHEDRAL TRAIL

LOST LAGOON

pool

MEADOW

SECOND BEACH

CEPERLEY PLAYGROUND

PITCH AND PUTT GOLF COURSE

ENGLISH BAY

SHUFFLE-BOARD

BEACH HOUSE RESTAURANT

TENNIS COURTS

LAWN BOWLING

SEAWALL PROMENADE

PARK BOARD OFF.

STANLEY PARK

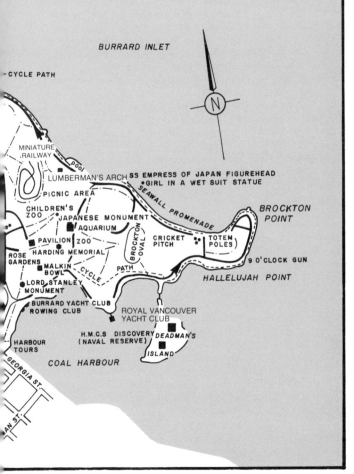

ARROWS

-CYCLE PATH

BURRARD INLET

N

MINIATURE RAILWAY

Pool

LUMBERMAN'S ARCH

SS EMPRESS OF JAPAN FIGUREHEAD

• GIRL IN A WET SUIT STATUE

PICNIC AREA

SEAWALL PROMENADE

CHILDREN'S ZOO

BROCKTON POINT

JAPANESE MONUMENT

AQUARIUM

PAVILION ZOO

BROCKTON OVAL

CRICKET PITCH

TOTEM POLES

ROSE GARDENS

HARDING MEMORIAL

9 O'CLOCK GUN

MALKIN BOWL

CYCLE

PATH

HALLELUJAH POINT

LORD STANLEY MONUMENT

BURRARD YACHT CLUB

ROWING CLUB

ROYAL VANCOUVER YACHT CLUB

HARBOUR TOURS

H.M.C.S DISCOVERY (NAVAL RESERVE)

DEADMAN'S ISLAND

GEORGIA ST.

COAL HARBOUR

AN ST.

are typical examples of a type of carving unique to the north-west coast of North America. Hallelujah Point is also the site of a former Vancouver tradition—the **Nine O'Clock Gun** which used to boom across Coal Harbour. Standing quietly among the trees to the left of the road is a memorial to Japanese Canadians who gave their lives in the First World War.

From **Brockton Point,** which points at the north shore of Burrard Inlet and bears one of the Park's original lighthouses, a beach stretches along the water to your right; the cricket fields lie to your left. At the end of the beach is a bronze statue of a girl which sits on a rock just offshore. It's called **Girl in a Wet Suit** and vies for attention in this section of the Park with the landlubbing wooden figurehead from the liner **Empress of Japan** which sank in the harbour in 1922.

Just beyond here on your left is **Lumberman's Arch,** made out of a giant cedar tree and paying tribute to one of British Columbia's major industries. The trail for **Beaver Lake** leaves the road a little further on.

Just after crossing over the causeway leading onto the Lions Gate Bridge, the Stanley Park road reaches **Prospect Point,** the highest point in the Park and site of its other lighthouse. Quite a prospect it is from here—out over the Lions Gate Bridge and down onto the ships moving in and out of the harbour. The totem pole here was carved by Chief Joe Capilano in the 1930s to commemorate the meeting of Captain Vancouver and the Squamish Indians in 1792. A memorial to the *SS Beaver,* the first steamship to sail the Pacific Northwest, stands above the rocks where the ship ran aground in 1888 after fifty-three years of service.

After Prospect Point the forest becomes almost primeval as the road follows the south side of the Park. On your left is a picnic area with tables, washrooms, and a water supply. On your right, a little further along, is the short trail to **Siwash Rock.** This was a favourite spot of the writer E. Pauline Johnson, who retells, in *Legends of Vancouver,* the story associated with this unusual geological formation. It commemorates an Indian who defied the gods so that his unborn child might have a bright and promising future.

On your left shortly after passing the Siwash Rock trail is the **Hollow Tree,** a shadow of its former self. It was once one of those mammoth west coast tree trunks, big enough to house a family or drive a car through. Earlier in the century, it was a favourite spot for group or wedding photographs.

Just before **Ferguson Point** at the eastern end of Third Beach, a quietly bubbling fountain stands as a memorial to E. Pauline Johnson. You can see this site if you turn off the road at the sign which directs you to the Teahouse. At the **Teahouse** itself are lawns on the heights looking over English Bay and westward out towards Vancouver Island.

Continuing on from here, the road will lead you to **Second Beach,** the **Ceperley Playground,** the lawn bowling grounds and acres of tennis courts near the Beach Avenue entrance, or back towards Georgia Street past **Lost Lagoon.** E. Pauline Johnson was responsible for naming this now-pond but one-time tidal pool where she used to paddle. She named it for the fact that at low tide she would lose her canoeing pond. After a causeway into the Park was built in 1911, sealing off the pool, it was no longer affected by the tide. Today, its water is fresh and hosts all sorts of birds and ducks. The fountain in its middle was erected in 1936 for the city's Golden Jubilee celebrations.

GETTING IN AND AROUND

The Park can be reached on foot from any number of streets running west from Denman Street. But **cars** headed into the park must use the **entrance off Georgia Street,** which runs through the Park and onto the Lions Gate Bridge. From the right-hand lane of Georgia Street westbound, the road for the one-way circuit around the Park's shore veers off to the right. Pipe Line Road to the left of the Georgia Street entrance cuts across the middle of the Park for quick access to the Park's south side.

The **Beach Avenue entrance** on the Southeast corner of the Park provides access only to the facilities in that area (tennis, pitch and putt, lawnbowling, shuffleboard), the Beach House Restaurant, and the Vancouver Parks and Recreation Board offices.

As you enter the Park by way of Georgia Street past Lost Lagoon, you will likely see gaggles of the Canada geese that hang out there. Some days they're real show-stoppers, and traffic may have to wait while they file across the road with a dignified lack of haste.

Throughout the Park, there are plenty of **parking** lots, and you may, at your own risk, park at the right-hand side of the road. Many easily visible trails cross the road, and there are lots of directional signs for the zoo, the restaurants, the Points, and other spots.

Between April and October, on Sundays and holidays, you can ride a **city bus around the Park.** A special "Sundays and Holidays" Pass which can be purchased on the bus (adults, $2; children and seniors, $1) allows you to get on and off the bus at various locations. The bus leaves from the Stanley Park Loop on Lost Lagoon at Chilco Street near Georgia, but you can get on at any bus stop along the route. On rainy days, buses are less frequent, so if the weather is poor, check the schedule posted at the Loop.

If you want, you can bike around the Park. **Bicycles** are allowed on the roadways, and there's also a designated **Bike Path** along the seawall in a counterclockwise direction. You are asked to dismount in the few narrow sections where you might collide with pedestrians. The whole circuit takes about an hour, even with stops to gaze at the scenery.

You can rent a bike from **Stanley Park Rentals** at 676 Chilco Street by Lost Lagoon (681–5581). A 3-speed bike for the tour or a small tyke's bike or a kid's seat costs $4/hour; $14/day. This shop also rents mountain bikes ($6/hour; $25/day), roller skates ($3/hour; $10/day), and ski equipment.

Or you can **hike** it around the Park. Circling the whole shore is the **Seawall** path. For thirty-two years of his life, James Cunningham designed and worked on this project, which both protects the foreshore from erosion and provides a magnificent tour of the forest, sea and harbour. Recently completed, after forty years in the making, the whole Seawall promenade is about 11 km (7 mi) long. There are plenty of resting places, and binoculars might come in handy for birdwatchers. The blue heron is often seen stalking about in the tidal flats.

A favourite shorter **walk** (about 5 km or 3 mi) is between English Bay and Siwash Rock along the south side of the Park. There's a path from the seawall up to the Teahouse at Ferguson Point, if you want to rest your feet there.

Criss-crossing the Park are various **trails.** Some were originally paths used by the Squamish, some were logging skidroads. Most of them are easy on the legs. Near Prospect Point, however, Hanson Trail is a steep one-kilometre climb towards the Lions Gate Bridge road, and Avison Trail descends in its course very steeply from Prospect Point to the Seawall. The Eldon Trail demands a bit of a climb for its excellent view of the entrance to the Burrard Inlet, but the rest of the trails are pretty level.

Cathedral Trail, to the cathedral-like grove for which it is named, is the shortest and prettiest. The Old Bridle Path is the longest. It loops through the centre of the Park's forest to Prospect Point, past Hollow Tree and back to Lost Lagoon. At the Lagoon, four trails begin, and the 1½ kilometre walk around the Lagoon itself is a lovely stroll. Another more secluded walk on thehalf-kilometre shore of Beaver Lake may afford you a sight of the trumpeter or whistling swans. In summer this freshwater lake is covered with pink, white, and yellow water-lilies. Merrilees Trail from Third Beach to Siwash Rock is another short waterside walk.

Dog-lovers and dogs love the Park too. In the spring, there is even an annual doggie walk, or should that be promenade? But note—for the protection of waterfowl in the Park—**dogs must be kept on a leash at all times.**

On your walks, you or your dog might come across a giant sequoia (some grow up to 300 feet), an arbutus (the native tree, protected from the saw by provincial law, which has the distinctive orange bark), a cedar of Lebanon, chestnut trees, spindly vine maples, towering red cedars, the dogwood (whose flower is the provincial emblem), hemlock, Douglas fir, holly or alder. Among the birds you might see are the Canada goose, various ducks, coots (that run along the water), the Great Blue Heron, bald eagle and the red-winged blackbird.

All in all, for walking there are 17 km (11 mi) of road and 43 km (27 mi) of footpath in the Park.

SPORTS

For both the sports fan and participant, there are various facilities in the Park. **Brockton Playing Fields** near Brockton Point on the north side of the Park host rugby, cricket and field hockey matches, and there is an old-fashioned cinder track around **Brockton Oval.** There are change-rooms and hot showers right at the playing fields.

In the English Bay corner of the Park, by the **Beach Avenue entrance,** there are lots of public tennis courts, pitch and putt (eighteen holes and golf clubs for rent), shuffleboard and lawnbowling.

The **Park Board office** (681–1141/2), just off the end of Beach Avenue on the southeast corner of the Park, can tell you about scheduled summertime events.

Also accessible from the Beach Avenue entrance is the **Ceperley Playground** beside **Second Beach.** Here there are swimming and wading pools (salt-water), and children love the old fire engine that stands at one end of the picnic ground. In the summer, there's dancing Mondays (Scottish), Tuesdays (Folk) and Thursdays (Square) from 8 to 10 pm, weather permitting. During July and August, the city's police department runs a **Traffic Safety Programme** for children. Mondays to Fridays, 2 to 4:30 pm, kids ages five to eight drive miniature cars through mock streets and traffic signals, get tickets, and are instructed in both car and pedestrian safety by the policeman in charge. It's free, first come first served, and very popular.

Third Beach, which can be reached only via the Georgia Street entrance or on foot, is more secluded, but like Second Beach, has both a concession stand and showers to rinse off the saltwater. Neither of these beaches came with the original Park, but have been manufactured from the generous sands of English Bay (First Beach).

Smack in the middle of the Park is a giant **checkerboard.** You may have to stand on a bench to survey your situation during the game.

For information on any of the Park's programmes and events, call the Park Board office at 681-1141/2.

MALKIN BOWL

For entertainment in the open air, there is Malkin Bowel, a theatre which was donated by former mayor, W. H. Malkin, in memory of his wife. When the Theatre opened in the early 30s, a company largely of volunteers was formed to put on a family programme mainly of musicals. Vancouver residents used to look forward to its summer shows. **Theatre-in-the-Park** still performs at Malkin Bowl, but today books shows for the theatre and concerts.

For information on scheduled performances, call 687–0174 in the summer or the Park Board at 681–1141/2.

THE ZOO AND THE VANCOUVER PUBLIC AQUARIUM

Both of these are big attractions in the Park. **The Zoo** isn't large, but it has a collection of monkeys, a variety of exotic birds and snakes, and several species of kangaroo and wallaby. We love the harbour seals, the more sedate California sea lions, and the penguins. The river otters put on a continuous show. The polar and black bears sleep most of the time. Peacocks strut about the ground freely, and the ponds are home to geese, ducks and emus.

For your own safety and that of the animals, please observe the NO FEEDING signs. Where feeding is permitted, try to ensure that your offering is suitable. Thanks.

The Zoo is open dawn to dusk all year, and it's free.

The **Vancouver Public Aquarium** is really something special. Moved here in 1956 from its modest premises on English Bay, it has grown to be Canada's largest aquarium and one of the biggest in North America. It displays both large and small, native and exotic species of marine life, including the Dover sole which looks as if it could be lying on your plate, piranhas, eels, octopuses, sharks, salmon, and that evolutionary oddity, the lungfish. The Aquarium is not only popular and fun but a dynamic part of the community, as it provides facilities for aquatic research and an educational centre for both children and adults.

The **whales** are among the most popular of the Aquarium's residents. They are also among the longest-living in captivity. Hyak, a killer whale who came to the Aquarium in 1968, is now 19 years old. Finna and Bjossa are the juvenile killer whales who came here from Iceland in 1980. White-Wings, the Aquarium's dolphin, shares the Beluga whales' pool. There is only one Beluga whale in residence at the moment, but the Aquarium is hoping to have two more shortly. They particularly like to study those who are studying them through the windows of the underwater viewing areas, which both killer whale and Beluga whale pools have.

In May of 1986, a new killer whale facility will be opening at the Aquarium to be called the **Marine Mammal Centre.** Here, at one of the largest killer whale exhibits in the world, viewers will be able to see the whales in something approaching their more natural setting. There will be rubbing rocks and beaches as well as deep pools for swimming.

At present both Beluga and killer whales demonstrate their grace, agility and intelligence all year round in the Aquarium's pools during opening hours between 10 am and 6 pm. Admission to the Aquarium and to the shows is adults, $5; children 13–18 yrs, $3.75; children 5–12 yrs, $2.50; families of up to five in number, $13. Memberships to the Aquarium allow admission to the centre at any time. For information on memberships, the Aquarium, or on whale show times (which vary), call 682–1118.

Other very popular residents of the Aquarium are the **sea otters.** With the birth of its first baby sea otter on the premises, the Aquarium scored a first; never before had a sea otter been born in captivity. A public contest chose the name of Clam Chops for this first one, and since then another one has been born in the Aquarium's pools.

In the Aquarium's new **Graham Amazon Gallery,** you walk through the exhibit itself, experiencing the sights, sounds and smells of the lush tropical rainforests of South America. One exhibit allows you to "witness" a tropical storm. In the trees and pools, you will catch sight of tropical birds, iguanas, caymans and other creatures you might find if you were in South America itself.

Outside the Aquarium, at its entrance, is a sculpture, *Killer Whale,* donated by Mr. and Mrs. James and Isabelle Graham after whom the Amazon Gallery is named. The whale sculpture is a striking piece of work by local artist Bill Reid. Cast in bronze, it reaches 20 feet in height, the elongated fin and heavy body cantilevered over a reflecting pool and arching from the tail which alone touches the ground. Only recently installed, it is already the most photographed attraction in the Park.

The **Children's Zoo,** beside the main zoo's emu and Arctic wolf exhibits, is open in the summer months from 11 am to 5

Killer Whale by Bill Reid, Vancouver Public Aquarium

pm, in winters only until 4 pm. As the name implies, this Zoo is designed with children in mind. Here, youngsters wander among and handle small or baby members of the animal world, patting young Peter Cottontail or holding one of the Three Little Pigs. The residents of this Zoo don't usually stay long. Some are only borrowed, some just grow up.

For children the admission price is small (75¢). For adults it's a little more ($1.35).

Across from the entrance to the Children's Zoo is the Stanley Park Junction Station for the **Miniature Train.** During the summer months, weather permitting, this train chugs along its circular track past streams, Indian villages, a gold-mining waterwheel, a miner's hut, a beaver pond, and several wild animals. Children, 75¢; adults, $1.35.

It runs between the first week of spring and mid-autumn from 10 am to 6 pm, and in winter, on weekends from 11 am to 4 pm, weather permitting. Just beside the train station are the always popular **pony rides.** The mounts are quiet, and the kids can take themselves or be led around the track. Pony rides are available only in the summer months.

EATING IN THE PARK

And now for some refreshment. If popcorn at the Zoo isn't enough, there are **concession stands** at several locations selling drinks, hot dogs, and good fish and chips: at the Children's Zoo, by the Zoo's duck pond, at Lost Lagoon, Lumberman's Arch, and at Second and Third Beaches.

The **Pavilion Restaurant** is large and cafeteria-style, near the Zoo, and beside Malkin Bowl and the Rose Gardens. **Prospect Point Restaurant and Café** (669–2737), halfway across (or around) the Park, has fine dining, a patio, and a view of the Lion's Gate Bridge. It is open for dinner, Fridays and Saturdays from 5:30 pm to 9:30 pm.

For elegant dining, The **Beach House Restaurant** on Beach Avenue (681–9951) has a long-standing reputation. It's open for lunch weekdays, 11:30 am to 2:30 pm, and for dinner from 5:30 pm to 11 pm, seven days a week, for brunch on Sundays from 11 am.

The **Teahouse** at Ferguson Point (669–3281) isn't really a teahouse at all. It's a beautiful dining-room with continental cuisine, walls of glass, and an excellent and popular Sunday brunch. In winter, dessert and a Polar Bear (coffee) by the fire are enjoyable. Some say their pecan pie—regular or chocolate—is the best in town. It's always busy and never cheap. Reservations are advised, as well as care in finding the entrance to the restaurant. Once you've passed it, it's very difficult and annoying to have to try to back up.

LEAVING THE PARK

If, instead of leaving Georgia Street westbound to drive around Stanley Park, you stayed on it, the three-lane road would take you right through the centre of the Park and onto the **Lions Gate Bridge.** Built in 1938, this suspension bridge which connects the Stanley Park peninsula to North and West Vancouver, is over a mile long and hangs 200 feet above the water. It was at first a toll bridge, costing vehicles a quarter, pedestrians five cents, until bought by the Province of British Columbia for $5,700,000 (the original cost of building the bridge) in 1962. At its Stanley Park end are two 12-foot lions. Since the bridge and its access causeway through the Park have only three lanes, the centre-lane, depending on the time of day, is barred to traffic driving one way. Watch for the overhead orange warning light in this lane, which lets you know that the direction of traffic is changing.

From about halfway around the circuit road in Stanley Park, there is an access road to Georgia Street westbound and the Lion's Gate Bridge. If you continue on the Stanley Park road, you will cross over Georgia Street and head down the Park's south side.

At Second Beach as you come toward English Bay, the road forks. The left fork will take you on around the eastern end of the Park to Lost Lagoon and **Georgia Street eastbound.** The fork to the right leads to **Beach Avenue and English Bay.**

Parking is allowed in most areas on the roadway itself within the Park, if you wish to stop and gaze or take a walk on one of the Park's trails.

For further information on any of Stanley Park's facilities or activities, call the **Park Board office** at 681–1141/2, Mondays to Fridays between 8:30 am and 4:30 pm. In summers, this office is also open on weekends.

Granville Island Public Market

9 *Granville Island*

One of the most exciting and vibrant projects going on—and on—in the city is on Granville Island. These 37 acres under the girders of the Granville Street Bridge were originally dredged up on the False Creek tidal flats in 1913 for an industrial park. From the outset, the area was considered an irritating eyesore.

Today, the once-shoddy collection of deteriorating factories and warehouses has undergone a facelift, and in the blending of extremes—old and new, commercial and recreational, land and sea, industrial and artistic—a lively harmonious environment is emerging.

Plans for the redevelopment of Granville Island took shape in 1976 with the formation of the Granville Island Trust. This body screens all projects or enterprises applying to set up on the island in order to maintain the direction for the Island that was originally intended. In terms of urban design, the project of Norman Hotson and Joost Bakker, Architects, was an award-winning one.

Initially, engineers inspected every one of Granville Island's industrial structures to determine which ones were still structurally sound. The rest were condemned and cleared. Then, to maintain the renovated industrialism theme, buildings were repaired without changing their characters. Corrugated metal was used to cover old structures; as much as possible of the original

features of a building—doors, cranes, windows, and wooden
beam supports—were conserved. Interlocking concrete paving
stones were used in the repair of the roads.

For modern utilities, thick squared posts, much like those
used in the original construction of the buildings, were erected

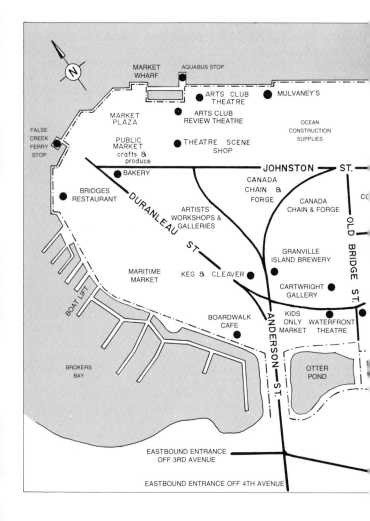

along the streets to carry electrical wiring and light fixtures by means of a pipe and lintel system. All the metal parts of theseutilitarian structures then got a dose of bright new paint. From them stretch the canopies of the island's shops and markets. Everything looks new and fresh and yet familiar.

Of the firms that once crowded the island, only the cement

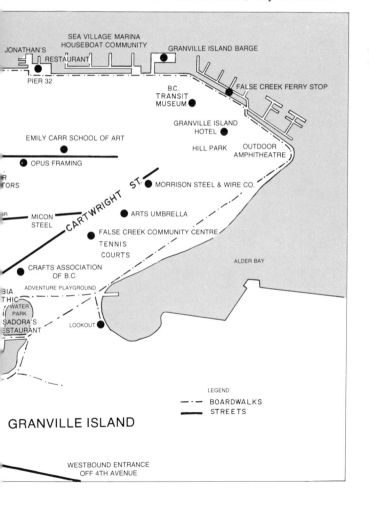

plant of Ocean Construction Supplies and their fleet of cement trucks remain. Until very recently, Morrison Steel, then the island's oldest industrial tenant, continued to make nails there. Canada Chain and Forge (est. 1922 and the only company in North America to produce hand-forged steel chain) moved out as late as 1984.

In their place, the island has taken on a whole new range of industry. Lawyers, architects, engineers, travel agents and realtors have hung out their shingles. The arts and specialty shopping—for fish and vegetables, boats and marine accessories, kidswear and toys—have found a home. A fleet of 12-foot brigantines, built by **The Small Ships Society,** 982 West 2nd Avenue (738–1952), docks behind Cartwright Street opposite the condominium developments of False Creek's shores. Between June 1 and September 6, 1986, they will be offering tours of their dockyard and putting on special shows. **West Coast Whale Research** (681–7092) lives here too, on Duranleau Street, and gives public presentations by request. **Outward Bound** (669–9196), also on Duranleau Street, gives courses in canoeing, kayaking, mountaineering, and the like. And the **False Creek Community Centre,** Cartwright Street, has its quarters here.

Among the businesses located on the island are many associated with the arts. **Kroma Industries** (669–4030) manufactures acrylic paints on Duranleau Street. **Blackberry Books** nearby (685–4113 or 685–6188) features books on art, architecture, cooking. They also have a large stock of books of British Columbia. **Opus Framing** (688–0388) sells more than it sounds. They carry a wide selection of artists' supplies— paints, papers, canvas—as well as framing materials and skills. **Gemini Photo and GI Plastic Laminating** (688–7433) specialises in commercial photography.

Studio, gallery and retail space has also been provided for artists and craftspeople. Painters, printmakers, sculptors, potters, weavers, jewellers and woodworkers are listed among the tenants. Haida artist Bill Reid has a workshop at 1659 Duranleau Street. It was here that the forms for the Aquarium's "Killer Whale" were made. **The Cartwright Gallery** (687–8266), named for its street, exhibits works of B.C. craftspersons. At **Studio Glass** (681–6730), you can watch David New-Small blow molten glass into delicate and delightful forms. **Grace Gallery,** 1406 Old Bridge Street (669–9606), is new and regularly shows the work of its co-operative of some two dozen British Columbia artists. **Circle Craft,** 1651 Duranleau Street (669–8021), represents its over 250 members.

The grey and industrial-looking structures on the island's northeast corner house the **Emily Carr College of Art.** Formerly the Vancouver College of Art, the school changed its name when it began classes in these new quarters, built to look like more original island buildings. Large windows line the north walls to allow in as much light as possible. Facilities for study are very good, and the school is both very contemporary and very energetic. In the central entrance corridor, student works are usually on display, and the college's **Charles H. Scott Gallery** (687–2345) hosts travelling exhibitions.

Behind the college, Pier 32 is the address of another ingenious set—the residents of Granville Island's houseboat community.

One of the big attractions of Granville Island is the **Granville Island Public Market,** opened in 1979 in a renovated structure formerly owned by the B.C. Equipment Company. Its 46,000 square feet of indoor marketplace are supported by the original wooden beams, and the old overhead cranes from the building's industrial days are still in place. All, however, has been brightly painted; new floors and lighting systems have been installed. And the largest selection of fruits, vegetables, meats and fish under one Vancouver roof is to be found here. Besides the permanent stalls of regular vendors, there is temporary space available for crafts and seasonal foods. Hand-stirred fudge and chocolates are made right on the premises. Bulk teas and coffees, health foods, breads, herbs, cheeses and cut flowers abound.

Among the many fishes and meats available, the patés at the **Boulangerie Française** are terrific (we haven't had the nerve to try their quails' eggs). If shopping for salmon, it's a good idea to check the prices of several stalls. One vendor sells nothing but turkey products (including turkeyburger). In muffins, the **West Coast Muffin Granny** makes an unusual assortment. The truffles at **House of Brussels Chocolates** can make your day (they are reputedly addictive), and, if calories don't count, you can pick up Devonshire Cream from **The Milkman. Attilio's** makes fresh pasta.

The Public Market also has a smoke shop which carries *The New York Times,* a post office, and bicycle racks at its doors.

For deliveries, trucks unload at the market's wide side entrances; fishing boats pull up to the wharf at the back. Public moorage is available here too but limited to three-hour tie-ups. Musicians, jugglers, mime artists and other entertainers can often be found "doing their thing" on the wharf to good-sized audiences.

Definitely a "people place," the Market is open 9 am to 6 pm, Tuesday through Sunday and on holiday Mondays. Usually closed Mondays, the Market may not open on the Tuesday following a holiday Monday.

Another high traffic area is the **Kids Only Market,** opposite the Granville Island Brewery at the corner of Anderson and Cartwright. Here, on two floors but under one roof, some thirty shops cater to the whims and needs of children . . . and no two stores sell exactly the same thing. Toy shops may have party favours, kites and puppets, wooden toys, stuffed animals, dolls, construction toys, models, educational and computer games, records and tapes. Among the clothing outlets is a stall for girls only, another for the sports-minded, one that specializes in leg coverings and one that sells anything you need for the water or when it's wet. There's a shop for linen, another for comics, one for art supplies and a bookstore as well as food counters designed to appeal to young appetites. Even the sinks and fountains are low for easy use by youngsters, and there is a changing area for Mums with small infants. The Kids' Market also houses a bicycle repair shop—for small fry.

Children also love the **Adventure Playground** next door to the False Creek Community Centre on Cartwright Street. On hot days, they line up for the slide in **Water Park.** Both Adventure Playground and the Water Park are operated jointly by the Vancouver Parks Board and the False Creek Recreation Association, and both provide supervision during the summer months. At the Water Park, however, children under 8 must always be accompanied by an adult.

On Anderson Street, **Over the Rainbow Playcare Centre** (683–2624) offers services which will allow Mums to shop in solitary efficiency, while their young ones play in a supervised environment. Or you can wheel your child, as well as your shopping, around the island in a little red wagon rented from **Kids Wheels** (688–9130). Another solution would be to enroll your youngsters in a course with **Arts Umbrella** (681–5268) on Cartwright Street. They specialise in teaching ages 2 to 18.

A spot worth stopping at on your way onto the island might be the **False Creek Flea Market.** It's open weekends and holidays from\10 am to 5 pm, and is housed in a tent.

Being all but surrounded by water, the Island has also become a centre for boat dealers, boating shops and sea-going, ocean-concerned activity. Around the corner from the Public Market, on the southwestern portion of the Island between Duranleau and the waterfront, is an area called the **Maritime Market.** On land, no less than fifteen boat brokers and retailers deal in zodiacs, canoes, kayaks, power craft, and sailboats and accessories. The boats you see moored offshore in ''Broker's Bay'' are for sale. Here too, you might see the 15-ton boat lift in operation particularly during the spring and summer when boaters clean and repair their vessels. If you need it, you can get marine insurance and tug boat services here.

If you don't own a boat, and don't want to buy one, but would like to spend some time on the water, there are a number of companies that organize charters and expeditions: scuba diving weekends, fishing trips and white water rafting. For local water, you could rent a kayak from **Ecomarine Ocean Kayak Centre** (689–7575), a canoe from **Vancouver Canoe and Kayak** (688–6010) or a rowboat from **Red & White Rowboat Rentals,** J Dock, Maritime Market—and paddle around False Creek for an hour or two.

At the Granville Island Hotel's ''Boatel,'' you'll find overnight, short-stay moorage. This marina will also rent you a boat, then berth it, and accommodates several charter companies. The hotel itself is small, recently opened, and certainly different. Its lounge, **''Pelican Bay''** (683–7373), and glassed-in dining-room, are popular evening haunts, looking to Fairview Slopes on one side and at Expo on the other. During the day, you can catch the scene from the outdoor patio of the hotel's **Island Bistro** with a soup and salad lunch.

Next door to the Hotel, off Johnston Street, **Computer Learning Centre** (685–0729) has found a berth on a barge.

Public Market Wharf, Granville Island

This company runs a series of computer classes for all age groups. On Cartwright Street, across from the entrance to Pelican Bay, restoration of **Canadian Pacific Locomotive #374**, which pulled the first passenger train to Vancouver, is underway. For more information on this project, call 683–0706.

Theatrical endeavours have also found sorely-needed space on Granville Island. Early on, the very successful Arts Club Theatre of Seymour Street opened a second **Arts Club Theatre** (687–1644) on the wharf between the Public Market and Mulvaney's Restaurant. The Seymour Street location continues to put on Arts Club productions, but the company now has room for further productions as well. Their new 480-seat theatre occupies a building that once housed a chain and forge company. Its glassed-in licensed lounge overlooks False Creek, and during intermission you can wander out to the waterside boardwalk.

Across the street, tucked into the back of the Public Market, the **Arts Club Review Theatre** (687–1644) features cabaret-style reviews. With tables for two and four, this theatre can accommodate a crowd of 225.

The 240-seat **Waterfront Theatre** (685–0707) now represents two companies. The **New Play Centre** (682–6228), dating back to 1970, concentrates mainly on works by B.C. authors and provides a script evaluation service as well as seminars and workshops. **Carousel Theatre** (683–9373) caters to children, with school productions and weekend matinees. Its theatre school has sessions for both children and adults.

Anytime of the day or night, if you're hungry, you've come to the right place. For a quick bite, the fast food outlets in the **Public Market** offer a variety of portable meals. Beside the indoor public seating area, the **Blue Parrot** makes some of the best coffees in town. Other outlets serve up fish and chips, fresh fruit salad, real Italian ice cream or baked goods. Whatever your fancy, you can take it out to eat on the wharf or sit at one of the indoor tables.

Foresightful **Mulvaney's Restaurant** (685–6571), next door to the Market, was a tenant here even before the Island became a project. Tucked in behind the Creekhouse Gallery, in the shadow of a bridge support pillar, the entrance to the restaurant is unique. New Orleans overtones dominate its decor and dining, and it has become a popular meeting spot.

At the Burrard Street Bridge end of the Island, **Bridges** (687–4400) is actually three restaurants in one. Depending on your pleasure, you can get fish and chips or a substantial burger in their **Pub,** a light repast in their glassed-in **Bistro,** or spend an elegant evening in their upstairs dining-room. The view from upstairs takes in the city's skyline and the North Shore Mountains. Downstairs, during the warm weather, the water-side outdoor patio opens and is always packed.

Isadora's Co-operative Restaurant (681–8816) serves healthy, reasonably priced meals and breakfast as well as high tea. Homemade soups, simmered avocado and mushrooms on a croissant, nut burgers and a kids' menu make this a great family spot. Breakfasts are self-serve, Mondays to Fridays; brunch is available from 9 am to 3 pm, Saturdays and Sundays; and dinners are served only from Tuesday through Sunday.

The atmosphere at **The Keg** (685–4735), a steakhouse, is casual. **Jonathan's Seafood House** (688–8081), a little more formal, features fruits of the sea. The **Boardwalk Café** (689–3455) is the newest eating-spot on the Island. Here, you can get a table overlooking Brokers Bay.

A relative new-comer to the industrious scene is the **Granville Island Brewery** (688–9927), on Cartwright Street at the corner of Anderson, just as you drive on to the Island. Made without preservatives or chemicals, their premium lager beer can be purchased between the hours of 10 am and 1 pm, including Sundays. Tours of the brewery are also available, but it is best to phone for times.

To reach the Island from Burrard Street, drivers going east on either 3rd or 4th Avenues turn left under the Granville Street Bridge. If travelling west along 4th Avenue, turn right under the bridge.

If possible, *don't* drive to the Island at all. Parking can be a frustrating experience.

By city bus, one has to transfer to a #51-Granville Island bus at the northwest corner of Granville and Broadway. (This bus doesn't run Mondays when the Public Market is closed.) For a reasonable fee, the **Granville Island Express** bus (669–1578) will take you to the Island from downtown. This bus departs from mid-block outside the Vancouver Art Gallery (on Howe

Granville Island, False Creek

Street between Robson and Georgia) every half hour between
9:15 am and 5:45 pm. The returning bus leaves from the Public
Market on the hour and the half-hour, 9:30 am to 6 pm.

A more scenic route to the Island is aboard one of the little
False Creek Ferries (684–7781), 1804 Boatlift Lane, Granville
Island, which run between the Maritime Museum in Vanier
Park, the Aquatic Centre on Beach Avenue and Granville Island. Stops are made at Bridges by the Public Market, Mulvaney's, Jonathan's, the Granville Island Hotel and Isadora's
until 8 pm. The **Aquabus,** which also crosses False Creek,
travels from the Jib Set Sailing Club Dock on Beach Avenue to
The Arts Club Theatre dock, 7:30 am to 8 pm.

Redevelopment of Granville Island continues to evolve with
no definite completion date in mind. What remains is the fact
that this is a place—once an industrial eyesore—where Vancouverites like to be these days.

Hotel Europe, Gastown

10 *Gastown*

by Ina Lee

East of Vancouver's downtown and backing onto the railway tracks, Gastown is an old Vancouver story with a happy ending.

It begins in 1867, with the arrival of Captain John Deighton, known to the city as "**Gassy Jack,**" a New Westminster, riverboat captain and notorious drinker. He set up Gastown's first establishment, the Globe Saloon. Quickly it was surrounded by a ramshackle cluster of general stores, gambling halls, saloons and so on.

By the turn of the century, Gastown as a name for the new westcoast city and terminus of the railway had been rejected, but the area was thriving as the commercial heart of Vancouver. During the Depression and in the decades following, Gastown's fortunes plunged steadily downwards. By the 1960s, it was the worst "skid row" in the country.

The city came to the rescue of its origins in 1974 with a plan to rehabilitate Gastown. Its turn-of-the-century buildings were restored to their original elegance, new buildings were built in keeping with the old, and sidewalks and courtyards were installed and upgraded. Merchants, business people, restaurant and club owners took a new look at Gastown, and set up shop along its cobblestone streets. Gastown was once again open for business.

Today, Gastown is home to designers and artists, art galleries and the arty, theatres and restaurants, music and dancing, and shops to suit all tastes and budgets. It begins at Cordova and Richards Street to the west, with the **Sears Harbour Centre Tower,** and extends east from there along Water and Cordova Streets. Its eastern end, where the district merges with the warehouses of Alexander, Powell and Cordova Streets, is less distinct.

Two landmarks will put you squarely in the heart of Gastown. At the corner of Cambie and Water Streets is the world's first steam-powered clock, designed and built in Gastown by a local resident, Ray Saunders. The **Steam Clock** 'blows its top' every 15 minutes to the familiar Westminster chimes tune. Further east, where Water Street converges with Alexander, Powell and Cordova Streets all at once, is **Maple Tree Square.** This was the original site of ''Gassy'' Jack's Globe Saloon, and here stands a statue to this boozing pioneer.

Many artists today make their home in Gastown as do designers and architects. Naturally some of the city's most interesting galleries are here. **Diane Farris Gallery,** 65 Water Street, in a luxurious third-floor setting, offers high-profile exposure to young Vancouver artists. This gallery is fairly new but has already established a reputation for quality showings. The **Coburg Photographic Gallery,** 314 West Cordova Street, is the only gallery in the city devoted exclusively to showing photography. Again, the gallery, even though fairly new, has already made its name internationally.

For something more on the cutting edge of the avante-garde, **Pitt International Galleries,** 36 Powell Street, is accommodating. This is the city's ''alternate space'' gallery, and it also hosts new wave musical evenings, performance art, and other way out events.

For Canadian traditions, you can find some fine examples of Inuit carving and printmaking at the **Inuit Gallery,** 345 Water Street. At the back of this gallery resides an unexpected and fascinating collection of artifacts from New Guinea.

The specialty shops give Gastown shopping its special flavour. For instance, **R.J. Clarke Tobacconist,** 3 Alexander Street, is old-fashioned, has a life-size, walk-in humidor, and carries the largest selection of tobacco blends in town. **Tout Sweet Chocolates,** in Le Magasin Mall, 322 Water Street, makes gourmet chocolates before your eyes. At 175 Water Street, **The Calico Cat** and **The Gingham Dog** carry novelty children's toys. **Inform Interiors,** 97 Water Street, is a high-tech design emporium for furniture and household wares. Leather fashions are the thing at **Neto,** 347 Water Street, and at **Minus Zero,** 348 Water Street, across the way.

All along Water Street, you will find souvenir shops selling standard Vancouver memorabilia. The most prestigious shops, such as **Hill's Indian Crafts,** 165 Water Street, carry genuine, westcoast Indian wood carvings, leather goods, and Cowichan sweaters. The latter as well as Cowichan knitted hats and mitts are a local specialty. **Canadian Impressions,** 321 Water Street, specialises in fine woollens, both Canadian-made and imported from the British Isles.

If you are seriously in search of high-style, flamboyant wear, on Cordova Street you will find 'up-beat', reasonably-priced fashion boutiques. **The Block,** 350 West Cordova Street, is a combination coffee-bar and fashion store, with a limited but distinctive selection of locally-designed creations and accessories. While contemplating, you can drink coffee around their artist-designed, new wave table.

Morning Star, 311 West Cordova Street, has changed its image, having replaced hippie-style cottons with "British street fashions." This is strictly vanguard fashion clothing, for women. Men go downstairs to **Boystown. Peter Fox,** 303 West Cordova Street, can supply the designer shoes. They're certainly not cheap, but do come in exotic styles and wonderful colours. Next door at **Colourbox,** you can have your hair cut and dyed to match. **Pitti's,** 2 Powell Street, carries exclusive Italian fashions; **Sara Boutique,** 10 Water Street, custom-designed bridal wear.

Two popular second-hand stores—**Cabbages and Kinx,** 306 West Cordova Street, and **Deluxe Junk,** next door at 310 West Cordova—are stocked with 50's styles for the 'new wave' look of the 80's. Gastown's two largest antique stores, among the many in the area, are **Antique Village Market,** 21 Columbia Street, and the **Gastown Emporium,** 49 Powell Street.

And, although Gastown is primarily known for its specialty shopping, two of Vancouver's most frequented department stores are also here. The **Army Navy Store,** 27 West Hastings Street, sells clothing, household items, and all the raingear you might suddenly need, at bargain-basement discount prices. **Woodward's,** 101 West Hastings Street, is the oldest department store in the city. Its ''Food Floor'' is famous, and the whole store, Vancouver's answer to Harrod's.

It's easy to find an inexpensive lunch or snack in Gastown. At the back of The Courtyard, 131 Water Street, is the **Cottage Deli,** where you can sit outside over a splendid harbour view with soup and a sandwich. **Frannie's Deli,** 325 Cambie Street, which opens at 6:30 am, is popular for breakfast as well as lunch. **The Windsor Tea, Coffee and Chocolate Shoppe,** 73 Water Street, combines an English sweet shop with a comfortable cafeteria-style dining room in the back. The scones are delicious, and while you eat you can have your Tarot cards read.

With its international selection of restaurants, Gastown is also a favourite for evening dining. **Umberto Al Porto** (683–8376), 321 Water Street, at the end of a long corridor, looks out over the harbour from the north side of Gastown. Being one of Umberto Menghi's restaurants, its Italian fare is excellent; more surprisingly, in this case, it's moderately priced. **Brother's,** (683–9124), 1 Water Street, is known for its steak, seafood and waiters dressed as monks. Another eating experience is to be had at the **Mediaeval Inn,** 50 Powell, where buxom lasses serve customers feasting communally at long tables.

Sophie's (669–2649), 32 Abbott Street, a cozy pub/restaurant for Greek and Italian food, is popular with the late night opera crowd. **Le Brasserie de l'Horlage** (685–4835), 300 Water Street, has a reputation for its reasonably-priced, French provincial style; the **Maharajah** (685–6714), 137A Water Street, is one of Vancouver's oldest Indian restaurants; and the **Kilimanjaro** (681–9913), 308 Water Street, serves very spicey east-African cuisine. Tucked away beside the railway tracks north of Water Street is **Le Railcar** (685–6252), 106 Carrall Street, which is just that, converted into a small but delightful French restaurant, more romantic than expensive. To top off this tour of international specialty eating is **La Brochette** (684–0631), 52 Alexander Street, the first French rotisserie-style restaurant in North America. The rotisserie itself, on which food is prepared in an open front kitchen, is 218 years old. After dinner you can relax downstairs around a huge,

Steam clock, Gastown

stone fireplace. The restaurant boasts, by the way, Vancouver's largest wine cellar.

At night Gastown stays awake not only to eating but to the sounds of music. In an area of about one block, there is more choice in evening listening than on your AM radio dial. **The Town Pump,** 66 Water Street, has both a dance hall which hosts live rock bands as well as a lounge, comfortably detached from the dance-floor's vibrations, with old English furniture and a fireplace. At Abbott Street and Water, is **The Lamplighter Hotel,** where another pub has dancing to top 40s records. **The Savoy Cabaret,** 6 Powell Street, above the street level, pumps out rock and roll until the wee hours, and around the corner at the **Blarney Stone,** 216 Carrall Street, you'll find the best in Irish entertainment.

At **The Classical Joint,** 231 Carrall Street, the listening is more intense, coffee imbibed, and the reputation of this longtime establishment secure. It has a loyal following of listeners, chess players and late night coffee drinkers for the blue-grass, jazz, and excellent musicians that this club draws.

For nightclubbing, **Punchlines** at 216 Water Street is into laughs with acts from Los Angeles, Toronto, and hometown; Tuesday nights are reserved for amateurs. We are eagerly awaiting the opening of a new club, **Ammnesia,** 99 Powell, which claims it will be "a nightclub you will never forget."

Theatre has also taken up residence among Gastown's nighttime crowds. **The Firehall Theatre,** 280 East Cordova Street, houses several companies and has an active schedule of musical and theatrical events. More on the fringe (of both theatre and Gastown) is **The Actors Institute of Vancouver,** 102 Powell Street, which is refurbishing this warehouse as a centre for creative productions. The building promises to be intriguing; while under reconstruction, it is still a little rough around the edges.

So there it is. Complete with **Wax Museum,** 21 Water Street on Maple Tree Square, short-term and emergency daycare at **Crabtree Corner** (689–2808), 101 East Cordova Street (sponsored by the YWCA and for youngsters 6 weeks to 5 years old), and **Visitors Bureau** branch in Le Magasin Mall. It's true that Gastown is an old story, but one with, in fact, no ending at all. As new shops, businesses and clubs open there every year, Gastown continues to grow, specialising by day in shopping and atmosphere, by night in eating and musical ambience of your choice. "Gassy" Jack himself would have thought that his town had done him proud.

11 *Chinatown*

by Ina Lee

With its turn of the century buildings painted shades of red, street lamps of the same vintage, dancing neon signs, temple-style phone booths and bustling tempo, Chinatown is as unmistakable as it is inviting.

It's also as old as the city itself. Carrall Street on the south side of Pender is the site of what was once **Shanghai Alley,** where the Chinese first settled in the 1880's. (It's marked with a sign on Pender, 50 feet west of Carrall.)

These early settlers were mostly men who had left their villages in southern China to work in British Columbia's gold and coal mines, on the Canadian Pacific Railway or as farm labourers. In these early days the Chinese were denied citizenship and the right to vote, Chinese immigration was taxed and employment of Chinese was restricted. It wasn't until the end of World War II that attitudes improved. From then on Chinatown has flourished, expanding eastward along Pender and continuing to grow today.

Though most of Vancouver's 100,000 Chinese residents live outside Chinatown, its Chinese schools, banks, churches, newspapers, cultural and athletic clubs, movie theatres and live entertainment make it the central focus of the community.

Visitors and Vancouverites in general flock to Chinatown for its festivals and special events, not to mention some of the best, most reasonably priced shopping and dining in town.

To get acquainted with Chinatown, walk its three main blocks east along Pender, from Carrall to Gore, up 1 block to Keefer and west back to Carrall again.

The Pender and Carrall Street intersection is both the historic and modern day heart of Chinatown. No. 9 Pender, on the northwest corner is the original and still functioning head-quarters of the **Chinese Freemasons.** In the early 1900's it was frequented by Dr. Sun Yat-Sen, father of the Chinese Revolution.

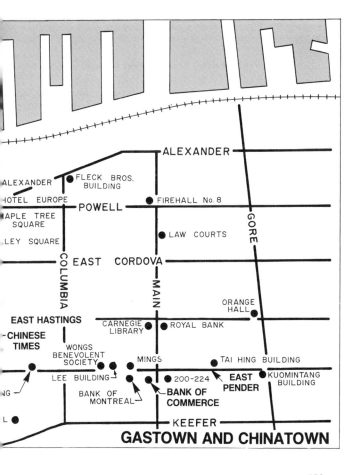

GASTOWN AND CHINATOWN

Directly across the street on Pender is the **Chinese Free Press** where, since 1907, the Freemasons have published Canada's oldest, daily newspaper, in Chinese only. Today its circulation extends to Chinese communities throughout western Canada.

No. 8 Pender, on the southwest corner, being 5 ft. in width, is reputedly the world's narrowest building.

Across the street (on the southeast corner) is the complex housing the **Chinese East Cultural Centre,** with administrative and educational facilities, commercial space and new Multipurpose Hall.

Adjacent to it is the **Dr. Sun Yat-Sen Park,** complete with man-made lake. its walled classical Chinese garden is the first full-scale Ming Dynasty garden to have been built either in or outside China since 1492. Designed after the 15th century garden compound of Suzhou, China's foremost 'garden' city, it's a showpiece of landscaping artistry with framed views, intimate spaces, rockeries, bridges, temples and a profusion of plants and trees. The gardens were recently constructed, in time for Expo '86. For more details contact the Chinese Cultural Centre (687–0729) or the Dr. Sun Yat-Sen Garden office (689–7133).

East from here along Pender is Chinatown's shopping district where curio shops sell their standard wares of incense burners, carved Buddhas and perfumed fans. It is also the place to look for silks, lacquerware, embroidery and chinaware. **Ming Wo Ltd,** 23 East Pender, is packed full of just about every kitchen utensil imaginable. The bamboo steamers used in preparing dim sum are sold here.

China West Merchandise, 41 East Pender, is a cheerful clutter of singing toy birds, kites, chimes and cleverly made trinkets—a great place for children's treats. Don't leave without giving the paper yoyo a go.

Universal Arts, 49 East Pender, is a wee and crowded shop where you can find inks, brushes, rice paper and a 'how to' booklet on Chinese ink painting.

Cathay Importers, 104 East Pender, is well stocked with rattan and bamboo products, and **Gim Lee Yuen,** 75 East Pender, is another good all-purpose store selling that most comfortable of shoes, the Chinese slipper. As do many of these shops, it carries specialty food items—dried octopus, lotus root, and one that caught my eye, canned, pickled lettuce.

Ripley's Shallowest ("Narrowest") Building, Chinatown

Speaking of food, this same stretch of Pender offers a good selection of restaurants. Most are Cantonese, the area of origin of many our city's residents. A few serve the spicier Mandarin and Szechuan cuisine.

At the won-ton and noodle houses you can watch the cook

prepare a quick and tasty meal from his store front kitchen. Then there's **Ho-In Chop Suey,** 79 East Pender, a great 'greasy spoon', early '30's style.

That most popular of dining traditions, dim sum lunch, meaning literally 'heart's delight,' is offered at **Ming's,** 147 East Pender. Steaming hot bamboo baskets are brought to your table with samplings of shrimp and pork stuffed dumplings, spicey spareribs, spring rolls and other sumptuous delicacies.

There are many good dim sum restaurants elsewhere in Chinatown. Try the **Golden Crown,** 124 West Hastings, the **King's Garden,** 238 Keefer, or the **Park Lock**, 544 Main Street.

When you come across an herbal shop, as you will along East Pender or Main, don't go by without taking a closer look. The art and science of herbal medicine is as ancient for the Chinese as it is strange to us. An herbalist on the premise will prescribe cures for his clients and make them on the spot from an amazing assortment of teas, raw or dried herbs and animal matter. The bill might well be added, by the way, with an abacas.

East of Main on Pender, you'll find yourself amidst grocery stores, meat markets and bakeries. The vegetables, teas, dried and canned foods sold here are found only in Chinatown. In the meat markets, the aroma of barbecued pork, duck and pig, and sausages that hang in the windows is irresistible, the taste testimony to China's 4000 years of barbecuing experience.

Chinese baked goods are really delicious. On Keefer just west of Gore, it's hard to resist **Loong Foong Restaurant and Bakery,** serving Chinese-style, cookies, cakes rolls and a particular favourite, the barbecued pork bun.

The largest and best known of Chinatown's special events is the **'Spring Festival,'** a celebration of the Chinese New Year, held on the lunar new year in mid-January or February. Lions perform their way down Pender Street to the sound of drums and firecrackers. Occasionally the parade includes the dramatic and colourful dance of the dragon.

Though historically rich and fascinating to see, Chinatown is no museum, nor is it strictly for tourists. It is a living heart of Vancouver's large Chinese community. Without the cultural and commercial vitality of Chinatown, Vancouver simply would not be the same.

12 *Vancouver and the sea*

THE WATERFRONTS

Founded on the proximity of water for logging and industrial purposes, Vancouver's waterfronts on Burrard Inlet, Coal Harbour, English Bay, both downtown and lapping the lengths of its North and South Shores, and False Creek today host ocean-going liners and freighters, airplanes, yachts, catamarans, windsurfers, swimmers and good tans. False Creek is hosting Expo.

Burrard Inlet

Early explorers, engaged in the search for a Northwest Passage, paid little attention to the superb landlocked harbour of Burrard Inlet. Nor, at first, did the city. Initially, Vancouver's growth stemmed from the forests and depended on the sea only for transportation between stump and sawmill.

But when the railway arrived from the east, the city suddenly became a port of note for the trans-shipment of western grain, and in 1911 the completion of the Panama Canal situated Vancouver's extensive, deep-water waterfronts at a crossroads of major trading routes of the world.

From **Lions Gate Bridge** to **Port Moody** extend the 19

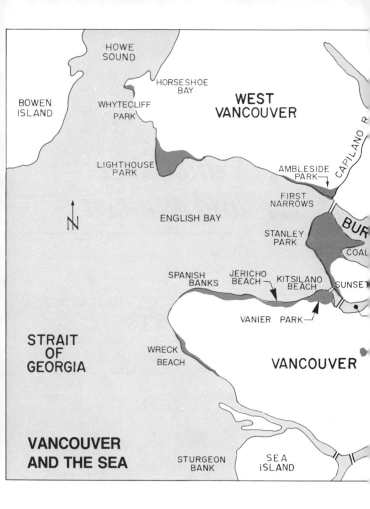

HOWE
SOUND

HORSESHOE
BAY

WEST
VANCOUVER

BOWEN
ISLAND

WHYTECLIFF
PARK

CAPILANO R.

LIGHTHOUSE
PARK

AMBLESIDE
PARK

FIRST
NARROWS

ENGLISH BAY

BUR

STANLEY
PARK

COAL

SPANISH
BANKS

JERICHO
BEACH

KITSILANO
BEACH

SUNSET

N

VANIER PARK

STRAIT
OF
GEORGIA

WRECK
BEACH

VANCOUVER

VANCOUVER
AND THE SEA

STURGEON
BANK

SEA
ISLAND

kilometres (12 mi) of Burrard Inlet, the Bridge itself crossing
what is known on the water as the First Narrows. The bridge
was built in 1938 by the Guinness family of beer-fame to enhance development of the British Properties in West
Vancouver—which they owned. In 1955 it was sold to the

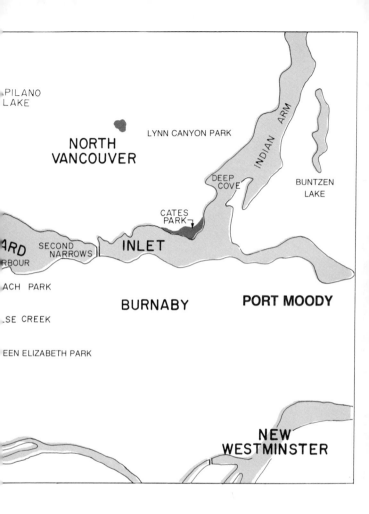

PILANO
LAKE

NORTH
VANCOUVER

LYNN CANYON PARK

INDIAN ARM

DEEP
COVE

BUNTZEN
LAKE

CATES
PARK

ARD
RBOUR

SECOND
NARROWS

INLET

ACH PARK

BURNABY

PORT MOODY

SE CREEK

EEN ELIZABETH PARK

NEW
WESTMINSTER

Provincial Government for $6 million but remained a toll-bridge until 1963. Cars were 25¢; pedestrians paid a nickle.

Two mountain peaks on the North Shore, **The Lions,** gave their name to the Bridge. Indian inhabitants of this area know The Lions as ''The Two Sisters''—ladies who insisted on inviting an entire enemy tribe to the party given in their honour. The Great Peace initiated by this potlatch immortalized their story, and they remain forever the twin peaks of Peace and Brotherhood looking over the city.

Further east, the Inlet is spanned by yet another bridge—at Second Narrows. The original bridge here was built in 1925 and accommodated both road and rail traffic. It was subsequently plagued with ups and downs. Several run-ins with passing freighters led to closures, and finally in 1957 steps were taken towards the building of a new bridge. On June 17, 1958, disaster struck, as the unfinished steel and concrete structure collapsed and nineteen men lost their lives. When the second **Second Narrows Bridge** opened in 1960, the ceremonies included sad reminders of a tragic event.

Throughout Vancouver's history, the site of the present Pacific National Exhibition grounds has been a recreational location. Early in the 1860s, Oliver Hocking settled at the mouth of the creek that now runs through Exhibition Park, and built Vancouver's first bridge across this ravine to connect travellers with the "End of the Road". Later, the area became known as Brighton or New Brighton, and the Brighton Hotel advertised itself as "The Most Fashionable Watering Place in British Columbia." Today, the New Brighton Pool carries on the tradition of seaside resort.

Historically, Vancouver's first export came from the North Shore of Burrard Inlet, from Pioneer Mill in 1864. The harbour really took root, however, on the south shore around Gastown and **Hastings Mill.** Since then, the Port of Vancouver has grown to cover a total water area of 555 sq km (214 sq mi), extending from Port Moody to Roberts Bank near the American border. It ranks first in size not only in Canada, but among ports along the North American Pacific seaboard.

Between Lions Gate Bridge and Port Moody, the **Inner Harbour** is lined with docking facilities and industrial maritime activity, particularly between the two bridges. Tugs push freighters around; giant cranes perch over vessels, and fork-lift trucks load and unload them; transports and trains pull up to discharge or pick up cargo.

Centennial Pier. At the foot of Heatley Avenue on the south shore of Burrard Inlet, east of Gastown, Centennial Pier (built in 1958) occupies the site of the old Hastings Mill and incorporates Ballantyne Pier, the oldest pier still in existence. All that remains of the Mill is the old office building now used by **The Missions to Seamen.** Although not open to the general public, this historic building is still very much a living part of the harbour. The original mill store was moved to the foot of Alma Street near the Vancouver Yacht Club and constitutes the Old Hastings Mill Store Museum.

Campbell Avenue Fish Docks. Immediately to the east are the Campbell Avenue Fish Docks, where the counter-style **Marine View Coffee Shop** lives up to its long-standing reputation for excellent fish and a view of the piers where the fishing boats unload. To get there, take the Heatley Avenue Overpass, veer right, and then turn left.

B.C. Sugar Museum. Beside the Fish Docks, at the foot of Rogers, is the B.C. Sugar Refinery. Here the B.C. Sugar Museum provides historical displays, a tour of the refinery, and a film, gratis. Open Monday through Friday, 8:30 am to 4 pm. For group arrangements contact someone at the refinery (253–1131).

Vanterm. The Port of Vancouver's Vanterm, next door at the north foot of Clark Drive, covers 76 acres of waterfront property. This terminus has a special public viewing area where you can watch the activities at the port facility. Open 9 am to noon and 1 to 4 pm during the summer; no admission charge. Parking is no problem. For group tours and information, call 666–6129.

The Cannery. Further along this south shore is the very popular dinner spot, **The Cannery Seafood Restaurant,** 2205 Commissioner (254–9606). To get there, it's best to take a cab. If you *insist* on driving yourself, Commissioner is a right-hand turn off Victoria Drive once you are past the railway tracks north of Powell Street. Follow along dockside a ways. You can't miss it.

Lynnterm and Seaboard. From any of these above spots along the south shore, you will see such North Shore terminals as Pioneer Grain, the Saskatchewan Wheat Pool, Seaboard and Lynnterm, the last two right beside the Second Narrows Bridge. Lynnterm, newest of the port facilities, includes 67 acres of dock space backed by a 29-acre industrial park. It handles steel and forest products in particular. **Seaboard,** immediately to the west, is famous. Presently this forest products facility is the largest of its kind in the world.

Freighters passing beyond the Second Narrows Bridge may be heading for the oil terminals situated up the Inlet or may be going the whole 7 miles (oops, 11 km) to the Pacific Coast Bulk Terminals at Port Moody for coal or sulphur.

Despite all the traffic, **Cates Park** at the Deep Cove corner of Burrard Inlet and Indian Arm in North Vancouver has lovely clear water for swimming. Looking up the deep fjord of Indian Arm on one side and out past the city and docks on the other, Cates Park has a picnic area, a playground for children, and a boat-launching site. Hiking trails are nearby.

North Vancouver, east of the Lions Gate Bridge as far as Indian Arm, is the birthplace of Vancouver industry. In 1865, Pioneer Mill was taken over by Sewell Prescott Moody and renamed Burrard Inlet Lumber Mills. Moody ran a tight ship of a lumber town and Moodyville flourished, for a time leading Hastings and Gastown in the population race.

Mr. Dollar, an American with a mill of his own, gives his name to the Dollarton Highway, east of the Second Narrows Bridge, which runs past Cates Park to Deep Cove and up along Indian Arm.

Coal Harbour

The shoreline curving from Canada Place near the foot of Granville Street west to Stanley Park delimits Coal Harbour on the downtown waterfront. When the Georgia Street causeway was built to allow access to Stanley Park, it cut Lost Lagoon off from the effects of Coal Harbour tides. That body of water had been the writer E. Pauline Johnson's favourite canoeing haunt, and she named it ''lost'' for the fact that it became no more than a shallow lagoon at low tide.

At the other and eastern end of Coal Harbour is the railway terminal where the first train to cross the west of Canada pulled in one hundred years ago. Today, the CPR station is the Vancouver terminus for the SeaBus which crosses Burrard Inlet to the North Vancouver landing at Lonsdale Quay.

Coal Harbour's relatively quiet waters are also the downtown landing site for a number of airlines that fly the British Columbia coast. Sea-planes for Victoria's downtown harbour take off regularly. Offshore, floating in the waters are the sea-borne gas stations that must fuel these and other flights.

With an ALRT station being built on the shore—Waterfront Station—and road access being improved, the face of the waterfront is changing. The Pan Pacific Hotel and Canada Place Pavilion stretching out into the water in front of it will give the shore an entirely new character. After Expo, Canada Place will become a trade and convention centre.

At the Stanley Park end of Coal Harbour, past the boat charter docks, marine supply outlets, and Keg restaurants, the Westin Bayshore Hotel has its waterfront berth. The entrance to the hotel and access to this waterfront area is to the left and right of the foot of Cardero Street. To reach the western end of Coal Harbour, take Burrard Street north to the shore.

False Creek

By the 1930s, some forty sawmills, a steel mill, and pulp factories thickly lined the shores of the False Creek industrial centre, and the ''creek'' had become one of the dirtiest bodies of water in Canada. At times, the smoke that rose from the area would block out the sun, and some mayoralty candidates even advocated filling the whole waterbody in.

The Creek takes its name from a canoe passage that used to appear only during high tides between this inlet and Burrard Inlet to the north. Since its industrial heyday's beginnings its size has in fact been reduced to one third of what it originally was.

Today, the sawmills are gone, the last lumberyard has just closed, and the waters are coming clean. The whole area has been re-zoned for the largest single urban development in Vancouver's history. The south side of the Creek has already gotten the treatment; Granville Island continues to find itself; and the north side of this inlet has leapt into the lime-light of Expo.

It was here in **Yaletown** in 1886 that the Great Fire of Vancouver started in a logging camp on the creek's shore. Factories and warehouses succeeded the lumbermen, and in the 1960s and 1970s there were plans to recycle them as living spaces. Then the city built its sportsdome, and plans got underway for the world fair.

From Pacific Avenue in the West End, you can reach Granville by "aquabus." It leaves the English Bay waterfront, west of the Aquatic Centre (at the Burrard Street Bridge) and stops at several points on the island. You can hop the aquabus until 8 pm; this is one way of avoiding Granville Island parking.

One unusual community "on" the island you might overlook is the houseboat neighbourhood. These seahomes roll on the gentle swells behind Emily Carr College of Art. The owners' ingenuity in living on their sea legs is worth a look.

English Bay

Beyond Burrard Inlet, in the Outer Harbour, freighters park on **English Bay.** It stretches from the Lions Gate Bridge at First Narrows and from the Burrard Street Bridge at the entrance to False Creek to the waters of the Georgia Strait. Landside, at Denman and Davie Streets in the West End, is the beach of the same name.

Vancouver's first beach-bathing facility was built here on **English Bay Beach,** also known as **First Beach,** in 1905. The beach has already been a popular haunt for sun-worshippers since the 1890s, when Joe Fortes set up house in Alexandra Park, where his statue now stands. Turning his back on a Gastown bartender's life, Joe devoted himself to caring for the beach, teaching bathers to swim, and rescuing those who couldn't. This popular beach has more recently been called "Waikiki with cold water."

On the shores of Stanley Park, and connected to them by walkways along the water from First Beach, are **Second Beach** and **Third Beach**, still waiting for more distinguished names. You can walk the several miles from the isolation of Third Beach in the Park all the way to the bustle of False Creek. Just outside False Creek itself (which begins with the Burrard Street Bridge), new beach has been added to the shore. It hasn't yet been named. At "it" is the **Aquatic Centre,** 1050 Beach Avenue (689–7156), a public, Olympic-sized, indoor swimming facility with salt water.

The South Shore

On the other end of the Burrard Street Bridge, across from the Aquatic Centre, is **Vanier Park,** location of the City Ar-

The West End, English Bay

chives, the Vancouver Academy of Music, the Burrard Street Civic Marina, the Coast Guard station, the Vancouver Museum and Planetarium, lawns for picnics and kite-flying, a bicycle path, and a boat-launch ramp.

From the Maritime Museum, parkland joins Vanier park to **Kitsilano Beach,** where suntanning, swimming, wind-surfing (and board rentals), basketball, beach volleyball, and hotdog-eating continue all summer long. The Kitsilano Swimming Pool, an immense, outdoor, saltwater pool is very popular. Winters it becomes home to local ducks and shorebirds. Summer evenings, bands play at the Kitsilano Show Boat by the pool, after it has closed and as the sun sets over Bowen Island. Near Kits Beach, there are plenty of eateries of all styles in "downtown" Kitsilano at Yew Street.

Further west again, between Kits and Jericho Beach, walking is possible at low tide (but in some discomfort) or necessitates taking to busy Cornwall Avenue for some blocks. At various places, public walkways lead down to the stoney waterfront. If you continue on past the corner at Alma Street, where the Old Hastings Mill Store Museum stands, past the Jericho Tennis Club, Vancouver Yacht Club, and Brock House, you will reach the eastern end of what is continuous parkland from there to Wreck Beach on the tip of this South Shore (Point Grey) peninsula.

The first section is **Hastings Mill Park,** where Jeremiah Rogers used to run a logging operation. Originally called Jerry's Cove, some say this name was abbreviated to Jericho. Now a park and picnic area of that name, this former golf course was taken over by the Department of National Defence, and became a boat and airplane base. In 1972, they turned it over to the city's Parks Board, and in 1978, much against the protests of those using the vacant hangar space, two of the old hangars were torn down. The others mysteriously burned down a year later. The cement wharves where these were are still here.

Next door to them is the Jericho Sailing Club, behind which are public tennis courts, soccer fields, and a baseball diamond. On Discovery Road here lives the Vancouver Youth Hostel.

From Jericho, right around the UBC peninsula through **Jericho, Locarno, Spanish Banks,** and **Wreck** (this last for the total tan enthusiast)—the beaches continue. The name "Spanish Banks" commemorates Captain Vancouver's 1792 meeting with the Spanish explorers, Galiano and Valdes. At low tide, the flats here stretch out as far as 250 metres. During the late spring and summer, smelt fishermen string their nets out into the water, and crab-catchers drop their traps off the piers. From anywhere along the shores here, the views of the mountains, Stanley Park and the city are grand.

Landside of Spanish Banks, N.W. Marine Drive leaves the water behind and climbs Point Grey. The section of beach beyond here will appeal to those who prefer to do their sunbathing in the buff. It used to be located discreetly around the

Horseshoe Bay, West Vancouver

corner, until the Parks Board decided to attack the erosion problem. New sand was poured over a foundation of cobble-stones to hold the old sand in place. One winter's weather blew it all away—down toward Spanish Banks—leaving the cobble-stones bare. Faithful sun worshippers have followed their sand.

South from Old Wreck Beach on the other side of the penin-sula, the Fraser River meets the sea. Log-booms line this side of the shore. And south of the river are the Vancouver Interna-tional Airport in Richmond, the flatlands of the Fraser delta, Roberts Bank (the major facility of the Outer Harbour), and the B.C. Ferry Terminal at Tsawwassen.

West Vancouver's Shore

Due (fairly) north of Point Grey, across the waters of English Bay, **Lighthouse Park** marks the entrance to Howe Sound. Its ninety acres of forest, looking much as it must have to the early explorers, surround this rocky point which juts out into English Bay. Built in 1875, the lighthouse was accessible only by water until 1928 when Marine Drive reached Horseshoe Bay. The forest today is a public park, and the rocky shores good for fishing, sunbathing, or practising rock-climbing.

Horseshoe Bay, around the corner on Howe Sound, is now the terminus for ferries to Nanaimo, the Sechelt Peninsula

(Sunshine Coast), and Bowen Island. Even though technically in West Vancouver, this intimate community is removed from the big-city atmosphere. On the main street, **Troll's Seafood Restaurant**—a family business—has been in operation since 1946. A few doors away is the **Troller's Pub,** which makes its own beer. On the shore, another business, **Sewell's Landing Horseshoe Bay Marina,** was founded in 1919 and is still owned by the same family.

West of Horseshoe Bay on Marine Drive is the little community of **Whytecliff,** where fascinating homes hang on the cliffs and blend with the natural woods setting. A little park on the shore here affords an excellent view of English Bay and the entrance to Howe Sound. Ferries bound for Vancouver Island pass directly in front of its shores. A Colonel Whyte was originally responsible for this subdivision early in the century and hoped that the planned University of British Columbia would be established there. It is said that he changed the spelling of Whitecliff Bay a touch.

The district of **West Vancouver**—not to be confused with downtown's West End—extends along the lower slopes of the North Shore mountains from Howe Sound to the Capilano River at the Lions Gate Bridge. The slow and scenic route along here is Marine Drive. On the shores of English Bay east of Whytecliff, are several beaches—Steerman, Caulfield Park and Tiddly Cove. Walkways between them are not continuous, but each does have an access from Marine Drive. These lovely, privately public shores between the rocky outcrops of the feet of the mountains are excellent for swimming and study of an intertidal zone.

From Dundarave on Marine Drive, the first shopping district east of Horseshoe Bay, to Ambleside Park at 13th Street near the Lions Gate Bridge, a continuous seawall called Centennial Walk follows the shore. At **Ambleside Park** itself, there are playing grounds, tennis courts, pitch and putt as well as swimming or salmon fishing. Across the way one can see the Stanley Park heights of Prospect Point, and the Park's seawall which continues around its shore toward Third Beach and the West End's beach at English Bay.

For recreation programmes on the beaches of the City of Vancouver, call the **Parks and Recreation Board,** 2099 Beach Avenue (681–1141). For activities in West Vancouver, call that municipality's **Parks and Recreation Administrative Office,** 750–17th Street (922–1211).

CHARTERS

Several of the city's numerous marine charter companies have their docks right on Coal Harbour. Overall they range from vessels which can be chartered for wedding parties, cruises, and conferences to those which can be had for a day's sail or a fishing trip.

The commodious stern-wheelers owned by Harbour Ferries, at the foot of Denman Street, used for touring the harbour and for the False Creek runs between the waterfront gates of Expo, are available for charter when not being used on their regular runs. This company also owns the *MV Britannia* which ferries the Royal Hudson train passengers between Vancouver and Britannia Beach up Howe Sound all summer. When not in service, this vessel is also available for charter. You can write **Harbour Ferries,** #1 North Ft. Denman Street, Vancouver, B.C. V6G 2W9, or call them at 687–9558 to make arrangements.

The *Malibu Princess* also docks in Coal Harbour, two blocks west of Burrard Street at the Barbary Coast Yacht Basin. This company runs "Summer Sunday Picnic Cruises" to Keats Island, Bowen Island, and up Indian Arm. For information, call them at 685–8468, or write **Malibu Yacht Charters Limited,** North Ft. Bute Street, Box 1199, Postal Station A, Vancouver, B.C. V6C 2T1 about chartering this boat.

The *MV Norsal* docks at the Tradewinds Yacht Charters pier, north foot of Jervis Street. The sixty-year-old, 137-foot *Norsal* has seven staterooms and can graciously accommodate twelve passengers overnight. During the summer months, it becomes a floating hotel, anchored north of Vancouver Island in the Haida Pass area. For a minimum of three days, you can fly up there from Coal Harbour and fish off the boat. Food and gear are provided, as well as help in packaging your catch for transporting home.

To book on the *Norsal* or arrange to charter it at other times of the year, you can talk to Captain-owner Jack Fournier (669–0475), or write **Norsal Executive Cruises Ltd.,** P.O. Box 1077, Postal Station A, Vancouver, B.C. V6C 2P1.

Westin Bayshore Yacht Charters, 1601 West Georgia Street (682–3377), will arrange charters for harbour cruises, fishing, or touring Alaska. **Tradewinds Yacht Charters,** north foot of Jervis Street (683–1686), Box 2224, Vancouver V6B 3W2, has over 50 yachts and boats available. **Barbary Coast Yacht Basin Ltd.** (669–0088 or 682–8150), at the north foot of Bute Street, Box 1199, Station A, Vancouver V6C 2T1, advertises "one of B.C.'s largest charter fleets."

From **Dauntless Charters** (685–8820), 505 Broughton Street, P.O. Box 48644, Bentall Centre, Vancouver V7X 1A3, you can charter a 70-foot, privately skippered yacht for a 50-guest gathering or a 12-person cruise. They will arrange and cater harbour cruises, scenic cruises, and fishing trips.

If you would like to sail for from half a day up to a week on a comfortable (hot and cold running water) sailing vessel, you can charter the C & C40 *Vltava* from **Westcoast Productions Ltd.** (689–4805 or 669–6284), 501 West Georgia Street, Vancouver, V6B 1Z5.

In North Vancouver, **Indian Arm Charters** (929–2268), 2156 Banbury Street, has a variety of boats at moderate rates. And in West Vancouver, **Sewell's Landing Horseshoe Bay Marina** (921–7461), 6695 Nelson Street, will supply you with everything you need for a day's fishing, with or without skipper.

In False Creek, **Admiralty Yachts** (685–7371), 1812 Boatlift Lane, arranges chartered lunch and dinner cruises. A 40-foot sailboat *Redonda* (681–3474 or 291–1633) can be chartered for day sails with up to 12 people or cruises (sleeping four) to the Gulf Islands. **Artemis Charter Service** (683–0027) has the *MV Kristina Rose* for cruises or sport fishing.

On Granville Island are **Cassidy's Yacht Charters** (681–3474), 1253 Johnston Street, for day or longer cruises in sail or power boats; **Cooper Yacht Charters** (687–4110), 1625 Foreshore Walk, for sailing lessons and luxury cruises; **Pacific Quest Charters** (669–3361), 1811 Maritime Mews, for vacation charters, sail or power; and **Sea Wing Charters** (669–0840), 1818 Maritime Mews, which has 60 power and sail vessels, with or without skipper. **North South Travel,** 1664 Duranleau Street (683–5736) arranges world-wide charters and customized tours.

From the **Jib Set Sailing School** (689–1477), 1020 Beach

Avenue, next to the Aquatic Centre, you can charter keelboats for day-sailing, with or without skipper. As might be expected from its name, this company offers a programme of sailing instruction and cruise and learn vacations.

BOAT RENTALS

If you have your own boat or have rented one, there are public **boat-launching facilities** at Cates Park in North Vancouver, Vanier Park on English Bay in Kitsilano, Woods Island in North Richmond, Ferry Road in Delta, and Rocky Point in Port Moody.

In the False Creek area, you can rent power boats from **Granville Island Boat Rentals** (662–7225), in front of Bridges Restaurant; canoes for paddling in False Creek from **Vancouver Canoe and Kayak** (688–6010), 1666 Duranleau Street on Granville Island; kayaks from **Ecomarine Ocean Kayak Centre** (689–7575) 1668 Duranleau Street; rowboats from **Red & White Rowboat Rentals** at the Maritime Market on the southwest side of Granville Island; and inflatable boats from **Pak a Boat Rentals** (685–5738), 997 Beach Avenue near the Aquatic Centre.

Outward Bound (669–9196), #206–1656 Duranleau Street, Granville Island, offers courses in canoeing, kayaking (basic and ocean), and sailing. The **Jib Set Sailing School** (689–1477), 1020 Beach Avenue, will rent you a boat and/or teach you to sail it.

In the Horseshoe Bay area, **Sewell's Landing Horseshoe Bay Marina** (921–7461), 6695 Nelson Street, will both rent you a boat and supply all you need for fishing. **Bay Boat Rentals** (921–7654), 6395 Bay Street, in Horseshoe Bay, has thirty power boats suitable for four people, for rent. They are open March to the end of September. **Whytecliff Marina** (921–7242), 7120 Marine Drive, nearly in Horseshoe Bay, also has boats available.

MOORAGE

On anchoring in English Bay if you are coming to Expo, the long and the short of it is—YOU CAN'T. There are no facilities for landing from your boat, and city concerns about

Vanier Park, English Bay. Coast Guard Station

sewage as well as the large volume of commercial and recreation traffic make it impossible for the Outer Harbour to also host visiting boats.

There is, however, a moorage booking service, with hundreds and hundreds of slips listed — **B.C. Marine Reservations** (687–7447/SHIP), 1000 Beach Avenue, Suite 202, Vancouver, B.C. Canada V6E 1T7. A $10 placement fee is charged for each booking.

Also available in 1986 will be a special supplement to "Notice to Mariners," containing information about services for boaters, customs facilities and requirements, charts, and so on. "**The Expo 86 Marine Advisory**" will be available wherever marine supplies and information regularly are. You can also obtain it by sending an *address label* with your address clearly marked to Project Expo 86, Canadian Coast Guard, 224 West Esplanade, North Vancouver, B.C. V7M 3J7. "Written Notices to Shipping" can be obtained from the Canadian Coast Guard, 25 Huron Street, Victoria, B.C. V8V 4V9 or marine stores in Vancouver; "Notices to Mariners" from the Canadian Coast Guard, Transport Canada, Ottawa, Ontario K1A 0N7 or Bovey Marine Ltd, 570 Seymour Street, Vancouver (683–7475). For maps and charts, call Canadian Hydrographic Services, Victoria, B.C. (656–8348).

At the **Kitsilano Base of the Canadian Coast Guard,** 1661 Whyte Avenue, right outside the entrance to False Creek, there will be a marine information booth. Check with them about safety regulations, navigational hazards, and the like.

For those who would like a rest from cooking in their galleys, **Off the Cuff Provisioning Service** (734–3119), #1–1927 West Broadway (around the back), Vancouver, B.C. V6J 1Z3, specialises in catering to the cruising crowd. They can handle special diets, have a wide variety of menus, and will be happy to direct you to what best suits your needs in a charter outfit.

The following are companies that regularly have moorage available for visiting boats.

Bay Boat Rentals (921–7654), 6395 Bay Street, Horseshoe Bay. 3 or 4 dockside spaces at $10/day.

Benick's Marina (942–6698 or 942–6696), 1770 Freemont, Port Coquitlam. Room for 50 boats at $1.75/foot/month; $.50/foot/day.

Captain's Cove Marina (1978) Ltd (946–1244), 6100 Ferry

Street, Ladner. $.30/foot/night.

Cassidy's Yacht Charters (681–3474), Granville Island Marina, 1253 Johnston Street, Granville Island. 1 or 2 spaces regularly; 3 or 4 on weekends. $.75/foot/night; $1.50/foot/night during Expo. By reservation only.

Condo Marina Ltd (435–5247), 4178 Winnifred Street, Burnaby. Provides accommodation on shore, transportation to ALRT or airport, chauffeured shopping tours, and private moorage.

Jib Set Cruising Club (689–1477), 1020 Beach Avenue, False Creek. 4 or 5 spots available for 30- to 34-foot boats; $1.50/foot/day. Club facilities, showers, laundry available. Reservations necessary.

Pitt Meadows Marina (465–6969), 14179 Riechenback, Pitt Meadows. $.30/foot/day; $4/foot/month; $2.95/foot/month if paid 3 months in advance.

Reed Point Marina (931–2477), 850 Barnet Highway, Port Moody. 30 spaces; $180/month; $52.50/week; $9/day.

Sewell's Landing Horseshoe Bay Marina (921–7461), 6695 Nelson Street, Horseshoe Bay. Small amount of moorage at $.30/foot/night.

Shelter Island Marina (270–6272), 21260 Westminster Highway, Richmond. Space for 40 to 50 boats and for lengths up to 100 feet. $.25/foot/day; $4.50/foot/month. Dry-land and water moorage. Reservations required for larger vessels.

Whytecliff Marina (921–7242), 7120 Marine Drive, West Vancouver. Open moorage, especially for sailboats. $150/month; $50/week; $10/day.

False Creek Fisherman's Terminal (731–5913), 1505 West 1st Avenue, Vancouver, normally moore fishing boats but will be making open moorage available for temporary occupancy off the shore of Granville Island during Expo. Rates are $1.06/metre/day.

The following marinas have moorage available on an *ad hoc* basis, i.e., when permanently occupied berths are vacant.

Bayshore West Marina (682–2143), 1755 West Georgia Street, Vancouver. For smaller boats at $.50/foot/day.

Burrard Bridge Civic Marina (733–5833), South end Burrard Street Bridge, False Creek.

Granville Slopes Marina (687–6874), 1650 Granville Street, Vancouver. May have a couple of slips available during Expo.

Heather Civic Marina (874–2814), 600 Stamps Landing, False Creek. As a last resort and only if a member is away on his/her boat. Call in advance.

Spruce Harbour Marina (733–3512), 1015 Ironwork Passage, False Creek. May have moorage in slips temporarily vacated by members.

Tradewinds Yacht Charters (683–1686), North ft. Jervis Street, Coal Harbour. Have a few places depending on the size of the vessel. $6/foot/month; $.50/foot/night.

WHERE TO FISH
by Lee Straight

For sanity's sake—and because a nine-kilogram salmon doesn't sound half so impressive as a 20-pound salmon—poundage has won this conversion battle. If you do get mixed up in differences, just remember that one kilogram equals just over two pounds.

Famous though British Columbia is for trout and salmon fishing, it is mostly **salmon** that interest tourists—certainly on the coast. **Licences,** both annual and short-term, are required for either tidal waters or non-tidal fishing and each type is separate. Tidal waters are managed by the federal Department of Fisheries and Oceans, while management of non-tidal angling is delegated by the federal department to the provincial Fisheries Branch of the Ministry of Environment. For information on the respective kinds of angling, or their regulations, call the Department of Fisheries and Oceans at 666–3169, in Vancouver, and the provincial Fisheries Branch at the nearest office. The provincial phone numbers in the two largest centres of British Columbia are 584–8822 in Vancouver and 387–1724 in Victoria. Copies of the provincial **"Sport Fishing Regulations Synopsis"** (non-tidal) and the **"Tidal Waters Sport Fishing Guide"** (tidal) are available free at most sport shops and department stores, and list regional offices and phones.

The mail addresses for the departments are: Department of

Lee Straight with 14 1/2-lb steelhead trout

Fisheries and Oceans, 1090 West Pender St., Vancouver, B.C. V6E 2P1 (tidal) and Fisheries Branch, Ministry of Environment, Legislature, Victoria, B.C. V8V 1X5 (non-tidal).

Stream and lake fishing is seriously depleted and highly competitive within 240 km (150 mi) of Vancouver on the mainland. There is some trout fishing in spring and fall, for which a provincial licence is required (available at sport shops). Try the lakes in the area we call the Sunshine Coast, a ferry-ride across Howe Sound northwest of West Vancouver from Horseshoe Bay.

There's a spot of trouting available, if guided by a knowledgeable resident, up the Fraser Valley, 96 km (60 mi) to Harrison River (using waders), or in the Skagit River, south of Hope, 225 km (140 mi) from Vancouver's centre. Here fall trouting, again in waders, is challenging.

Other river fishing prospects in the area include barfishing with bait along the Fraser River at well-known access points, all months except June to August, and river-fishing for **steelhead rainbow trout** from Christmas to May.

Steelhead (sea-run rainbow trout) are also badly depleted. There is an ongoing salmon and sea-trout enhancement programme, however, which is rebuilding some stocks. The best prospects, and only if assisted by a resident or guide, are the Chilliwack-Vedder Rivers, 105 (65 mi) east of Vancouver, for winter-runs; and the Squamish and Cheakamus Rivers, 80 km (50 mi) north of Vancouver, between Squamish and Whistler Ski Village, for spring-run steelhead. The latter is heavily fished, best in March and April, and has special tackle restrictions.

There is some fair **coho** salmon spinfishing in the Squamish River, and coho bait fishing on the Fraser bars, in October. From August to October, there is exciting sport with hatchery-stocked cohoes in the Capilano River, right in West Vancouver, near the north end of the Lions Gate Bridge over the First Narrows.

Tackle used for trout fishing is the light spinning or fly tackle used throughout North America and Europe. Tackle used for river fishing for steelhead or salmon is heavy spinning or casting rods and reels.

There are five species of Pacific salmon, all of which may be encountered in rivers. But only two fresh-water species may be kept by anglers. All may be kept if caught in the sea. The two legal fresh-water catches are the coho and chinook.

The risk of mistakes is not great when river-fishing. You almost never catch a **sockeye** there, or in the sea. Only occasionally does a **chum** or **pink salmon,** which complete the list of the three illegal catches, take a lure. The latter two usually are accidentally snagged in the skin or a fin, though they occasionally strike at lures. If in doubt about the species of your catch, ask a nearby angler, or release the fish.

The main fishing around Vancouver is in the sea, and prospects are good—not as wonderful as tourist publicity may imply, but a top prospect for visitors who like to angle. There is sea-angling all year round here—better in winter than in summer. The waters of outer Burrard Inlet and Howe Sound, which supply most of our angling, are heavily silted by the Fraser and Squamish Rivers in the tourist months from June to early August. The visitor's chances of catching a salmon, guided or unguided, are best here from August to May.

In winter, the quarry are silver-bright, tasty, immature **chinook salmon,** running from 2 to 12 pounds in fall and winter, and up to 30 pounds in spring and summer. The odd lunker of 40 pounds is caught around here, but not nearly as often as further up the coast, or over on Vancouver Island.

Take-off points for fishing are Horseshoe Bay in winter and the marinas in West Vancouver from Fisherman's Cove to Lions Bay—the centre of the action being Horseshoe Bay and Sunset Marina. The action can start as soon as you pull away from the wharf. It's usually trolling, with rental tackle, unless you charter a boat. Charters may be arranged by phoning marinas at Horseshoe Bay, or by calling the Bayshore Inn Marina (689–7371). Check the listings earlier in this chapter for marinas, rates and boats available.

Visitors with more than a day to spare and who seriously seek salmon are advised to visit Secret Cove, Pender Harbour, or Egmont on the Sunshine Coast. These excellent spots are just two or three hours from the city centre—either busing or driving—by way of the Horseshoe Bay-Langdale ferry across Howe Sound.

There are boat rentals and charters at all three centres and salmon fishing the year round. A visit to Egmont is particularly exciting for fishing near the Sechelt Rapids of Skookumchuck Narrows. This area is always sheltered from heavy winds or seas.

Pender Harbour fishing is also attractive to those who don't relish tall seas. Most fishing is with light tackle and live herring bait, still-fishing in calm waters. The many arms of the harbour are a maze unless you keep a chart handy.

Tackle used for salmon is in two classes: nine- to eleven-foot limber rod and single-action reel carrying 300 yards or more of 20-pound-test line, for ''mooching'' (still-fishing with strip-cut, plug-cut or live herring or anchovy); or a stiff, six- to nine-foot rod and the same reel and line, for trolling a large

Lee Straight with 14-lb. chinook salmon

flasher-blade and lure or bait, held down by a heavy sinker. Marinas will explain the terminal hookups and supply what you don't have. Live bait is often difficult to obtain and its use is technical, but it is the most effective single bait. Trolling is a better prospect for the newcomer.

Bottom fish are more easily caught and often deliberately avoided by guides but are tasty and interesting. They can even be exciting to a visitor, who should understand that he won't offend a guide or charter skipper by asking to catch a few. Bottom fish considered delicacies are **snapper, rockfish (rock "cod"), sole, flounder, greenling, lingcod** and **perch.** Interesting, though seldom eaten, are **ratfish, dogfish, whiting, hake** and even the small **shiner perch** that can be caught on bits of seaworm or mussel meat from floats or wharves. The bottomfish can be caught on herring or shiner baits, dead or alive, by fishing on the sea-floor or near it, from boats or steep shores.

There is no public information bureau on fishing spots, itineraries or methods, but the **Fisheries and Oceans Depart-**

ment has a twenty-four hour answering service (666–3169), for sea-fishing reports on where the fish are biting. During office hours specific information is given. At other times, including the weekend, there's a recorded message. These reports cover the Vancouver, Victoria and Pender Harbour areas in winter, and other parts of the Strait of Georgia as well from spring to fall.

Freshwater licences are available at sport shops, by calling 435–4137, or by writing to **B.C. Fish and Wildlife Branch,** 4240 Manor Street, Burnaby, B.C. V5G 1B2.

The B.C. Wildlife Branch can also supply you with a list of freshwater fishing locations. This office and Woodward's Department Store, 101 West Hastings (684–5231), carry the **B.C. Sport Fishing Regulations.**

Lee Straight *is the recently retired recreational fisheries advisor to the Federal Department of Fisheries and Oceans, Pacific region. He was full-time outdoors editor for thirty-three years with the* **Vancouver Sun** *newspaper.*

Fees, non-tidal waters

If you live outside Canada: $23 annually; a six-consecutive-day licence, $12; for steelhead the licence is $15. If you are a Canadian but live outside of British Columbia: $15 annually; steelhead $15. Residents of British Columbia: $13 annually; steelhead $6.

Fees, tidal waters

Non-residents of Canada: $20 annually; $10 for three days; $3.50 per day. Residents of Canada: $5 annually; $3.50 per day.

13 *Vancouver above sea level*

VIEWPOINTS

Flying into Vancouver on a clear day, you will have a chance to see the setting for which the city is justly famous. Mountain ranges rise straight from the north shores of English Bay and Burrard Inlet, giving nearly everyone in town remarkable mountain views. The waters of the Georgia Straight and Vancouver harbour are protected from the open Pacific by Vancouver Island. It's rare to see whitecaps on the water here.

At night, you will be able to pick out the lights of **Grouse Mountain,** on all year and for nighttime skiing in winter. Grouse is 4,100 feet high, looks down on the heart of the city, and has a completely enclosed, multi-passenger gondola skyride to its top, all of twenty minutes from downtown Vancouver. From here, on a clear day, you can see Vancouver Island, the Fraser Delta and some of the peaks of Washington State. A short walk on the trail to Camel/Crown Mountains will show you the crowded mountain-range scenery to the north.

Cost of the Superskyride, open 10 am to 10 pm, seven days a week, is adults $7, seniors $4.50, children $3.50, families $18. A Summer Season's pass ($9.95) allows you to bring guests for 50 per cent off the regular fare. Up top are cafeterias and a dining room (the gondola ride is free if you have a reservation at The Grouse Nest), nature trails and mountain meadows, picnic areas and barbecue pits.

You can drive to the foot of the Superskyride by Capilano Road in North Vancouver. By bus, take the #246-Highlands bus going west on Georgia Street to Edgemont Village in North Vancouver where you transfer to a #232-Queens bus to Grouse Mountain. You can also pick up the #246-Highlands bus at the Lonsdale Quay SeaBus terminal in North Vancouver.

For general information and reservations on Grouse Mountain, call 984–0661; for special events and ski reports, call 986–6262; for the Ski School, call 980–9311.

East of Grouse, **Mount Seymour** looms over Burrard Inlet, Burnaby, and the whole of the lower mainland. Mount Seymour Provincial Park, thirty minutes from downtown Vancouver, is open 7 am to 11 pm, daily. The cafeteria and chairlift (weather permitting) are open 11 am to 5 pm seven days a week in July and August, weekends in September and October. They are naturally open for skiing when the snow arrives.

You can reach the Mount Seymour Parkway from Highway #1 in North Vancouver (the Upper Levels Highway) or from the north end of the Second Narrows Bridge via the Keith Road exit. There are plenty of picturesque picnic sites along the route up the mountain.

For information on Mount Seymour Provincial park, call 986–2261, 24 hours a day, or the Provincial Park office for Mount Seymour at 929–1291.

Cypress Bowl Provincial Park in West Vancouver comprises 12,645 acres and rises from the alpine valley floor of the bowl (itself at 3,000 feet) up the sides of Black, Strachan, and Hollyburn Mountains to elevations of up to 4,800 feet. The ten-mile Cypress Parkway to the bowl switchbacks up the West Vancouver mountain face, affording magnificent views of the Lower Mainland and the water between Vancouver and Vancouver Island. Access to the Parkway is from the Upper Levels Highway (Transcanada #1) near Horseshoe Bay in West Vancouver.

For information on Cypress Bowl Provincial Park, call their office in the park at 926–0314, or Hollyburn Ski Lodge at 922–0825, or for information on skiing, Cypress Park Resort at 922–4558.

Vancouver Art Gallery, Robson Square and Law Courts

Back in town, more modest but still outstanding heights rise to Simon Fraser University on Burnaby Mountain, to the Bloedel Conservatory in Queen Elizabeth Park (at 33rd Avenue and Cambie Street), and to the University of British Columbia on **Point Grey.** This latter plateau is fairly modern, having risen as glacial pressure retreated some 10,000 years ago. Simon Fraser University on its part sits beside mountain ranges 80 million years old. Its "mountain," **Burnaby Mountain,** although unprepossessing, has the air, scenery and vistas we associate with more spectacular altitudes.

The height of **Queen Elizabeth Park** may also seem insignificant—at a paltry 500 feet—but this elevation affords a quite spectacular 360° view of the city surrounding its peak. On top stands the **Bloedel Consevatory,** a glass dome housing plants and birds and some of the freshest air in the city.

For another 360° view, you can sit in the lounge on top of the **Sheraton-Landmark Hotel,** 1400 Robson Street (689–9211), 42 storeys above the street. A comfortable seat in this high spot will show you the sights starting at some point in the following sequence: Lions Gate Bridge, Grouse Mountain behind North Vancouver, Second Narrows Bridge and the mountains of Seymour Provincial Park beyond, Burnaby Mountain on which Simon Fraser University stands, East Vancouver, False Creek and the three bridges which cross it, Mount Baker, the International Airport, the city's South Shore from the dark green peninsula of UBC to Kitsilano, the Planetarium, English Bay and its ships, Stanley Park, Lighthouse Park across the water, the mountains of West Vancouver (Cypress and Hollyburn), the British Properties, and again the Lions Gate Bridge.

For a rising view of the city scene, you could take the external, glassed **Skylift elevator** of the **Harbour Centre Tower,** 555 West Hastings Street, to its 44th-storey observation deck. The deck is one of the pancakes you see sitting on top of this distinctive, downtown office tower. It is open seven days a week, 10 am to 10 pm, Fridays and Saturdays until midnight. Adults $1.50, seniors and children $1.

For information on the Skylift elevator and Observation Deck (which can be booked for parties or receptions), call 689–0421 or 683–5684. For the Harbour House Revolving Restaurant, in another of the horizontal, sky-riding pancakes, call 669–2220.

In lots of other places in town, a rise in the ground may suddenly surprise you with a striking scene. For instance, heading east from the University of British Columbia on 8th Avenue, at Sasamat the whole prospect of the North Shore, English Bay, downtown Vancouver, Burnaby, and even Mount Baker in the United States opens up to your view.

Everywhere you turn in this seaside/mountainside city, the environment will tend to pop out in unexpected ways with startling presence. You could meet a gull in mid-town, suddenly come upon the whole Fraser River delta, or catch a mountain looking over your shoulder. There are countless spots in which to contemplate its space or fly a kite.

If you want to fly yourself, try **hang-gliding**—now there's a view! Safer still, watch someone else set up and take off from the top of Grouse Mountain some Sunday afternoon in the nice weather.

Up in the mountains, you'll probably meet one of our best friends—the **whiskey jack.** This bird hangs out in groups in mountain woods, is a student of human nature, and seems particularly fond of peanut-butter cookies. He's bold once he knows you're a friend or a soft touch, and will land on your hand to eat.

Here's to sharing the view with a friend!

HIKING THE LOCAL HEIGHTS
by Fedor Frastacky

Mount Seymour

This is my personal (lazyman) favourite for a superb view with little effort. From the higher lookouts on Mount Seymour Parkway, the panorama sweeps from Indian Arm and the Fraser Valley in the east, past Mount Baker (always majestic when visible) in the south, to Georgia Strait and Vancouver Island (pray for a clear day) in the west. Below lies Vancouver, sometimes shrouded in mist (smog is something other people get) but always an impressive sight.

The road ultimately leads to several unspectacular parking lots and to a chairlift. The area is sub-alpine, mostly clear of trees, and therefore excellent for summer walking and winter skiing.

The chairlift operates daily in winter and summer, ferrying visitors up to Mystery Peak. While the view from the top of the chair is rewarding, those more physically-inclined may want to venture beyond on a well-marked trail to Brockton Point—or even further to the 1,454-metre elevation of Mount Seymour some 4 km (2½ mi) away.

Inexperienced walkers should be warned that the trail between Brockton and the summit is not well-marked and that the terrain includes rock scrambles and steep slopes. Great caution is required or you'll get lost. Nonetheless, for those who reach the summit, a superb view in all directions makes the effort worthwhile.

Beside the Mount Seymour Trail, there are eight others starting from the various parking lots. All the trails are well-marked and the majority of them are considerably less arduous than the trail to the summit. An easy walk with very little elevation change is the Goldie Lake Loop trail. This 2 km (over a mile) "trek" starts near the First Aid Building and winds around to Goldie Lake and back.

Overnight stays for self-contained recreational vehicles are allowed in Parking Lot 3 only. Alpine camping is permitted north of Brockton Point.

For further information contact District Superintendent, Mount Seymour Provincial Park, 1600 Indian River Drive, North Vancouver, B.C. V7G 1L3. Tel: 929–1291.

Hollyburn Mountain

This "neighbourhood mountain" in West Vancouver probably has some of the most pleasurable alpine trails on the North Shore. Cross over the Lions Gate Bridge and turn off in the direction of West Vancouver. Turn right at the first stop light, Taylor Way, and continue past the Upper Levels Highway into the British Properties. Follow Eyremount Drive to the parking area at the end of the road. Just beyond, visitors will find a logging road—this is the best starting point.

The logging road continues for several hundred yards and then forks. The right fork heads uphill and is the access to various well-marked trails leading to such delightful spots as Lost Lake, Brothers Canyon, and Blue Gentian Lake. The trails are not onerous and are often the scene of family outings complete with small children and dogs.

Fortunately, for those of us who like our comforts, most trails lead to Hollyburn Ski Lodge, Hollyburn Ridge, West Vancouver (922–0825), which is open year round. Beyond the lodge, trails tend to focus on Hollyburn Peak, winding through a mixture of treed areas and open meadows. The wide trails are well-marked and make for a pleasant countryside walk. The area directly around the summit has rocky outcrops—excellent spots for a picnic.

The rangers will give you more details. Contact the Holly-burn Ranger Station, Hollyburn Ridge, West Vancouver. Tel: 922–7933.

Cypress Bowl Provincial Park

Access to the hiking trails of and beginning in this Provincial Park is from the cross-country skiing parking lot, the first one you come to at the top of the Cypress Parkway, about 8 miles (13 kms) from the Upper Levels Highway and just past the Cypress Park Resort. The main trail from here goes to Holly-burn Mountain, from where, at 4,345 feet, you can ski to the downhill runs on Black and Strachan mountains.

For summers, the hiking trails to Deeks Lake and the Lions, whose peaks reside in the park, are being developed, and the brand-new Howe Sound Crest trail looks as if it will be a popular sub-alpine favourite. This trail begins at the logging slash between the chairlifts on Black and Strachan, and is part of a proposed hiking route to go all the way to Mount Garibaldi in the vicinity of Squamish. As far as The Lions, the trail is well-groomed and comfortably graded. Beyond this point, about an hour's walk from the start, it's a wilderness trail, at present only for serious and experienced hikers.

For information, phone or write the District Superintendent (929–3911), Cypress Provincial Park, 1600 Indian River Drive, North Vancouver, B.C. V7G 1L3 or the provincial park office in Cypress Park at 926–0314.

Grouse Mountain

The sometimes-marked trail to Goat Mountain begins to the left at the bottom of the chairlift and leads around Grouse's summit by a pointless but beautiful road. Just beyond is a bit of a rock scramble which should take you only a few minutes to traverse and which opens on to a very walkable trail. That's not

Downtown Vancouver looking east

to say it's flat. The trail actually climbs steeply, but the mountain must extort its small price for the richness of the views it offers. While by this time views of Vancouver and even Mount Baker may be old-hat to the visitor, few vantage points are better. Grouse-Goat also offers one of the few spots from which to view the mountains to the north. And just think — after a couple of hours of hiking, you can be back relaxing at the Grouse Nest, leisurely enjoying refreshments while waiting for the gondola ride back down the mountain.

For further information, contact Grouse Mountain, 6400 Nancy Greene Way, North Vancouver, B.C. V7R 4K9, telephone 984–0661.

Baden Powell Trail

Winding through the trees above the houses of North Vancouver, this trail provides easy walking and occasional glimpses of Vancouver spread out below. It connects with Capilano Canyon Regional Park and can be reached from there or from many of the North Vancouver roads which head up the mountains.

The Baden Powell Trail affords some of the safest hiking for the inexperienced. A **North Vancouver volunteer rescue group,** if notified by the police that someone is missing, can be out at the drop of a hat. They are well organised and experienced at looking for people on the mountainside. You can call them directly at the North and West Vancouver Emergency Program, 165 East 13th Street, North Vancouver—985-1311.

An avid skier, determined hiker, and agile rock-climber, **Fedor Frastacky** *misses the westcoast exhilaration of wilderness heights. He now does high finance in Toronto but spent eight years in Vancouver, hiking up and down mountains all over the province.*

WINGS OVER THE CITY
by John Rodgers

If you want to see at least some of Vancouver's remarkable bird-life—about 300 species are sighted in the city and its environs throughout the year—get out your walking shoes.

You should certainly become acquainted with the city's specialty, the **crested mynah,** which lives nowhere else in North America. Ornithologists come from all over to see this member of the starling family which sports a bushy crest, white patches on its wings, and a yellow bill. Locally, it is known as the Japanese or Chinese starling, because it was introduced here from Asia in the early years of this century. Our crested mynahs live in the streets, where they nest in trees, telephone poles and buildings. In recent years, its numbers have decreased, probably because the **starlings** have taken over some of its haunts. The best place to see them is in the southern areas of the city bordering the Fraser River.

Walking the **Stanley Park seawall** (a #11 downtown bus takes you to the Georgia Street entrance, or Robson and Davie Street buses will take you to the Davie Street entrance at Lost Lagoon), you could see **Barrow's goldeneyes, scaups,** and **surf scoters** in the hundreds, **wigeon, harlequin ducks, black**

turnstones, western grebes (5,000 have been counted in one flock at Ferguson Point), **horned grebes, glaucous-winged gulls, herring gulls, mew gulls, sanderlings, double-crested cormorants, pelagic cormorants, red-breasted mergansers, great blue herons, pigeon guillemots,** and our beach-combing **northwestern crows.**

On a good day, **common** and **red-throated loons, dunlins** feeding on the shore, or some **oldsquaw ducks** might be spotted. At migration time in the spring and fall, **western sandpipers, common terns,** and **Bonaparte gulls** stop for a while.

Along the woodland trails of Stanley Park, in summer listen for the "Quick—three beers" call of the **olive-sided flycatcher,** and in winter for the two haunting notes of the **varied thrush,** rarely found in Canada outside British Columbia. **Black-capped chickadees, chestnut-backed chickadees, rufous-sided towhees, downy woodpeckers, common flickers,** **Swainson's thrushes** (in summer), **white-crowned sparrows, golden-crowned sparrows, fox sparrows** (in winter), **golden-crowned kinglets, brown creepers, dark-eyed juncos, purple finches,** and **pine siskins** also live in these woods. In spring, **song sparrows** tirelessly sing their "Maids, maids, maids, pick up your tea-kettles, -ettles" song.

Several species of brightly-coloured **warblers,** the flighty troubadours of the woodlands, are seen at migration times.

Stanley Park's **Lost Lagoon** and **Beaver Lake** have a reputation for hospitality to winter-visiting water birds and others on migration. Among these are some already mentioned as well as **buffleheads, common goldeneyes, hooded mergansers, coots, ruddy ducks,** and **canvasbacks.** The local residents are **Canada geese, mallards, wood ducks** ("clad in wedding raiments"), and **red-winged blackbirds.** In summers, a pair of **ospreys** has been seen fishing in Lost Lagoon.

In a colony near the **zoo,** in two trees overlooking the open-air theatre of Malkin Bowl, the **Great Blue Herons** have nested for many years. This is one of the city's great wildlife spectacles.

At **Jericho Beach** (a #4 bus will take you there from downtown) and as far as Spanish Banks, you are likely to see **common murres** and **marbled murrelets** among the other birds in the winter.

In the forests of the **University Endowment Lands,** on the south side of English Bay (a #10 bus goes there), you could encounter species you may not have seen elsewhere—**rufous hummingbirds, goldfinches, cedar waxwings, Steller's jays, band-tailed pigeons, winter wrens, solitary, warbling and red-eyed vireos.** Another heronry is resident here, and **bald eagles** are not uncommon near the sea. Don't be surprised if you hear the squawk of a **ring-necked pheasant.**

Hummingbirds love the flowers of **Queen Elizabeth Park** (a #15 bus goes there), and along the edges of any of the city's golf courses, you can try to find a **killdeer's** nest. These plovers build on the ground, and will entertain you with their "wounded wing" act in an effort to decoy you away from their eggs if you should come too close.

Why not look for that sign of spring, the **robin.** Here they stay in town all year 'round. Amid the downtown uproar, you can admire our **house finches** and maybe even catch their songs. From early June to August, you could also see and hear **common nighthawks** "booming" and pirouetting above the streets. They nest on the tops of West End high rises.

Winter-visiting **red-tailed hawks** are seen in the Fraser Delta area, and even the occasional birdwatcher will want to visit the **Reifel Migratory Bird Sanctuary,** known throughout North America for its waterfowl. In the fall, **snow geese** from Soviet Siberia arrive to rest and feed on their way south. At this season, flocks on wing, thousands strong, fill the skies with their resonant calls. Here one can see **northern harriers,** sometimes in winter a **peregrine falcon,** and more rarely a **gyrfalcon. Marsh wrens** nest in the reeds.

The Sanctuary offers walks and nature talks, kits and birdseed. There are trails throughout, but some are closed at certain times of the year to protect the domestic privacy of the flying guests.

Reifel Migratory Bird Sanctuary is located at 5191 Robertson Road, R.R. #1, Delta (946–6980), less than an hour's drive from Vancouver. There's a small charge for admission. To get there, take Highway 99 over the Oak Street Bridge, turn off at the posting to Ladner, and continue along River Road for 2.9 km (1.8 mi). Cross the bridge on to Westham Island, and stay on the main road for 4.8 km (3 mi). Westham Island is visited by **snowy owls** from the Arctic even during the coldest days of most winters.

Among the many places close at hand, I also recommend the mountainous North Shore of Burrard Inlet. **Lighthouse Park** (the bus for Horseshoe Bay from Granville and Georgia streets will take you there) is a good spot, and **Mount Seymour Provincial Park** has the **blue grouse** among its many winged denizens.

On Sundays, the **Vancouver Natural History Society** (687–3333) makes birding trips. You would be welcome to join. At any time, if you should want information about our birds, I would be pleased to answer your questions (266–1939), providing, of course, I am not away on one of my own expeditions.

John Rodgers *wrote a weekly column,* **Wildlife,** *in the Leisure supplement of* **The Vancouver Sun.** *His book,* **The Birds of Vancouver,** *is now out of print. He has led birding parties to southern California, Hawaii, Texas, Bermuda, Scotland, and the Netherlands.*

14 *Vancouver in the rain*

If it's pouring, why not do what Vancouverites do—dress for it and forget it's happening. You'll be surprised at how many residents, accustomed to the ample annual rainfall, simply ignore it. Some keep a couple of green garbage bags in their cars in case of sudden downpours, but you can get more sophisticated rainwear at the **Army and Navy Department Store,** 27 West Hastings Street. And good rainboots too, if you want to keep your feet dry. Lots of Vancouverites don't bother.

One store is devoted entirely to the provision of umbrellas—**Vancouver Umbrella Ltd.,** 424 West Hastings Street (681–5271). Umbrellas always sell well, probably because they're the easiest thing in the world to lose, especially if the sun comes out during lunch. A distinguishing feature will help locate yours if you happen to leave it behind somewhere. (Have you ever seen two umbrellas trying to pass on a narrow sidewalk? It can often lead to comedy worthy of W. C. Fields.)

When you are in the city for only a few days and it's pouring buckets on one of them, some of the following indoor sights might keep the family off the streets and entertained. Details on museums and other centres appear in Chapter 6.

In the rain, you could ''get into'' west coast anthropology, starting with the **Museum of Anthropology** at the University of British Columbia. It has the most extensive displays, but good points of comparison can be seen at **Vancouver Museum,** or by looking at the totem poles in Stanley Park—on a sunny day. At Vancouver Museum, you can also study the history of European inhabitation of the area and compare that with what you'll find at **The Old Hastings Mill Museum.**

Appetite whetted, how about a drive out to New Westminster to see **Cap's** collection of settler memorabilia? **Irving House** and the **Royal City Museum** are nearby. From there, it's a short drive to **Fort Langley** and the **antique shops** in the Fraser Valley.

It would be an appropriate day to look at the boats inside at the **Maritime Museum**. Behind the building is another totem pole—quite a tall one.

Although the mountain view may not be too clear in a downpour, Simon Fraser University should be included on an anthropological (for the Museum) or architectural tour. Nearby, you could look into an oil refinery at **Gulf Oil of Canada Ltd.,** 1155 Glenayre Drive, Port Moody (939–3333). Call to make arrangements to be shown around. Not far from here, the **Coquitlam Shopping Centre** is architecturally interesting, has 100 and umpteen stores in it, and is the second largest in western Canada. To get there, carry on out Hastings Street around Burnaby Mountain. The first traffic light is for the oil refinery. At the second, a few kilometres along (St. John Street in Port Moody), turn left. You'll see the Coquitlam Centre on your left across from K-Mart.

On an art theme, you could start at the **Vancouver Art Gallery,** then study works at smaller galleries which are mentioned in Chapter 6. Check the newspapers for special showings.

The stars are indoors at the **Planetarium,** but remember it's closed on Mondays. At the **Aquarium** in Stanley Park the fish—and they're fascinating—are inside, although the whales are out in the rain. Often there are films or lectures here as well. The **Lynn Canyon Ecology Centre** has a roof and lots of interesting displays. Kids could spend hours intrigued by the story of the forest cycles at **MacMillan-Bloedel Place** in the VanDusen Botanical Gardens. But wear your rain gear to get there. You have to walk half way across the park.

At the **Bloedel Conservatory,** the garden is under glass.

But, if it is raining, you'll miss the marvellous 360° view.

A rainy day might be a good time for a tour of **B.C. Place,**
Vancouver's new air-supported, multiple-use dome. The
Stadium is 10 acres itself and can seat 60,000 for football and
soccer. It converts to use for concerts, baseball, and other
events. Guided one-hour tours of the inner working of the dome
(kept up by 16 fans) leave Gate A off Beatty Street at 11 am, 1
pm and 3 pm during the summers. Adults $2.75, seniors and
students (13 to 18) $2, children (6 to 12) $1.25, under 6 free.

Canada Place, when this whole harbourfront complex is
completed and Expo has gone, would be ideal to explore. It has
an IMAX theatre which will be running special film shows.

The Arts, Sciences and Technology Centre, 600 Granville
Street at the corner of Dunsmuir, invites participation in its
exhibits for "hands on" discovery. It's open Monday to Saturday from 10 am to 5 pm, Sundays and holidays from 1 to 5 pm.
Adults $3, students, seniors and children $1.50.

Out at the University of British Columbia, the **TRIUMF**
(Tri-University-Meson-Facility), cyclotron—a nuclear ac-
celerator which can split atoms—is open to the public. One and
one-quarter hour tours take place on weekdays at 11 am and at 2
pm, from May to August, at 1 pm Wednesdays and Fridays,
during the winter. They are not recommended for children
under 14, nor for pregnant or handicapped persons. For further
information, call the TRIUMF Information Office, 4004 Wes-
brook Mall, University of British Columbia (222–1047, ext.
435).

Robson Square Media Centre, under Robson Street behind
the Vancouver Art Gallery, has an active calendar of art showings, film, talks, exhibitions, and special events—much of it
free. For programme information, call 660–2487. You can pick
up their monthly calendar of events at the British Columbia
Buildings Corporation, 800 Robson Street, or at the office of
Tourism B.C. in Robson Square.

In North Vancouver, **Maplewood Children's Farm,** 405
Seymour River Place (929–5610), is indoors and out, but suitable for a family visit on a rainy day. Open 10 am to 4 pm,
closed Mondays. To get there, take the Deep Cove exit on the
other side of the Second Narrows Bridge, and veer left at the
second stop light. The farm is a block up this road on your left.

Something that always fascinates kids (and about which they

usually know a lot more than anyone older) is the **B.C. Sports Hall of Fame** (253–2311). It is at the Pacific National Exhibition Grounds by Second Narrows Bridge, and open Monday to Friday, 9:15 am to 4:45 pm, Sundays and holidays, noon to 5 pm. Closed Saturdays.

If you want to catch up on your reading you are always welcome at the **Vancouver Public Library,** 750 Burrard at Robson Street (682–5911). It's open from 9:30 am to 9:30 pm, Monday to Thursday, Fridays and Saturdays til 6 o'clock. On Sundays, the library is open from 1 to 5 pm, but there is no telephone reference service on those days. For information on opening times on holiday weekends, call 665–2276. Other branches of the city's public library system are listed in the phone book under "Vancouver Public Library."

For getting wet *indoors,* there's the **Aquatic Centre,** 1050 Beach Avenue (689–7156). The specially-designed and decorated children's pool is supervised at certain hours, so the bigger folk can use the giant pool or the Olympic-style diving boards.

Industrial and Educational Tours

For the following tours it is advisable to phone ahead to be sure the company is offering the tours on the dates and at the times listed. Some require that you make arrangements in advance to tour their facilities.

Alberta Wheat Pool, Rm 400 - 1111 West Hastings Street, Vancouver (684–5161). Tours of a grain elevator by arrangement only. Children 16 years and under are not admitted.

Andres Wines (B.C.) Ltd, 2120 Vintner Street, Port Moody (937–3411). Tours of the winery any day of the week between 2 pm and 10 pm, on the hour.

B.C. Packers, 4300 Moncton Street, Richmond (277–2212). Advance arrangements are necessary for this one-hour tour of the fresh fish and cold storage, cannery, reduction plant and warehouse. Tours are available between June and September; children must be over 10 years old and accompanied by an adult.

B.C. Sugar Museum, Ft. of Rogers Street beside the Fish Docks (253–1131). A tour of the museum and the sugar refinery, open Monday through Friday, 8:30 am to 4 pm. It is a good idea to call in advance, and necessary in the case of group arrangements.

Crown Forest Industries Limited, 15 King Edward Avenue, Coquitlam (521–1941). A two-hour tour of the sawmill and plywood plant, for groups of from 10 to 20 people, in July and August at 9 am and 1:30 pm. Advance arrangements are necessary; children must be 12 years old or older.

Granville Island Brewery, 1441 Cartwright Street, Granville Island (688–9927). A 20- to 25-minute tour of the brewery, at 2 pm and 4 pm, Mondays to Saturdays and at 1 pm, 3 pm and 5 pm Sundays, during the winter. Please call the brewery for summer tour times. For large groups, please make reservations.

Green Valley Fertilizer and Chemical Company, 12816 - 80th Avenue, Box 249, Surrey, B.C. V3W 6B6 (591–8461). Arrangements for touring this facility must be made 3 weeks in advance. Tours take place between 10 am and 2:30 pm,

An umbrella-built-for-two

Monday to Friday.

Gulf Canada Products Company, 1155 Glenayre Drive, Port Moody (939–3333). A two-hour walking tour of the oil refinery, 9 am and 1 pm, Monday to Friday, refinery conditions permitting. Tours must be booked in advance, and children accompanied by an adult.

Jordan and Ste Michelle Cellars Ltd, 15050 - 54A Avenue, Surrey (576–6741). Tours are scheduled Monday to Friday at 11 am, 1 pm and 3 pm. The winery is located near Highway 10, south of the Fraser Highway and north of Highway 99, and is reputed to have some of the largest aging cellars in North America.

Neptune Bulk Terminals Canada Ltd, 1001 Low Level Road, North Vancouver (985–7461). A half-hour tour of the bulk loading terminal operation, available to chartered bus tours only, Tuesday to Thursday at 9 am, 11 am, 2 pm and 4 pm.

Sayfrey's Salmon Run, 6438 Ash Street, Vancouver (324–6648). A five-hour tour (including lunch) of the Capilano Salmon Hatchery and Steveston harbour in Delta. Lunch (barbecued salmon) is served at the Granada Motor Inn in Richmond. Tours depart from the Hotel Georgia in downtown Vancouver and from the Granada Motor Inn in Richmond, Monday through Friday during July and August. Adults $35, children (5 to 12) $20.

Snow Crest Packers, 1925 Riverside Road, Abbotsford (859–4881). A half-hour tour of the food processing operation, July to September, Mondays through Fridays, from 8 am to 5 pm. Advance arrangements are necessary, and children must be supervised by an adult for safety reasons.

Vanterm, the Port of Vancouver's transshipment terminal, north foot of Clark Drive, Vancouver (666–6129). From a special public viewing area, you can watch the port's activities. Open 9 am to noon and 1 pm to 4 pm during the summer. Tours of the facility are also available.

15 *Vancouver after dark*

TICKETS

For many theatrical productions and concerts in Vancouver, tickets can be booked by phone through **Vancouver Ticket Centre/Concert Box Office** (locally known at **VTC/CBO**) and charged to Eaton's, Visa, Mastercard, or American Express credit cards. A small service charge (75¢) is added to each order. VTC/CBO will then either mail your tickets (if there is time) or hold them for you. They have 30 outlets in the city, including ones at Eaton's (fifth floor), Pacific Centre Mall (main concourse, lower level), Royal Centre Mall, Denman Inn Mall, and Oakridge (in the basement of Woodward's).

Their number for ordering tickets is **280–4444**. For information on events which they are carrying, call 280–4411. Their sports event number is 280–4400.

On the day of a performance, you can purchase a half-price ticket to many shows from **Front Row Centre,** 1025 Robson Street (683–2017). They are open Monday to Saturday from noon until 7 pm.

You can also book tickets at the **Gray Line** counters in some hotels (or with the Gray Line service through the hotel desk). This bus company also arranges dinner-and-theatre evening tours. Gray Line services are available at the Denman Inn, the Hotel Georgia, the Hyatt Regency, Ming Court, Sandman Inn—Howe, the Sheraton Landmark Hotel and Sheraton Plaza 500.

Special discounts for **preview shows** or sometimes matinées are offered by Vancouver Playhouse, City Stage, Studio 58, and UBC's Frederic Wood Theatre. Call the theatre in question to see when tickets are available.

Arts Plus, #302 - 5970 West Boulevard (266–6364), buys tickets at discounted group rates and arranges evening outings for its members.

The Dress Circle Club, 1025 Robson Street, Vancouver B.C. V6E 1A9 (683–2017) puts out a brochure called ''Vancouver Theatre Guide'' and arranges excursions, discounts, even tickets in other cities.

THEATRE

While theatre—of some sort—has always been a part of the Vancouver scene, it was not until the 1960s and 70s that government funding helped to place it on the stage. Today, more and more people are going to the theatre to see top-quality music, dance and theatrical productions, the tried and true as well as the new and innovative.

In 1959, the **Queen Elizabeth Theatre** (683–2311; offices at 649 Cambie Street), opened its doors onto Georgia Street (between Cambie and Hamilton Streets). This is Vancouver's largest theatre, with a seating capacity of 2,820 and space for three wheelchairs. The programmes of the multi-purpose theatre include those of the **Vancouver Opera Association,** concerts, plays, dance, music, musicals, and guest performers. Such internationally-renowned names as Julian Bream, Eugene Fodor, the Peking Opera, Yul Brynner, and Martha Graham have played there.

Adjoining this complex is the **Vancouver Playhouse** (683–2311), at the corner of Dunsmuir and Hamilton Streets, sharing office space with the Queen Elizabeth Theatre. It seats 650, can accommodate four wheelchairs, and features plays and recitals.

To bring some of the international talent which Vancouver was to see in the 1950s and 1960s, Hugh Pickett founded Famous Artists Ltd. Over the years, he introduced audiences to European and American shows such as *Chorus Line, Death*

Trap, and *Chapter Two.* Currently, the **Vancouver Playhouse Theatre** (873–3311) continues to put on major plays.

The **Vancouver East Cultural Centre,** 1895 Venables Street at Victoria (254–9578), has—for one reason or another—caught the attention of every Vancouverite. Hardly a night, or day, goes by when this theatre is not in use. Formerly a Methodist church (built in 1907), this charming building was converted into intimate theatre space in 1975. **Tamahnous Theatre Workshop Society** (254–1555), the resident company, has been experimenting there with original works about contemporary issues since 1971.

In addition to a fine schedule of theatre, music, and dance, VECC offers classes in the theatre arts (669–0029) and shows films for children, Saturdays at 1:30 pm (pay what you can). Tickets for all their shows can be reserved by calling 254–9578, open Monday to Saturday from 10 am, Sundays from noon, until showtime. The box office will hold the tickets for you until 15 minutes before the show starts.

Vancouver East Cultural Centre

With few stages until recently, a search for theatrical space has not been an uncommon problem for companies in the city. In 1979, the opening of two theatres on Granville Island helped to alleviate some of the congestion. One was the offspring of the 200-seat **Arts Club Theatre,** 1181 Seymour Street (687–5315). The **Arts Club Theatre, Granville Island** has in turn spawned a third theatre—the **Arts Club Revue Theatre**—across the street from its Granville Island location. Whereas the other two theatres stage both plays and revues, this cabaret theatre has only the latter—and very good ones at that. Currently *Ain't Misbehavin'* is enjoying a long run and intends to continue right through Expo. We will also be seeing that year an evening of songs about the local scene in a revue called *Only in Vancouver*. Both shows are great fun.

Tickets for all Arts Club productions can be purchased through VTC/CBO, Front Row Centre, or at their box office on Granville Island (687–1644). For those interested in getting in on an act, the Arts Club runs a graduated series of classes during the fall. For information, call the Arts Club Drama Centre (263–1838).

Waterfront Theatre, 1405 Anderson Street at Johnston (685–6217), is the other main stage on Granville Island. Westcoast Actors (with a variety of plays), New Play Centre (with an emphasis on British Columbia authors), and Carousel Theatre (with a repertoire for children) solved their space problems by joining forces to open here.

City Stage, 751 Thurlow Street (688–1436), most of the week puts on short plays of all genres. Saturday afternoons, for the matinées, seats are sold at a price of two for one. Friday and Saturday nights after the show, their very popular Theatresports is on (11 pm). Tickets are $5, and the audience is in command. Two teams of actors ''contest'' in improvisation in response to cues and scenarios supplied by the audience.

At the University of British Columbia, productions at the 400-seat **Frederic Wood Theatre** (locally known as ''Freddie Wood''), 6345 Crescent Road behind the Faculty Club (228–2678), are looked forward to by Vancouver audiences throughout the year. Special discounts for preview shows are available. Around the corner, in a basement, the **Dorothy Sommerset Studio** offers more informal, often one-man or one-act plays. For information and season schedules, call the theatre box office.

At Simon Fraser University, the Centre for the Arts sponsors a series of dance, music and theatrical productions in the **Simon Fraser University Theatre** (291–3514). This theatre seats 450, has space four wheelchairs, and brings in major companies and individual talents from across the country. At least once a semester, students produce a dance or theatrical show. The university's theatre is located on the South Mall, across from the main library. Parking in Simon Fraser lots is free after 6 pm.

Studio 58 is the company associated with Vancouver Community College's Theatre Department. For information on and reservations for their productions, call 324–5227. Discounts for preview shows are available, and seats for Sunday matinées go at two for one.

The premises currently occupied by **Firehall Theatre,** 280 East Cordova Street, were built in 1906 and until 1975 housed working fire-engines. In 1982, the building opened as a theatre. Dance Centre, Axis Mime, and Touchstone Theatre regularly perform there as well as other theatre companies and musicians. The theatre already has a particularly active schedule of both experimental and familiar drama. For their box office, call 689–0926.

Out on the leading edge of contemporary theatre is **Western Front,** 303 East 8th Avenue at Scotia (876–9343). They concentrate on performance art and inhabit a building formerly that of the Knights of Pythias. A large and accoustically interesting hall is their main stage.

The recently-held First Fringe Festival in Vancouver, with over 70 groups performing on 10 days at 6 different locations brought to the city's attention a number of other hard-working companies in town. **Vancouver Little Theatre** (876–4165) performs at Heritage Hall, 3102 Main Street at 15th Avenue. This building was built in 1916 as Postal Station C and is a fine example of Beaux-Arts architecture.

The **New York Theatre,** 639 Commercial Drive, 639 Commercial Drive (254–5934) provides a stage for plays, concerts, and a wide variety of events.

Robson Square Media Centre, 800 Robson Street off Robson Square, provides a multi-purpose theatre for films, readings, concerts, fashion shows, and other events. For information regarding programmes, call the Visitors and Convention Bureau (682–2222) or pick up a Robson Square "Calendar of Events" at Tourism B.C. at Robson Square.

One company will be surprising us in 1986. **Headlines Theatre Company,** 2524 Cypress Street (738–2283), regularly offers up-to-date satire on contemporary political issues. Currently they are taking a look at the effects of a restrained economy. In 1986, they will be putting on "Guerilla Theatre," spontaneously doing shows on the street, in elevators, wherever they might find you. Only in Vancouver!

MUSIC

The Vancouver Symphony Orchestra (VSO) has been directed since 1972 by the vibrant Kazuyoshi Akiyama from Tokyo. More recently, an exciting Russian conductor, Rudolf Barshai, has joined him to share the work of directing the symphony orchestra. Formed in 1931, the VSO performs several series a season, and accompanies the Vancouver Opera and visiting ballet companies. It has gained a national and international reputation and has toured Canada, Japan and the United States. If you can't get a ticket, CBC broadcasts VSO Main Series performances on AM, FM, and the French stations. For complete programme information, call 689–1411.

The fabulous **Orpheum Theatre** (683–2311), 884 Granville Street on the Mall, is home to the VSO. Opened in 1927 with a silent film and vaudeville show, the premises were not updated until the 1970s. A gala programme in November 1977 honoured the opening of an Orpheum Theatre restored to the elegance of its Spanish renaissance style complete with sparkling chandeliers and a dome mural. Holding 2,788 people, with room for four wheelchairs, the acoustics are so sound, there isn't a bad seat in the house.

The Vancouver Opera Association (682–2871), 111 Dunsmuir, gave its first performance in 1960. Presently, performances are held at the Queen Elizabeth Theatre every season between October and May. For Expo, both the Vancouver Symphony Orchestra and the Vancouver Opera Association will be arranging special events. For information on these, call VTC/CBO (280–4444) or Expo at 660–3976/EXPO, or write Expo Info, P.O. Box 1800, Station A, Vancouver, B.C.,

Orpheum Theatre

Canada V6G 3A2.

Formed in 1961, the **Festival Concert Society** (736–7661), 3737 Oak Street, is the largest (including affiliates) concert-touring organization in Canada. Music ranging from folk to classical as well as theatre, dance and opera are all promoted by this society. It is a non-profit organization and includes a division called ''Young People's concerts.'' It is also the administrative body for the International Shawnigan Summer School of the Arts on Vancouver Island, the Victoria International Festival, and Canada Opera Piccola.

In Vancouver, Festival Concert Society has introduced **Sunday Coffee Concerts,** a series at which touring and local artists are invited to perform. Shows are held at the Queen Elizabeth Playhouse at 11 am Sundays and cost $2. Tickets are available at the door (box office opens at 10 am). Performances run about an hour, and baby-sitting can be arranged by calling the theatre 24 hours in advance. Tickets for Festival Concert Society's evening shows are usually sold through VCT/CBO outlets.

On Saturdays, the Festival Concert Society's Coffee Concerts are held at the **Richmond Gateway Theatre,** 6500 Gilbert Road (270–1812). The box office opens at the theatre at 10 am, tickets cost $2, the music starts at 11 am, and child care is available if you call in advance. This theatre also has a regular schedule of good Saturday-night concerts of music, dance, and family shows.

At the **Vancouver East Cultural Centre,** Masterpiece Music has entered its second decade. This series of 10 chamber-music concerts features the Masterpiece Trio, the Purcell String Quartet, and special guests performing classics from Bach to Gershwin.

Among choral societies, the largest in the city is the **Vancouver Bach Choir** (921–8012) which fulfills the large-scale choral requirements of the Vancouver Symphony Orchestra as well as performs a three-concert series of its own—by no means limited to Bach. Tickets can be obtained through VTC/CBO outlets, and information about what and where they are performing from the choir's office.

The **Vancouver Chamber Choir** (738–6822) performs here, in the Orpheum as well as at Ryerson United Church, 2195 West 45th Avenue at Yew Street. You can purchase tickets for either of these locations through VTC/CBO outlets.

Other musically active groups in town arrange performances in their areas of specialty. The **Vancouver Society for Early Music,** 1254 West 7th Avenue (732–1610) concentrates on medieval, renaissance and baroque works. It sponsors concerts at the UBC Recital Hall, the Orpheum and other theatres. Tickets are available at VTC/CBO outlets. This society also puts out a journal, *Musica*, which can be obtained by writing them (postal code V6H 1B7).

The **Vancouver New Music Society** (731–3511) sponsors concerts by and performs the works of serious contemporary composers. They are planning some special events for Expo.

At both the University of British Columbia and at Simon Fraser University, a lot of music goes on. Many of their concerts are free. Call the **Department of Music, UBC** (228–3113) or the **Theatre Box Office at SFU** (291–3514) for their schedules of concerts and musical happenings.

For lower-brow listening, there's good live rock (and dancing) at the **Commodore Ballroom,** 870 Granville Street (681–7838 or 683–9413). The entertainment is usually big name, the bar stocks lots of beer, and the 1931 dance floor is spring-loaded. Tickets for concerts are available through VTC/CBO, or at the door.

The **Hot Jazz Society,** 2120 Main Street (873–4131), blows its horns Tuesdays through Saturdays in Dixieland, New Orleans and big band swing styles. The dance floor is usually active. For members, week nights are free; guests pay $3 (seniors $2). Friday and Saturday nights, members pay $3; guests, $5 (seniors $3). Special events, usually held on weekends, may cost more. Tuesday nights are regularly "jam sessions." Considering the musical returns, the six-month membership fee of $10 is nominal.

The **Classical Joint Coffee House,** 231 Carrall Street (689–0667), also features jazz as well as blue-grass and just good music. When the music is there, there is usually a cover charge. Coffee and healthy sandwiches are on the menu. When there's no music, you can play backgammon or chess or read or write as most of the other patrons will be doing.

The **Savoy Cabaret,** across the street at 6 Powell Street (687–0418), and the **Town Pump,** 66 Water Street nearby (683–6695), will rock you at appropriately high, live decibel levels. At **Club Soda Cabaret,** 1055 Homer Street (681–8202), the rock is taped and the dancing lively.

Something a little quieter, but rocking good fun, is the music at **Carlos 'n Bud's,** 555 Pacific Avenue at Seymour nearly under the Granville Street Bridge. In this converted automobile garage, they serve "down home cooking and foot-stomping music'' most near every night of the week.

DANCE

Dance in Vancouver deserves special mention and gets lots of attention. Some of the city's interest has been generated by good local dance schools and companies. Simon Fraser University's dance programme has also had a lot to do with it. They are the first western university to offer a degree in this field and one of only two in Canada.

The Anna Wyman School of Dance Art, 1705 Marine Drive, West Vancouver (926–6535), made its professional debut in 1971. Since then, this contemporary dance company has travelled to Europe and toured extensively in British Columbia, Canada and the United States.

Paula Ross is the choreographer, driving force and inspiration behind the **Paul Ross Dance Centre,** 3488 West Broadway (732–9513). Founded in 1965, this is Vancouver's first and oldest contemporary dance company. Call her centre for information on when the company will be performing.

Edam Performing Arts Society, 303 East 8th Avenue (876–9559), works at the Western Front. It does some of the most innovative performances in town, and one dancer who performed with them now has her own touring company. **Judith Marcuse Repertory Dance Company of Canada,** 6754 Dufferin Street, West Vancouver (921–8436), will have a dance ensemble based at Douglas College and will be performing at Expo next year. Her company will also be performing at the Queen Elizabeth Theatre in upcoming seasons.

Mountain Dance Theatre, founded thirteen years ago, has now joined with **Dance Plus,** 39 West 5th Avenue (877–1910). This contemporary company performs frequently in schools. **Jumpstart,** the company now occupying the theatre where Mountain Dance started, 6450 Gilpin Street, Burnaby (299–4522), will be doing some of their thing at Expo.

Several dance studios offer classes and exercise sessions. **Arts Umbrella,** 1286 Cartwright Street, Granville Island (681–5268), concentrates on kids. **Harbour Dance Centre,** 518 West Hastings Street (684–9542), has good ballet. **Main Dance Place,** 2214 Main Street (874–7223), offers classes for all ages and levels in modern ballet and jazz. **Pacific Ballet Theatre School,** 456 West Broadway (873–5024), offers a complete range.

Immram Dance Studio, 337 West Pender Street (669–4497), both has daily classes and dance conditioning sessions (at convenient times) and gives performances. Call the studio for their schedule. **Karen Jamieson Dance Company,** 5552 Fraser Street (327–6088), also both teaches and performs.

We'll find out more about local dancing next year when **Vancouver Dance Centre,** 1 Alexander Street (682–8098), holds "Vancouver Dance Week," February 2 to 8, 1986. Local dance companies and choreographers will be performing then at Vancouver Playhouse and the Firehall Theatre. A series of dance films will be shown concurrently by Pacific Cinemateque.

During Expo, an **International Dance Critics Symposium** will take place at the University of British Columbia, August 11 to 17, 1986.

To find out what's happening at Simon Fraser University, call the Theatre Box Office (291–3514). The University's Dance Department recently hosted a Canadian choreographers Workshop, treating us to some fine performances.

MOVIES AND VIDEO

Vancouver has lots of theatres showing first-run movies, which are listed in the entertainment sections of the city's newspapers—the *Vancouver Sun* or *Vancouver Province*. For recorded information on what is playing at Odeon theatres in the city, call 687–1515. For "what's on" at Famous Players theatres, the number is 681–4255.

The only two independently-owned and operated first-run theatres in Vancouver are the **Hollywood** at 3123 West Broadway (738–3211) and **Studio Cinema,** 919 Granville Street at Smithe (681–1732).

Varsity Fine Arts, 4375 West 10th Avenue (224–3730), and **The Bay,** 935 Denman (685–9822), include some European, Japanese and other films in their programming.

The **Royal Centre Mall Cineplex,** 1055 West Georgia on the basement level of the mall (669–9791), usually has a good variety at its ten theatres.

The **Ridge Theatre,** 3131 Arbutus Street (738–6311), and **Vancouver East Cinema,** 2290 Commercial Drive (253–5455), are the two theatres where the annual **Vancouver International Film Festival** is held in the spring. For information on the Festival, call 732–0422 or 738–0400. At other times of the year, the Ridge shows first-run serious contemporary film or holds mini-festivals of classics. Tuesday nights, admission is at the discounted rate of $3 per show. Vancouver East Cinema usually has a double billing (single price) of contemporary foreign films.

Pacific Cinemateque, 1616 West 3rd Avenue (732–5322), brings unusual films on the arts to their small theatre on West Georgia Street and to Robson Square Media Centre. To buy a ticket to these films, you must have a Pacific Cinemateque card ($5 at the door). Flyers listing Pacific Cinemateque showings are available at Tourism B.C., at the Pacific Cinemateque offices, or at showings of their films. For information on what is showing, call 732–6119.

For home viewing, the **National Film Board,** 1161 West Georgia Street (666–0718) maintains a film library of 2,100 English and 1,700 French titles. You can order films in person, by telephone, or by mail (postal code V6E 3G4). Every borrower, however, must have an NFB Library Card, which can be obtained at the National Film Board office at the above address. There is no charge for borrowing their 16 mm films. There is a charge ($2/day) for the use of their videocassettes. To reserve a film or video, call 666–0718. For other information on the library, call 666–0716.

You can pick up a video movie for home viewing (and a machine if you need one) at **7-11 Stores** (open 24 hours) for 99¢ during the week. They cost a little more on weekends. Titles are pop ones. **The Future Shop,** 943 West Broadway (738–6565), has 500 titles, each going for $2 weekdays, $3 Friday and Saturday nights. The shop is open Monday to Wednesday from 10 am to 6 pm, Thursday and Friday from 10 am to 9 pm, Sundays from 11 am to 5 pm.

For foreign film videos, film festival productions, old movies and music videos, try **Videomatic Ltd,** 1829 West 4th

Avenue (734–0411), a welcome addition to the video marketing scene.

BOOZING

Pubs

The comprehensive guide for pubbing in Greater Vancouver, the Fraser Valley, Squamish, Whistler, and on the Sunshine Coast is *A Guide to Neighbourhood Pubs,* by Ian Kennedy, Vern Simpson, and Gordon R. Elliot, published by Gordon Soules Books. This compendium gives you descriptions, maps, and pub activities for 77 pubs. We will therefore just mention a few in town. Most close at 11 pm week-nights; by 1 am on Friday and Saturday nights.

Stamp's Landing, 610 Stamp's Landing, False Creek (879–0821). Their own brew is one the best beers in town.

Bimini's, 2010 West 4th Avenue at Maple (738–2714). A comfortable pub drawing crowds both after work and all through the evening. Off-license on their main floor. Food available.

Darby Dawes, 2001 MacDonald Street at 4th Avenue (731–0617). Noisey and sometimes with live music. Off-license.

Jerry's Cove, 3681 West 4th Avenue near Alma (734–1205). An interesting Kitsilano bar.

The Rose and Thorne, 757 Richards Street (683–2921). A downtown location for a quick one after the show.

Rusty Gull, 175 East 1st Street, North Vancouver (988–5585). A good local name and congenial.

Queen's Cross, 2989 Lonsdale Avenue at Queens, North Vancouver (980–7715). Really hopping on the North Shore.

Park Royal Hotel Pub, 440 Clyde Avenue (926–5511). Take the Lions Gate Bridge exit for West Vancouver, turn right off Marine Drive at the first stop-light (Taylor Way) and then right again at the first street (Clyde). You enter this long-popular pub through the hotel.

The Troller, 6422 Bay Street, Horseshoe Bay, West Vancouver (921–7616). They make their own beer and have live music Saturday afternoons from 3 to 6 pm.

The Grouse Nest Pub, 6400 Nancy Greene Way on top of

Stamp's Landing, False Creek

Grouse Mountain (984–0661). Open until 11 pm or 12 midnight or until the last Superskyride heads down the mountain.

Lounges

Garden Court Lounge, Four Seasons Hotel, 791 West Georgia Street (689–9333). An elegant and grand lounge, with piano music among the plants.

The Bacchus Lounge, Wedgwood Hotel, 845 Hornby Street (689–7777). Currently a favourite with the downtown crowd, it has d-j'd loud music Tuesday to Saturday nights.

Hi-Rigger Lounger, Hotel Vancouver, Georgia and Burrard Streets (684–3131). Mellow piano music in this lobby lounge at 5:30 pm. Upstairs on the **Panorama Roof,** there's live music to add to the view Friday and Saturday nights until 11:30 pm.

Il Giardino, 1382 Hornby Street (669–2422). An elegant lounge in a restaurant. Taped classical music and opera until 1 am.

The Arts Club Bar, Arts Club Theatre, Granville Island (687–1354). A quiet bar, pleasantly located by the waters of False Creek on the wharves of Granville Island's north side. Self-serve. Friday and Saturday nights, live music—jazz, blues, easy-going rhythm and blues.

English Bay Cafe, 1795 Denman Street on English Bay (669–2225). A bistro in actuality, so you have to order something. A light menu is provided. Open until 2 am, valet parking (free) until midnight.

At Restaurants

Bridges Pub, 1696 Duranleau Street, Granville Island (687–4400). Packed with people who might have just been skiing at Whistler—summers and winters.

Mulvaney's, Granville Island between the Arts Club Theatre and the cement plant (685–6571). Dancing in their window'd lounge from 9:30 pm to 1 am, Sundays excepted.

Pelican Bay, Granville Island Hotel, 1253 Johnston Street (683-7373). Music and dancing every night except Sunday.

Mama Gold's, 1516 Yew Street at Cornwall (736–8828). Live music every night. Discount meals after 10:30 pm.

Frank Baker's, 2975 Cambie Street at 14th Avenue (874–9119). Mellow piano Thursday to Saturday nights. Sundays, live jazz. No parking problems. Open until midnight.

Fogg on Fourth, 3293 West 4th Avenue at Blenheim Street (72B–EERS). Open until 11 pm week-days, until 1 am Friday and Saturday nights.

Orestes, 3116 West Broadway (732–1461). Greek music to go with the spanakopita, homous, and retsina.

Earl's Place, 4397 West 10th Avenue at Trimble in Point Grey (222–1342). Open til midnight during the week, until 1 am on weekends.

Broadway Earl's, 901 West Broadway (734–5995). Open and serving food until 11:30 pm weekdays, until midnight on weekends.

Bars

Landmark Jazz Bar, Sheraton Landmark Hotel, 1400 Robson Street (687–9312). Live music, mostly jazz, dance floor. Open until 1:30 am Wednesday through Saturday.

The Railway Club, 579 Dunsmuir Street (681–1625). Members pay an annual $10 membership fee. Guests pay $2 at the door. Open until 2 am.

Bombay Bicycle Club, Abbotsford Hotel, 921 West Pender Street at Burrard (681–4335). Live music 9 pm to 1 am.

The Spinning Wheel, 212 Carrall Street, Gastown (681–2814). Irish music. Bob Geldorf and his Booktown Rats used to play here.

Ammnesia, 99 Powell Street, Gastown (682–2211). A new one.

Billy Bishop Branch 176 of the Royal Canadian Legion, 1407 Laburnum Street, Kits Point (738–4142 or 738–4623). Members and guests only. The most talked about Legion bar around.

16 *Shopping*

Vancouver can be divided into shopping districts, each with a distinctive character. West Vancouver shopping is excellent and pricey. Kerrisdale Village, at 41st Avenue and East Boulevard (the south continuation of Arbutus Street), and Oakridge Shopping Mall, 41st Avenue and Cambie Street, are in this league. South Granville, south of the Granville Street Bridge, combines art, antiques, good clothing, and the unusual. On 4th Avenue west of Burrard Street, second-stores are interspersed with the eclectic.

The downtown area divides itself into Gastown for crafts, unusual clothing and souvenirs; Granville Mall at Georgia Street for the big department stores; Pacific Centre Mall for underground shopping; and Robson Street for the chic.

The following listings are not meant to be comprehensive but to suggest a few shops you might like to include in touring the stores of any of these areas. Other shops in Gastown are noted in this book's chapter on that district; video shopping comes into "Vancouver after Dark"; boat and marine shopping is good on Granville Island or on Coal Harbour at the foot of Cardero Street; sporting stores are mentioned in "Sports."

Haute Couture and Good Clothing, etc.

Edward Chapman, 833 West Pender Street (685–6207), and

at the Westin Bayshore Inn, Hotel Georgia and the Oakridge Shopping Centre. Vancouver's "leading importers of British woolens since 1890" for men. They also sell good cotton, linen, silk and cashmere wear. Sections for women called "Chapy's" are at the above locations with the exception of the Westin Bayshore.

Chapman's Collectibles, Pacific Centre Mall (688–6711), and South Granville at 10th Avenue, Oakridge Shopping Mall, and Marine Drive at 18th Street in West Vancouver. European imports for ladies.

The Scotch Shop, 674 Seymour Street (682–3929), and 2845 south Granville Street, and 1760 Marine Drive, West Vancouver. Fine imported tweeds and woolens.

Ferragamo, 918 Robson Street at Robson Square (669–4495). The only Canadian outlet for this sophisticated Italian line.

Mark James, 2941 West Broadway (734–2381). Good men's clothing.

Laura Ashley, 1171 Robson Street (688–8727). British fabrics, blouses and skirts of Laura Ashley's distinctive design.

Rodier Paris Boutique, 1025 Robson Street (681–1671), and in the Oakridge Shopping Mall. Expensive French imports.

Vanessa Boutique, 2015 South Park Royal, West Vancouver (926–7215), and Pacific Centre Mall, and 1075 Robson Street. Expensive.

Charmante's, 992 Park Royal, West Vancouver (922–1201). Beautiful clothes in classic styles.

Harmony, 1530 Marine Drive, West Vancouver (925–2770). Silks and wash 'n wear fashions by a local designer.

Angel Handpainted Fashions, 1140 Robson Street (681–0947). Wild and wonderful, for all ages.

Shop 41, 2658 south Granville Street (732–9111), and Park Royal South, West Vancouver. Good Scandinavian imports.

Bizo/Zo, 4440 West 10th Avenue (228–8812), and 760 Robson Street. Stylish and unusual fashions.

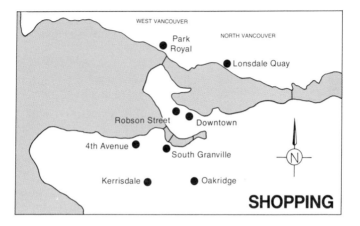

Wear Else, 2360 West 4th Avenue (732–3521). Stylish women's clothes and footwear.
Teeze Fashions, 3586 West 4th Avenue (733–1475). Clothing with esprit.

Cotton Ginny's, 990 Robson Street (685–5759), and Pacific Centre Mall. Cotton sportswear in fashionable styles.

Van Ley's, 2301 West 41st Avenue, Kerrisdale (266–2363). Accessories, hats, necklaces, gloves, purses.

Hermes Jewellery, 1189 Robson Street (688–8809). Extravagant costume jewellery.

Peter Fox Shoes, 303 West Cordova Street (662–3040). Very unusual, high-fashion footwear.

British Boot Shop, 541 Granville Street (684–6921). Good men's shoes.

Elle Fabrics, 644 Seymour Street (683–7466). Fine imports.

Cecil B. Makeup Studios, #112–1025 Robson Street (681–3043).

For the Younger Crowd

Kids Only Market, 1496 Cartwright Street, Granville Island (689–8447). An amazing array of clothing, toy, and equipment stores. Short-term, drop-in daycare available at Over the Rainbow Playcare Centre (683–2624).

Czar Nicholas and the Toad, 2375 West 41st Avenue, Kerrisdale (263–9313). Marvellous clothes and toys; pricey.

Bratz, 2828 south Granville Street (734–4344). Neat kids' clothing; quite pricey.

Windmill Toys, 2387 West 41st Avenue, Kerrisdale (261–2120), and 982 South Park Royal, West Vancouver. Quality toys.

The Toybox, 3010 West Broadway (738–4322). Complete line of high quality children's toys, special orders and imports.

Toy Carousel, 6111 West Boulevard, Kerrisdale (266–1227). Recycled toys and baby strollers, etc.

On The Go West Coast Styles, 2007 West 41st Avenue, Kerrisdale (261–6373). Clothing for teens.

Vancouver Kidsbooks, 2868 West 4th Avenue (738–5335), and at Kids Only Market, Granville Island (685–5741).

Hagar Books, 2176 West 41st Avenue, Kerrisdale (263–9412).

Shopping Malls and Department Stores

Park Royal Shopping Centre, Marine Drive and Taylor Way, West Vancouver (922–3211). Beside the Park Royal Hotel. Fashion, jewellery, furnishings on both north and south sides of Marine Drive. Eaton's, Woodward's, The Bay. Shuttle-bus service stops outside Birks, Woodward's, and the Canada Trust. Also two overpasses crossing the highway and a crosswalk at Marine Drive and Taylor Way.

Pacific Centre Mall, 701 West Georgia Street at Granville Street (688–7236). Below the Four Seasons Hotel. Fashion, shoes, specialty stores. Eaton's, Le Chateau, Holt Renfrew's. The Bay, joined by a short walkway and shopping centre called Vancouver Centre Mall. VCT/CBO outlet.

Royal Centre Mall, 1055 West Georgia at Burrard Street (689–1771). Below the Hyatt Regency Hotel. Fashion, jewellery, gifts. Cineplex (669–9791).

Oakridge Shopping Centre, 41st Avenue and Cambie Street, south Vancouver (261–2511). Fashion, gifts, Doggie Deli for pet-wear (?) and needs. Woodward's, Marks & Spencer, Edward Chapman and Chapy's.

Woodward's, main store, 101 West Hastings Street (684–5231). Vancouver's own department store. Also known for its supermarkets called ''Woodward's Food Floor.''

Eaton's, main store, 701 Granville Street at West Georgia (685–7112). Good quality department store, travel bureau, delicatessen, Visitors and Convention Bureau office at the Robson Street entrance during the summers. Useful brochure available from the store or the Visitors Bureau which includes maps and size conversions.

The Bay, main store at the northeast corner of West Georgia and Granville Streets (681–6211). Canada's oldest commercial interest, being a descendant of the Hudson Bay Company. An up-to-date department store.

Harbour Centre Mall, 555 West Hastings Street (689–7304). Sears.

Birks, main store, 710 Granville Street at West Georgia (669–3333). Top quality, full service jewellers. Appraisals, repairs, silverware, crystal, china. A Canadian company and the size of a department store.

Army and Navy Department Store, 27 West Hastings Street on the edge of Gastown (682–6644). Discount department store.

Gifts

Vancouver Museums and Planetarium Gift Shop, Vanier Park (731–4158). Beautiful jewellery by native peoples, books, prints.

Vancouver Aquarium Gift Shop, Stanley Park (685–3364). Children's toys, novelties, books, prints, particularly having to do with marine life.

225

The Gallery Shop, Vancouver Art Gallery, Robson Square (682–5621). Books, prints, post-cards, novelties.

Georg Jensen, 790 Robson Street (688–4744). Fine dinnerware, flatware, kitchenware, jewellery

Bowerings, Park Royal, Pacific Centre and Oakridge malls, Canada Shop at Royal Centre Mall (685–1811). Household gifts.

Puddifoot, 2350 West 41st Avenue, Kerrisdale (261–8141). Fine china and gifts.

The Legh Shop, 2279 West 41st Avenue, Kerrisdale (266–9168). Fine china and crystal.

Chachkas, 1073 Robson Street (688–6417). Great fun, not cheap. Adult greeting cards.

Treemendous, 2384 West 4th Avenue (731–5368). Novelties such as fashion erasers, for all ages.

The Unbirthday Store, 3472 Cambie Street (875–1554).

Edgemont Gifts, 3115 Edgemont Boulevard at Lonsdale Avenue, North Vancouver (980–1727). Unique things, greeting cards.

Specialty Shopping

Pappas Furs, 449 Hamilton Street (681–6391). Sylvester Stallone poses for their ads.

Furs by Jacques, 720 Burrard Street at the Hotel Vancouver (684–9041, local638).

Hill's Indian Crafts, 151 and 165 Water Street, Gastown (685–1828 or 685–4249). Authentic and on the coast for 38 years.

Heritage Canada, 650 West Georgia Street in the Vancouver Centre Mall running between The Bay and Pacific Centre Mall (669–2447), and 356 Water Street, Gastown (669–0121). Cowichan goods.

Canadian Impressions at Hudson House, 321 Water Street (689–2024). Cowichan goods.

Arctic Loon Gallery, 3095 South Granville Street (738–9918). Top quality crafts by native peoples artists.

Canada West Antiques, 3790 West 10th Avenue near Alma Street (224–4818).

Country Furniture, 3097 Granville Street at 15th Avenue (738–6411).

Sylvan, 3080 Edgemont Boulevard at Lonsdale Avenue, North Vancouver (986–4863). Excellent local pottery.

Shindler & Co, 2415 south Granville Street (734–4856). Persian and oriental carpets.

Kimono-Ya, 3600 West 4th Avenue (734–0223). Japanese imports of silk and cotton kimonos, clothing, gifts.

Thomas Hobbs' Florists, 2127 West 41st Avenue (263–2601).

Mayhew-Sherwood Flowers, 3691 West Broadway (736–6565).

Robson Square

The Flag Shop, 2081 West 4th Avenue (736–8161). Carries—and knows about—flags from all over the world.

The Comicshop, 2089 West 4th Avenue (738–8122). New and used.

The Write Place, 3063 Granville Street (732–7777). Great stationery.

European News Import House, 1136 Robson Street (683–0616). Newspapers, magazines.

James Inglis Reid Ltd, Ham Curers, 559 Granville Street (683–2632). An old-fashioned and specialty butcher.

George Jackson Meats, 2211 West 4th Avenue (733–9165). Seven days a week.

Galloway's Specialty Foods, 1084 Robson Street (685–7927), and Pacific Centre Mall. On Robson Street since the 1930s.

Murchie's Tea and Coffee Ltd, 1200 Homer Street, head office and wholesale (662–3776), and 850 North Park Royal, West Vancouver (922–3136). A Vancouver establishment dating back to the 19th century.

House of Brussels Chocolates, 2257 West 41st Avenue, Kerrisdale (263–3292), and Granville Island Public Market (684–9678). Their ''truffles'' are getting quite a reputation in town.

Le Chocolat Belge, 1133 Robson Street (688–9624), 980 Robson Street, 2260 West 41st Avenue (Kerrisdale), and 100 South Park Royal, West Vancouver.

Ping-Pong Ice Cream, 5611 West Boulevard, Kerrisdale (263–2430). Italian style.

Baskin-Robbins Ice Cream, Pacific Centre Mall, 866 Denman Street, 2 Water Street (Gastown), Cornwall and Cypress (Kitsilano), and more. Multiple-choice in good ice cream.

Books and Records

Duthie Books, 919 Robson Street (684–4496), and 4444 West 10th Avenue, their ''university'' branch (224–7012), and 4255 Arbutus Street in Arbutus Village Square.

Hager Books, 2176 West 41st Avenue, Kerrisdale (263–9412).

The Bookstore, University of British Columbia (228–4741). Across from the bus loop.

Banyen Books, 2685 West Broadway (732–7912). Huge selection of self-help, psychology, and the spiritual.

White Dwarf Books, 4374 West 10th Avenue (228–8223). Fantasy and science fiction.

Manhattan Books and Magazines, 1089 Robson Street at Thurlow (681–9074).

William Hoffer Bookseller, 60 Powell Street (683–3022). Rare and antiquarian books.

A & A Records and Tapes, 776 Granville Street (685–0405). All the rock.

Zulu Records, 1869 West 4th Avenue (738–3232). Up-to-the-minute rock.

Collectors RPM, 456 Seymour Street (685–8841), and 2528 Main Street (876–8321). Great selection of hard-to-find records, new and used. Beatles museum at the Seymour Street location.

Black Swan, 2936 West 4th Avenue (734–2828). Jazz.

The Magic Flute, 2100 West 4th Avenue (736–2727). Classical.

Re-Runs

The Vancouver Flea Market, 703 Terminal Avenue east of Main Street (685–0666). Saturdays and Sundays, 8 am to 4 pm; admission 50¢. 40,000 square feet of indoor space.

Ex-Toggery, 6055 West Boulevard, Kerrisdale (266–6744). Quality re-sale.

Deluxe Junk, 2600 West 4th Avenue (732–6331) and 310 West Cordova Street, Gastown (685–4871). Men's and women's clothing.

Turnabout Collections, 1453 West Broadway at Granville

Street (734–5313). Quality re-sale.

Second Hand Rose, 2951 West 4th Avenue (738–5844). Women's clothing, especially for party wear.

Jasmine, 1913 Yew Street (732–3418). Beautiful vintage clothing.

The Materialist, 2565 Alma Street at Broadway (738–3144). Women's clothing.

Gastown

17 *Sports*

An outdoor sports paradise, Vancouver is more into year-round get-active athletics than spectator sports. For information on activities associated with city parks and community centres—lawn bowling, pitch and putt, archery, swimming, ice skating, tennis, shuffleboard and jogging—call the **Vancouver Parks Board,** 2099 Beach (681–1141).

For other sporting activities in and out of the city, call **Sports B.C.,** 1200 Hornby (687–3333). Known by its street number, this building and one switchboard serves two organizations—B.C. Recreation and The Outdoor Recreation Council of B.C. The central switchboard can give you information on or put you in touch with local non-profit clubs, groups or associations involved in everything from hiking to hang-gliding, skiing to scuba diving, road racing to ocean kayaking.

For information on recreation throughout the province, but outside the city, contact **Tourism B.C.,** 800 Robson (660–2300). **The Vancouver Convention and Visitors Bureau,** Royal Centre Mall (682–2222), has a fairly comprehensive list of sports facilities as well.

A marvellous reference guide to the various sports facilities in the Greater Vancouver area is *The First Complete Recreation Guide*, by Dona Sturmanis and Karl Bergmann, now unfortunately out of print.

Primarily of interest to members, *The Hosteller,* a local publication, lists sporting programmes sponsored by the Canadian Hostelling Association. It comes out three times a year and can be picked up at the Pack & Boots Shop, 3425 West Broadway (738–3128).

If you are a jogger, you can run almost everywhere—sidewalks, beaches, and parks. A lovely course is along the dikes of the Fraser River. In several parks, there are special **running tracks.**

Balaclava Park — Carnarvon and 29th
Camosun Park — Discovery and 16th
Kerrisdale Park — East Boulevard and 45th
Killarney Park — Kerr and 45th
Memorial Park South — Prince Albert and 41st
Stanley Park — Brockton Oval

For general information on running, contact the Track and Field Association of B.C., 1200 Hornby (687–3333, local 259 or 283). For seaside jobs, there's the Seawall Running Society, P.O. Box 4981, Vancouver V6B 4A6 (669–3626) which organises road races and fun runs. For information call Don Basham there.

You'll find fitness circuits in Stanley Park (behind Brockton Field House), in Ambleside Park, in Parc Verdun in West Vancouver, and at the Burnaby Lake Regional Park sports complex.

For a drop-in fee, you can work out at the following fitness centres or gyms.

YWCA, 580 Burrard Street (683–2531). Women only.

Dyna-Fit at Park Place, 666 Burrard Street (662–3110)

Vancouver Nautilus Fitness, 971 Richards Street (669–2002)

Olympic Fitness Centre, #4 - 2627 Arbutus Street (736–2308)

Ron Zalko's Fitness Affair-Fitness Connection, 2660 West 4th Avenue (736–0341)

World Gym, 444 West 6th Avenue (879–7855)

Western Gym Co-ed Fitness Centre, 244 East Broadway (879–2719)

Harbour Dance Centre, 518 West Hastings Street (684–9542), **Immram Dance Studios,** 337 West Pender Street (669–4497), and at **Anna Wyman School of Dance Arts,** 1705 Marine Drive, West Vancouver (926–6535) all offer conditioning sessions.

BICYCLING

In a time of energy awareness, more and more people are applying foot power to their own pedals. In the city, a new 19 kilometres of trail (for both cyclist and walker) will soon be open along the route of the city's Light Rapid Transit System. This parkway will stretch from New Westminster through Burnaby and Vancouver to False Creek, eventually connecting with Stanley Park and Kitsilano Beach. It will touch on or traverse 32 existing parks and have plazas, fitness stations, drinking fountains, rest areas, displays, and flowers and flags along its way. Miles of tulips are planned. For city bicycling, it will be a welcome addition.

Other good city locations for cycling include the Stanley Park seawall and the University Endowment Lands on Point Grey. In the latter, the area called Southlands, south of Marine Drive, takes you along quiet roads by golf courses and fields of horses which board in this area.

On the North Shore, the air is admittedly fresh but the roads decidedly steeper.

To meet this last challenge, the "mountain bike" is the latest in cycling comfort. Developed for 'off-road' riding, this bicycle has lots of gears (12, 15 or 18), chubby tires to handle potholes and sewer grates, and good suspension to cushion the ride. Take one for a leisurely city tour, to the more rigourous countryside, or to one of the Gulf Islands for a day. If you plan to cycle the Islands, remember they are not flat.

In the city, there are some restrictions. At first it didn't look as if bicycles were to be allowed on the Sea Bus at all, but a demonstration at its opening party brought the media into the fray. Bicycles can now be taken on board—but only on weekends and statutory holidays and for the price of one regular adult fare.

Riding bicycles on the sidewalks anywhere in the city is illegal, except on the Burrard Street Bridge. On the Lions Gate

Bridge, you cannot ride on the street and should walk your bike across. On the paths of the city's beaches, bicycling is usually prohibited, and this, while annoying to those on wheels, is a blessing to the stroller. For a stretch on the narrow southern side of the Stanley Park seawall, bicycles are prohibited, but you can ride on the rest of this path as well as on others throughout the Park. Watch out for some real wheel-bending holes on the "bike routes."

The George Massey Tunnel under the Fraser River poses a major difficulty to cyclists in getting out of town and to Tsawwassen. There are no sidewalks in the tunnel, and it took some public pressure for bikes to be allowed through it at all. Four times a day, between the end of May and the last weekend in September, a bus now shuttles between the north end of the tunnel and the Town & Country Inn on the other side. Pick-up spots, for cyclist and cycle, are poorly-marked. For specific details, call the highways office in New Westminster (277–2115).

Of course getting to the tunnel in the first place is an adventure as bicycles are not allowed on Highway 99. When heading south from Vancouver, the cyclist must chart a more circuitous route through Richmond. Nowhere in the province are bicycles permitted to travel on expressways (defined as 'limited access highways' usually involving the maintenance of speeds of 60 km/hr or more). For help getting through Richmond, call the New Westminster Department of Highways (277-2115).

If you want to explore on your own, two books by Tim Perrin will help. *Exploring by Bicycle* travels only outside Vancouver and into the Gulf Islands. *More Exploring by Bicycle* deals with the metropolitan (Lower Mainland) area.

For those who prefer a more organized excursion, the **Vancouver Bicycle Club** tours the city and surrounding area. To find out the schedule of outings, the B.C. Bicycling Association at 1200 Hornby (687–3333) can tell you how to reach the Vancouver Bicycle Club.

Unless you have the appropriate licence, **Road Racing** is only a spectator sport. Again, the B.C. Bicycling Association can provide you with a list of races and locations, or put you in touch with someone who knows.

Bicycle Rentals

Stanley Park Bicycle Rentals, 1950 West Georgia (681–5581).

Robson Cycles, 1463 Robson Street (687–2777).

Bayshore Bicycles, 1876 West Georgia (689–5071).

Hertz Car and Bike Rentals, The Westin Bayshore, 1601 West Georgia (682–7117).

Dunbar Cycles, 4202 Dunbar Street (738–7022).

Kids Wheels Ltd., 1496 Cartwright Street, Granville Island (688–9130).

Bike rental charges are as varied as cycle selection. A 3-speed averages $14/day, while a 6-speed runs from $15 to $19 a day. Mountain bikes go for considerably more. If you crave togetherness, try a bicycle-built-for-two (the tandem) from Stanley Park Rentals or Bayshore Bicycles. Stanley Park Rentals also has baby buckets available, while Hertz will whip you up a picnic for a price that includes the cost of renting the bike. Instead of a bicycle, you may prefer to rent a little red wagon from Kids Wheels to transport your children, your groceries and your shopping while visiting Granville Island.

GOLF

At the public courses listed here, green fees range from $8 to $15 depending on the course and day of the week. Their pro shops rent clubs. Burnaby Mountain, Musqueam and Fraserview also have driving ranges.

For those who belong to clubs elsewhere, a list of private clubs in the city is included. Most will let you play there with a member, or on a reciprocal privilege basis if you have your home club's membership card. Phone ahead for tee-off times. Capilano Golf and Country Club has an unusually spectacular view from its mountain-clinging location.

Public Golf Courses Within Easy Reach

Burnaby Mountain Golf Course, 7600 Halifax, Burnaby (421–7355). 18 holes, par 71)

Fraserview Golf Course, 7800 Vivian, Vancouver (327–3717). 18 holes, par 71.

Gleneagles Golf Course, 6190 Marine Drive, West Vancouver (921–7353). 9 holes, par 35.

Green Acres Golf Course, 5040 No. 6 Road, Richmond (273–1121). 18 holes, par 70.
Langara Golf Course, 290 West 49th, Vancouver (321–8013). 18 holes, par 71.
McCleery Golf Course, 7170 MacDonald, Vancouver (261–4522). 18 holes, par 72.
Musqueam Golf Centre (Par 3), 3904 West 51st, Vancouver (266–2334). 18 holes, par 60.
Seymour Golf and Country Club (open to the public Monday and Friday), 3723 Mt. Seymour Parkway, North Vancouver (929–2611). 18 holes, par 72.
University Endowment Lands Golf Course, 4701 University Blvd., Vancouver (224–1818). 18 holes, par 69.

Public Golf Courses a Little Further Afield

Carnoustie Golf Course, 533 Dominion, Port Coquitlam (941–4076). 18 holes, par 71.
Delta Golf Course, 11550 Trunk, Delta (594–1414). 18 holes, par 72.
Hazel Golf and Tennis Club, 18150 8th, Surrey (538–1212). 18 holes, par 72.
Meadow Gardens Golf Course, 19699 Lougheed Highway, Pitt Meadows (465–5474). 18 holes, par 71.
Newlands Golf and Racquet Club, 21025 48th, Langley (533–3288). 18 holes, par 70.
Peace Portal Golf Course, 16900 4th, South Surrey (531–4444). 18 holes, par 72.
Squamish Valley Golf and Country Club, 2458 Mamquam, Brackendale (898–9691). 18 holes, par 72.
Surrey Golf Course, 7700 168th, Surrey (576–8224). 18 holes, par 72.
Whistler Golf Course, Box 1700, Whistler V0N 1B0 (932–4544, summers only). 18 hole Arnold Palmer Championship course, par 72. On the west side of Highway 99, opposite Whistler Village. Manager's office (year-round), 932–3928.

Private Golf Clubs

Beach Grove Golf Club, 5946 12th, Delta (943–9381). 18 holes, par 71. $12.
Marine Drive Golf Club, 7425 Yew, Vancouver (261–8111). 18 holes, par 71. $30 unsponsored.

Point Grey Golf and Country Club, 3350 S.W. Marine Drive, Vancouver (261–3108). 18 holes, par 72. $45 unsponsored.

Quilchena Golf and Country Club, 3551 Granville, Richmond (277–3138). 18 holes, par 72. $20 sponsored.

Richmond Country Club, 9100 Steveston Highway, Richmond (277–6266). 18 holes, par 72. Non-members $40 on Mondays, Wednesdays and Fridays only.

Shaughnessy Golf and Country Club, 4300 S.W. Maine Drive, Vancouver (266–6248). 18 holes, par 73. Guests with members only.

Vancouver Golf Club, 771 Austin, Coquitlam (936–3404). 18 holes, par 72. $15.

Pitch and Putt

There are pitch and putt courses in a number of the city's parks: Ambleside in West Vancouver (922–3818); Central Park in Burnaby (434–2727); Queen Elizabeth Park (874–8336); Rupert Park (253–2530); and Stanley Park (681–8847).

Green fees range from $3.80 to $4.50 for adults, $2.05 to $2.50 for children and $1.90 to $2.50 for seniors. Clubs can be rented at all driving ranges and cost from 15¢ to 50¢ a club.

TENNIS ANYONE?

Tennis courts under the supervision of the **Vancouver Board of Parks and Recreation** (681–1141) are open to all at no charge. And you never have to wait for more than half an hour to play. Sit by the court of your choice and those on it (unless it is being used for lessons) must vacate within 30 minutes.

There are 21 courts in **Stanley Park,** Beach Avenue entrance; 20 in **Queen Elizabeth Park,** 33rd and Cambie; and 10 courts in **Kitsilano Beach Park,** Cornwall at the foot of Yew Street.

In addition, there are little pockets of courts all over the city. Here are just a few of them.

West Side

Almond Park (2 courts), Dunbar and 12th
Elm Park (2 courts), Larch and 41st
Granville Park (4 courts), Burrard and 14th

Heather Park (4 courts), Heather and West 18th
Jericho Beach Park (6 courts), Trimble and 4th
McBride Park (4 courts), Collingwood and 4th
Memorial West Park (6 courts), Dunbar and 33rd
Tatlow Park (3 courts), Point Grey Rd and MacDonald
West Point Grey Park (4 courts), Trimble and 6th

South Central Vancouver

Eburne Park (4 courts), Oak and 71st
Langara Golf Course (4 courts), Cambie and West 49th
Oak Park (2 courts), Oak and Park Drive

East Vancouver (near PNE Grounds)

Burrard View Park (2 courts), Wall and North Penticton
Pandora Park (4 courts), Pandora and Nanaimo
Hastings Community Park (3 courts), Pender and Renfrew
Strathcona Park (4 courts), Campbell and Prior
Grandview Park (3 courts), Commercial and Willian

LAWN-BOWLING ET AL.

Lawn Bowling

Visitors can arrange games at the following clubs.
Dunbar Lawn Bowling Club (228–8428). Memorial Park
West, 33rd and Dunbar.
Kerrisdale Lawn Bowling Club (266–1116). Elm Park, 41st
and Larch.
Stanley Park Lawn Bowling Club (683–0910). Stanley Park,
Beach Avenue entrance.
Terminal City Lawn Bowling Club (731–8422). Granville
Park, Fir and 14th.
Vancouver Lawn Bowling Club (879–8916). Queen Elizabeth
Park, 37th and Ontario.
Vancouver South Lawn Bowling Club (874–3038). Grays
Park, 33rd and Windsor.

Checkers

The locations in brackets are where you'll find the equip-
ment? pieces? necessary for this game? sport?
Cedar Cottage Park, Clark and 11th. (Trout Lake Community
Centre)

Connaught Park, Larch and 10th. (Kitsilano Community Centre)

Kerrisdale Centennial Park, 42nd and West Boulevard. (Kerrisdale Community Centre)

Memorial South Park, 41st and Prince Rupert. (Killarney Community Centre)

Oppenheimer Park, Powell and Dunlevy. (Carnegie Library, Downtown Eastside Rear Project)

Victoria Park, Victoria and Grant. (The caretaker)

Stanley Park, Upper zoo area near the Pavilion Restaurant via Pipeline Road. (Not on the board? Try the Parks Board office, 2099 Beach.)

Shuffleboard

Kerrisdale Park, 41st and Knight.

Stanley Park, next to the tennis courts near the Beach House Restaurant.

HORSEBACK RIDING

For between $10 - $14 for one hour, you can enjoy B.C.'s great outdoors on horseback. Along with the one- and two-hour outings, the following stables offer a variety of half-day, full-day, guided and unguided rides atop reliable mounts.

Alpine Riding Academy, 3170 Sunnyside Road, Ioco (461–7111). Lessons, hayrides and day-rides.

Beach Grove Riding Stables, 9230 Ladner Trunk Road, Ladner (946–9408). Beach-rides and day-rides, hayrides and lessons.

Cheekye Stables, Fernwood Road, Brackendale (898–3432). Half-day picnic rides, full-day mountain rides with lunch.

Horseshoe Stables, 21617 128th Avenue, Maple Ridge (463–3852). Rides into Golden Ears Park.

Mustang Stables, 13920 224th Street, Maple Ridge (467–1875). Lessons, fishing and pack trips, nature photography anywhere you want to go, ponies, barbecues.

Grouse Mountain Horseback Trail Rides, Grouse Mountain, North Vancouver (984–0661). Guided trail rides, pony rides for children and wagon rides. Complementary Skyride with trail ride reservations.

As described by Tourism B.C., **dude ranches** must have saddle horses available on the property, may be in remote locations, and can offer lodge-type accommodation or housekeeping units. A complete list of these holiday-in-the-country places is available from Tourism B.C., 800 Robson (660–2300).

One riding school, right in the city, welcomes beginners and has an out-of-town clientelle that tends to come back every time in town. **Canterbury Stable,** 53rd Avenue and Blenheim Street (266–5316), offers riding instruction at $17/hour; no rentals.

SKIING

If you'd like to ski, you've come to the right place—that is, if it's winter. And winter for skiers here usually lasts from mid-December to late-April. Even in *summer,* however, there's skiing on the Whistler glacier.

Whistler Mountain and its recent neighbour, Blackcomb Mountain, are a two hour drive from Vancouver. With the greatest vertical drop in North America, Whistler has over 60 marked runs and several serene powder bowls. Blackcomb offers at least 26 runs and boasts the longest uninterrupted fall-line skiing (up to 5 km) on the continent. Between these two giants, there is something for everyone—from novice to expert, mogul bashing to powder skiing.

Mount Baker's picture-postcard, snow-capped heights are visible from the city. It is across the border in Washington State—about half-way to Seattle. Less developed, it has a shorter vertical drop, but is favoured by many Vancouver skiers. It gets lots of snow.

Then there are Grouse Mountain and Cypress Park—minutes from downtown Vancouver, lighted for night skiing, and accessible by city bus. How lucky can we get?

Lift tickets for downhill skiing usually cost $16 to $23 a day.

In some cases, special rates include half-day or night skiing tickets, discounts for weekday skiing, children and senior citizens, or several-day package prices. Whistler and Blackcomb Mountains have a 2-Mountain Pass.

The **Canadian Hostelling Association,** 3425 West Broadway (738–3128), organizes excursions for downhill and cross-country skiing and snowshoeing.

To check on weather conditions, call **Mountain Forecast,** 276–6112 in Vancouver, listen to **Weatheradio Canada,** 162.4

Blackcombe Mountain, Whistler

Mhz, or watch Channel 14 on cable TV during the ski season.

*A tip in time: When car tire chains are required for driving to ski areas, snow tired are **not** an acceptable substitute.*

Downhill (Alpine) Skiing

The following ski areas all provide ski shops, full rental facilities, a selection of group ski programmes to match all levels of ability, and private lessons.

Grouse Mountain. In North Vancouver, at the top of Capilano Road (984–0661). To get there by city bus, catch the #246-Highland on Georgia, transfer at Edgemont Village to a #232-Queens. 2 gondolas, 4 double chairlifts, 2 T-bars, 3 rope tows, snow-making and night skiing. Complete facilities at the top include baby-sitting, day lodge, restaurants, cafeteria, lounge, beer garden and evening entertainment. For ski reports, call 986–6262.

Cypress Bowl. To reach this ski area behind West Vancouver on the North Shore, take Upper Levels Highway to Cypress Park turn-off, 12 km (7½ mi) west of the Lions Gate Bridge. Chains or snow tires may be required. For information, phone 687–5539. For snow reports, call 926–6007. 2 chairlifts, 1 rope tow and night skiing. First Aid station, dining lounge, 'ankle biters' programme and toboggan area. Snowshoe and hiking trail connects with parking lot. The alpine ski area is 2 km beyond the Hollyburn parking lot, 16 km (10 mi) from the highway. There is a bus service to and from the area on weekends and holidays from points within the city on a reservation basis (926–8644 or 687–5539).

Mount Seymour. For Mount Seymour, above North Vancouver on the North Shore, cross over the Second Narrows Bridge and follow the signs for the Mount Seymour Parkway. The ski area is 14.5 km (9 mi) from downtown. Chains are sometimes required. For info or road reports or snow conditions, phone 986–2261. 3 chairlifts, 2 twin rope tows. First Aid station, cafeteria, snowshoeing and tobogganing.

Hemlock Valley. Hemlock Valley Recreation Limited, Box 7, Site 2, R.R. 1, Agassiz, B.C. V0M 1A0 (797–4411 or Vancouver 524–9741). 1 triple chairlift, 2 double chairlifts, 1 handle tow, night skiing and heli-skiing. Day lodge, accommodation, camper hook-ups (propane filling station), children's centre, teen centre, and great view. For snow reports call 520–6222. Children 8 and under and seniors ski free. Take Lougheed Highway (#7) east through Mission; turn left at the Sasquatch Inn. The hills are 20 minutes to half an hour from here. Chains sometimes needed.

Gibson Pass. Gibson Pass Resort Inc, Manning Park, B.C. V0X 1R0 (840–8822). 232 km (145 mi) east of Vancouver via Highway 1 to Hope, then Highway 3 to Manning Park. 2 chairlifts, 1 T-bar, 1 rope tow. Day lodge, cafeteria, accommodation at Gibson Pass Resort Lodge (reservations required, 840–8822), sleigh rides, tobogganing, ice skating and snowmobiling. For snow conditions, call Vancouver 926–6071. Greyhound buses travel to Manning Park from the Dunsmuir Bus Depot in Vancouver (662–3222), four times a day beginning at 6:40 am.

Whistler. Site of both Whistler Mountain and Blackcomb Mountain. 120 km (70 mi) north of Vancouver via Highway 99 to Squamish and beyond through the Cheakamus Canyon on a greatly improved stretch of road. Both mountains have day lodges, licensed restaurants top and bottom, recreational racing, a selection of ski packages, day care with or without ski instruction and guided tours for the newcomer. Heli-skiing and telemarking (equipment rentals and lessons) are available from the town centre. For information on either mountain or accommodation, phone the Whistler Resort Association (604–932–3928). For reservations, call 604–932–4222 in Whistler, 222–2554 in Vancouver, 467–7554 in Seattle or 249–1446 in Portland.

Whistler Mountain facilities include 1 gondola, 7 double chairlifts, 3 triple chairlifts, 2 T-bars, 1 platter lift, 2 two-handled lifts. For further information or snow reports, call Whistler Mountain (685–0521). For heli-skiing, call 932–4105.

Blackcomb Mountain facilities include 5 triple chairlifts, 1 double chairlift, 1 T-bar. For more info and snow conditions, contact Blackcomb Mountain (932–3141).

B.C. Rail (984–5246 or 986–2012) leaves daily for Whistler. During the winter only, Maverick Coach Lines (255–1171 or 662–3222) also runs daily scheduled service to and from the area.

From the Vancouver Airport, Perimeter Transportation (261–2299) which runs the airport Hustle-bus will take you directly to Whistler Mondays, Wednesdays, Fridays, Saturdays or Sundays. Buses leave the airport at 1 pm on these days and also at 4 pm Saturdays and Sundays. Fares are $19 for adults, $9.75 for children 3 to 12 years. Tuesdays and Thursdays, a connecting bus leaving the airport at noon will take you to the Vancouver Bus Depot for a Whistler bus. If you wish to stay in Vancouver overnight, Perimeter will arrange to pick you up at 6 am for a Whistler bus.

Cross-country (Nordic) Skiing

B.C. offers 100s of kilometers of well-groomed, track-set cross-country touring. Most of the major ski resorts have complete facilities (including rentals and lessons) for cross-country as well as downhill skiing. In addition, there are spectacular trails in most of B.C.'s national parks and many of its provincial parks. Within easy driving range of Vancouver, there is Nordic skiing available at **Whistler, Alice Lake** and **Brandywine Falls** north of the city via Highway 99, **Diamond Head** in Garibaldi Provincial Park near Whistler, **Hemlock Valley** and **Mount Baker.**

A little further away in Manning Park, **Gibson Pass** has 157 km of marked trails, 30 km of which are track-set, and part of which is lit.

Closer to town on the North Shore, **Hollyburn** (922–0825), part of Cypress, and **Mount Seymour** (986–2261) provide trails within a 20 minute drive from the Lions Gate Bridge. All have full rental facilities and offer instruction.

For a province-wide list of areas specializing in cross-country touring, contact Tourism B.C., 800 Robson (660–2300), or the Ministry of Lands, Parks and Housing, Parks and Outdoor Recreation Division, 1019 Wharf Street, Victoria, B.C. V8W 2Y9.

Helicopter and Snow-Cat Skiing

For both cross-country and alpine skiing, **Whistler Heli Skiing Ltd.,** Box 368, Whistler, B.C. V0N 1B0 (932–4105), can organize one-run, one-day or two-day excursions. **B.C. Powder Guides,** Box 258, Whistler, B.C. V0N 1B0 (932–5331 or 894–6994) leaves Whistler and Bralorne for daily, three-day and weekly outings into the Spearhead and Chilcotin ranges.

A slightly less expensive way to beat the lift line-ups and get away from the crowds is snow-cat skiing. **Selkirk Wilderness Skiing,** General Delivery, Meadow Creek, B.C. V0G 1N0 (366–4424), and **Great Northern Snow Cat Skiing Ltd.,** Trout Lake, British Columbia, Business and Reservation Office, P.O. Box 2763, Salmon Arm, B.C. V0E 2T0 (832–9500), offer a variety of trips.

For helicopter and snow-cat skiing in other areas of the province, contact Tourism B.C., 800 Robson (660–2300).

SKATING

Since winter here in the city is very short and not very cold, outdoor skating rinks have a limited life-span. If it does freeze, an area of **Lost Lagoon** in Stanley Park is roped off for skaters. A small artificial rink appears during the winter months in **Robson Square,** downtown. (No charge at either.) Other than that, you'll have to go indoors to flash the silver blades.

A large number of rinks are run by the Vancouver Parks Board. They all have schedules which include sessions for Adults Only or for Parents and Children. Most allow hockey at times. Some have a Teen Night, Children's Specials, and Beginners Only. On Sunday mornings, the **West End** rink has a Handicapped Skate sponsored by the Optimists Club. Admission is adults $1.90, seniors and children 85¢. Skate rentals are available. Other community rinks include:

West End Community Centre Ice Rink, 870 Denman (689–0571)
Kitsilano Ice Rink, 2690 Larch (734–4974)
Killarney Ice Rink, 6260 Killarney (437–9167)
Kerrisdale Arena, 5670 E. Boulevard (261–8144)
Britannia Ice Rink, 1661 Napier (253–4391)
Trout Lake Ice Rink, 3350 Victoria (876–2625)
Sunset Ice Rink, 390 E. 51st (324–4115)
Riley Park Ice Rink, 50 E. 30th (879–6222)

Other Rinks

Public sessions are limited at the following rinks, but you can usually skate sometime on Friday, Saturday or Sunday. Phone for schedules. Skate rentals are available.

UBC Thunderbird Winter Sports Centre, UBC (228–6121).

Karen Magnussen Arena, 937 Lynn Valley, North Vancouver (984–9341).

Burnaby Lake Rink, 3676 Kensington, Burnaby (291–1261).

Municipal Ice Arena, 786 22nd, West Vancouver (926–8621).

WATER SPORTS

Swimming

The Parks and Recreation Board of Vancouver manages nine indoor pools throughout the city.

Britannia Pool, 1661 Napier (253–4391)
Kensington Pool, 5175 Dumfries (327–9401)
Kerrisdale Pool, 5670 E. Boulevard (261–8518)
Killarney Pool, 6260 Killarney (434–9167)
Lord Byng Pool, 3990 West 14th (228–9734)
Percy Norman Pool, 30 East 30th (876–8804)
Renfrew Pool, 2929 East 22nd (434–4712)
Templeton Park Pool, 700 Templeton (253–7101)
Vancouver Aquatic Centre, 1050 Beach (689–7156)

Their schedules are complicated and cater to various interests, ages and abilities. Call the pools for further information. Water at the **Aquatic Centre,** 1050 Beach Avenue (689–7156), is salt, and the facilities there include a diving pool, a children's pool, sauna, whirlpool, and exercise gym.

The **YMCA pool,** 955 Burrard (681–0221), is open only to members, but anyone can buy a pass for the pool at the **YWCA,** 580 Burrard (683–2531). And the facilities of the **UBC Aquatic Centre** (228–4521) are open to the public at certain times.

There are outdoor saltwater pools at **Ambleside Park, Second Beach** in Stanley Park, and **Kitsilano Beach** (731–0011). The latter is 137 feet long and heated, and all have change-rooms and showers.

On the following beaches, there are lifeguards on duty from

11 am to 9 pm, Victoria Day to Labour Day: English Bay Beach, Second and Third Beaches in Stanley Park, Kitsilano Beach, Jericho Beach, Locarno Beach, Spanish Banks, Trout Lake Beach and Sunset Beach.

Dogs are prohibited on all beaches.

Scuba Diving

Because of the nature of British Columbia's coastline, the Pacific waters here are protected and considered clean, clear and very safe for diving. Avid divers tell us that winter is the best time of the year for diving, since temperatures, except on the surface, remain around 40° F all year.

The diver's guidebook is Betty Pratt-Johnson's *141 Dives in the Protected Waters of Washington and British Columbia.* Most dive shops and bookstores in the city stock it.

There are at least 29 excellent dive sites very close to Vancouver, but the Harbour, between the Lions Gate and Second Narrows bridges, is *closed* to divers. Elsewhere within harbour waters, permission must be obtained from the **Port of Vancouver, Harbour Master's Office** (666–3326) before diving.

Diving parks in the greater Vancouver vicinity include **Whytecliffe Park** in West Vancouver at the entrance to Howe Sound, **Porteau Cove** further up the Howe Sound toward Squamish, **Saltery Bay,** and **Ogden Point Breakwater** in Victoria.

For further information, ask at one of the many dive shops in Vancouver, at a local club, or read *Diver Magazine,* 8051 River Road, Richmond, B.C. V6X 1X8 (273–4333).

Dive shops supply rental equipment, but most expect you to provide your own personal gear—fins, facemask, snorkel, mitts, and boots. Also, to have your tank filled, you must have proof of your certification and of a current hydrostatic test for the tank. The following shops welcome tourists who would like to join in their organized dives.

Adrenalin Sports, 1512 Duranleau Street, Granville Island (682–2881)

Diver's World, 2828 West 4th (732–1344), or 5760 Cedarbridge Way, Richmond (273–2064)

The Diving Locker, 2745 West 4th (736–2681)

Odyssey Diving Centre, 2659 Kingsway (430–1451)

Capilano Divers Supply, 1236 Marine Drive, North Vancouver (986–0302)

Aqua Society UBC, Student Union Building, 6138 S.U.B. Boulevard, UBC (228–3329). Dives at least once a month on Vancouver Island or the Gulf Islands.

If you're looking for a partner to dive with, **Dive and Sea Sports,** 825 McBride Boulevard, New Westminster (524–1188 has a list—The Buddy Book.

For divers who wish to explore some interesting and unusual sites, **Oceaner Diving Charters,** 995 West 2nd Avenue, Vancouver, B.C. V5Z 2A2, runs scheduled scuba trips from February to November. Trips include destinations in the Queen Charlotte Islands, Alaska, Port Hardy, or the Gulf Islands, a study of local marine life and a look at old ship wrecks. Some don't start out from Vancouver, but the company will arrange connections when there is no regular flight to the point of embarkation. Boat charters run $75 to $105 per person per day and include meals, tanks, weights, air and accommodation. For more info, phone Oceaner Recreation (738–6811) or Diver's World (732–1344).

There are also several resorts that cater to scuba divers. **Beach Gardens Dive Resort,** 7074 Westminster Avenue, Powell River, B.C. V8A 1C5 (485–6267), and **Hotel Sydney,** 2537 Beacon Avenue, Victoria, B.C V8L 1Y3 (656–1131), provide for the total underwater holiday.

Scuba Clubs

The Diving Locker Association, 2745 West 4th Avenue (736–2681)

Richmond Aqua Addicts, P.O. Box 23452, Richmond, B.C. Vancouver AMF, V7B 1W1 (271–1756)

You'd Rather Be Sailing?

From **The Jib Set Sailing Centre,** 1020 Beach Avenue, Vancouver, B.C. V6E 1T7 (689–1477), you can arrange a charter, bareboat or skippered. Their craft are all cruising keel boats. A day-outing in a 27-foot boat for six people, plus skipper, costs approximately $135 to $149 depending on the day of the week. Four hours in a 20-foot boat costs from $50 to $70. They also have a variety of 'learn-to-sail' vacation cruises, ranging from three to six days.

Sea Wing Sailing School and Charters, 1818 Maritime Mews, Granville Island, Vancouver, B.C. V6H 3X2 (669–

Scuba diving in local waters

8040) has a large fleet of boats. From them, you can charter a boat for from a half-day to month-long excursion with or without skipper. Their five-day cruise of local waters costs $629/person, $589/person for 2 people. They also have yachting courses or cruise-and-learn vacations.

White Water Adventures, 1616 Duranleau Street, Granville Island, Vancouver, B.C. V6H 3S4 (689–7238) has a Maple Leaf 68 Sailboat which rents for $150 to $200/hour with skipper and one crew member.

Outward Bound, #206 - 1656 Duranleau Street, Granville Island (669–9196), among other things offers courses in sailing.

Ecosummer Canada Expeditions Ltd, 1516 Duranleau Street, Granville Island, Vancouver, B.C. V6H 3S4 (669–7741), organises expeditions.

Canoeing and Kayaking

On Burnaby Lake, kayakers and rowers train all summer for the World Championships and the Olympics. So, if you're into this sport, you're in good company.

Prices vary from hourly to weekly rates, but in general canoes and kayaks can be rented for roughly $15 to $20 a day. Most rentals include paddles and life jackets. Some, if necessary, have roof racks available.

Alouette Canoe Sales and Rentals, 1780 Freemont Street, Port Coquitlam (941–2822), **Cove Canoe and Kayak Rentals,** 2156 Banbury Road, North Vancouverr (939–2268) or **Deer Lake Boat Rental,** 5400 Sperling Avenue, Burnaby (255–0081) will rent you either.

For canoes, try **B & D Outdoor Equipment** (for lake use only), 6849 McPherson Avenue, Burnaby (437–4824), **Pack-a-Boat,** 1000 Beach Avenue (685–5738), **Vancouver Canoe and Kayak Shop,** 1666 Duranleau Street, Granville Island (688–6010).

Walter's Ski Shack, 1637 Marine Drive, North Vancouver (988–3937), and **Mountain Equipment Co-op,** 428 West 8th (872–7858), specialize in kayak rentals.

Pack-a-Boat also have a selection of zodiacs for rent ranging from $40 a weekend to $341 a week.

The **Canadian Hostelling Association** (736–3116) organizes kayak tours up the west coast of Vancouver Island for members, July to September, and day-paddles in the city area. Contact John Ruckwood (732–6637) for more info.

Canoe Sport B.C. is the umbrella organization for the Recreation Canoeing Association of B.C., the Whitewater Canoeing Association of B.C. and the Olympic Canoe and Kayak Association of B.C. Located at 1200 Hornby (687–3333), Canoe Sport can provide information on local groups, tours, courses and events.

Ecomarine Ocean Kayak Centre, 1666 Duranleau Street, Granville Island, Vancouver, B.C. V6H 3S4 (689–7575), has single-man ocean kayaks for rent at $8/hour or $20/day; doubles are $12/hour or $34/day. You can rent their kayaks for longer periods (at lower prices), but it is a good idea to book well in advance if planning an extended rental during the summer months.

Ecosummer Canada Expeditions Ltd, 1516 Duranleau Street, Granville Island, Vancouver, B.C. V6H 3S4 (669–7741), organises trips; **Outward Bound,** #206–1656 Duranleau Street, Granville Island (669–9196), gives courses.

Sailboarding

Seven days a week, you can take a course and rent a board, wetsuit or accessories from **Windsure Windsurfing School Ltd,** 1768 West Georgia (687–SURF or 687–WIND) or **Vancouver Surf-Sailing (1984),** 1352 Argyle Street, West Vancouver (922–7245). Rent by the hour, day, weekend, long weekend, week, with or without instruction.

Windsure has two further shops and one beach site—**Village Boardsailing** (summers only), 1845 Marine Drive, West Vancouver (926–7547), **Windsure Manufacturing,** 1793 West 4th Avenue (734–SAIL), and **Jericho Sailing Centre** at the foot of Discovery Road (224–0615). At any of these locations, one hour of instruction including rental costs $25, wetsuit plus board $10/hr, just wetsuit $5/hr, board only $10/hr. If you take a high-performance board out on demonstration, you can put the rental fee toward its purchase price.

At Vancouver Surf-Sailing (1984), a 3-hour lesson including rental costs $20, boards $7/hr, and wetsuits $3/hr.

There is also sailboarding at Whistler. On Alta Lake, **Whistler Windsurfing** (932–3389) will give you a lesson or rent you a board for $10/hr with wetsuit, $40/day or $70 for the weekend.

Rafting

This exhilarating and unusual outdoor vacation takes you down many of the rivers that early explorers travelled by canoe. Some of the rapids encountered are serious business, especially at low tide, and many of the trips take you through the infamous Hell's Gate. The companies listed here say they take every possible precaution to ensure your safety.

Whitewater Adventures Ltd., 1616 Duranleau Street, Granville Island, Vancouver, B.C. V6H 3S4 (669–1100 or 689–RAFT). Day trips on the Elaho, Thompson and Fraser Rivers; 2 days on the Thompson and Fraser Rivers; 6 days on the Fraser River. Longer trips (canoeing, sailing and rafting) include 12 days on the Nahannni River in the Yukon, 5 days on the Chilco-Chilcotin Rivers, 6 days sailing in the Gulf Islands, 9 days sailing the Inside Passage, ocean sailing cruises and yacht charters.

Kumsheen Raft Adventures Ltd., 281 Main Street, Lytton, B.C. V0K 1Z0. Call collect from outside B.C., 455–2296, or toll free within the province, 1–800–482–2269. They also have an office at 1730 Burrard Street, Vancouver, B.C. V6J 3G7 (736–0411). 3 hours on the Thompson River; day trips on the Thompson and Fraser Rivers; 1 day paddle-your-own-raft (with guide) on the Chilliwack River; 2 days on the Thompson River; 3 days on the Thompson and Fraser Rivers; 6 days on the Chilco-Chilcotin and Fraser Rivers; 7 days on the Fraser and Thompson Rivers.

Hyak River Expeditions, 1614 West 5th Avenue, Vancouver, B.C. V6J 1N8 (734–8622). Day trips on the Chilliwack, Elaho and Thompson Rivers; 2 days on the Thompson River; 7 days on the Chilco River; 13 days on the Firth River in the Yukon. Hyak also offers a 1-day, learn-to-paddle-a-one-man-inflatable-kayak/canoe experience.

Raft River Adventures, R.A.F.T. Inc., Box 34051, Stn. D., Vancouver, B.C., V6J 4M1 (261–RAFT). One- and two-day trips on the Chilliwack and Nahatlach Rivers.

Frontier River Adventures Ltd., 927 Fairfield Road, North Vancouver, B.C. V7H 2J4 (929–7612 or 867–9244). One-, two-, three- and eight-day trips on the Thompson and Fraser Rivers.

Whistler River Adventures Ltd., Box 202, Whistler, B.C., V0N 1B0 (or call The Leisure Connection, 932–5850). 2

hours on the Cheakamus River, 3 hours on the Birkenhead River, or 1 day on the Elaho River.

PARACHUTING, HANG-GLIDING AND SOARING

If you've got the nerve to jump out of a plane, contact **Horizon AeroSports (1982) Ltd,** 5112 Gladwin Road, Matsqui (854–3255) or 146 East 54th Avenue, Vancouver (327–3867). The drop zone is located 35 minutes from Vancouver on Highway 401, and there is free camping on the grounds on weekends. The cost is $75/person which includes equipment and instruction by members of the Canadian National Parachuting team. With a group of 20 or more, there is a free barbecue in the evening. The Vancouver office is open 10 am to 6 pm for pre-registration.

Universal Sport Ski and Hang-Gliding School, P.O. Box 227, Yarrow, B.C. V0X 2A0 (823–4273, or 298–4389 in Vancouver), can provide equipment, instruction, and hang-gliding excursions. They also arrange outings to deep powder skiing.

The Vancouver Soaring Association (263–3630) operates out of the airport in Hope at the junction of Highways 3 and 1. For $30 you can get a twenty-minute ride as a passenger any weekend between the beginning of April and the end of October.

SPECTATOR SPORTS

At **Brockton Oval** in Stanley Park, you might catch a cricket, rugby, field hockey or soccer match on the weekend. Call the Parks Board office (681–1141) to see what's happening there or to find out the baseball schedule in **Queen Elizabeth Park.**

There are viewing stands beside the **Burnaby Lake** rowing, canoeing and kayaking training site. The Burnaby Department of Parks and Recreation (294–7450) can give you specific details on when you should watch.

For a real lift, you might want to take the **Grouse Mountain** Super Skyride up to 3600 feet above sea level and watch the hang-gliding dare devils take off from yet a further 5000 feet up the slope. Hang-gliders take off most days during the good

253

B.C. Place, False Creek

weather and each summer Grouse Mountain hosts the Annual World Invitational Hang-Gliding Championship. Call 984–0661 or 986–6262 for more information.

At the Pacific National Exhibition (PNE) grounds (253–2311), the **Vancouver Canucks** ice hockey team plays in the **Coliseum** between early October and the Stanley Cup finals. For game times and tickets, call 254–5141.

The city's baseball team, the **Vancouver Canadians,** plays at **Nat Bailey Stadium,** 4601 Ontario Street at 30th Avenue (foot of Queen Elizabeth Park). For their schedule and tickets, phone 872–5232.

Between early July and the Grey Cup playoffs, the **B.C. Lions** kick around the pigskin under the 'Dome' of Vancouver's latest sports facility, **B.C. Place Stadium.** Located on the north shore of False Creek at No. 1 Robson Street, this multi-purpose amphitheatre is situated in the heart of the city. It has a seating capacity of 60,000 and is used for everything from rock concerts to religious gatherings, sports events to seminars and conferences, and tractor pulls. At the moment, the B.C. Lions are the only regular tenant. Tickets to all B.C. Place Stadium events are available through VTC/CBO outlets (280–4444). Guided tours can also be arranged. Call 661–DOME for more info.

Empire Stadium on the PNE Grounds, where the B.C. Lions used to play, could be devoted entirely to amateur sports in future.

For horse-racing there are two tracks. One is at the **PNE** grounds (254–1631), and the other is the **Cloverdale Raceway,** 6050 176th Street, Surrey (576–9141).

Port Mann Bridge, Transcanada Highway

18 Touring further afield

FRASER VALLEY

Fraser Valley — North Side

To reach the lower Fraser River Valley, drive east on Broadway (Highway 7) and the Lougheed Highway (7) to Port Coquitlam. Or follow the south shore of Burrard Inlet on East Hastings (Highway 7a) and the Barnet Highway (7a) to Port Moody, then travel the Lougheed Highway (7) for Port Coquitlam. The latter route is slower and takes you through a bustling residential district, past the PNE Grounds, Burnaby Mountain Park and Barnet Beach Park.

Port Moody. From here you are within easy reach, via Ioco Road, of recreational parks, camping facilities and the Alpine Riding Academy (461–7111) at Buntzen Lake. Also north via Ioco Road is Belcarra Park and Bedwell Bay.

Coquitlam. The huge Coquitlam Shopping Centre is at the junction of Barnet Highway, Pine Tree Way and the Lougheed Highway. It's close to the city of Port Coquitlam, Burke Mountain, and its recreational facilities. The Westwood Car Racing Circuit is also nearby. Races are held on summer Sundays beginning in April. Motor Sports B.C. (687–3333) can provide a complete schedule.

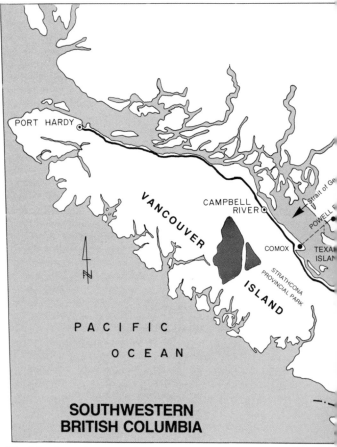

**SOUTHWESTERN
BRITISH COLUMBIA**

Pitt Meadows and Maple Ridge. These names refer not only to the towns, but also to the municipalities in which they are located. Moreover, the official name for the town of **Haney** is now Maple Ridge. Beginning about 40 km (25 mi) east of Vancouver, this area offers excellent shops for browsing, especially for antiques. There are scenic walks, boating, swimming, golf, tennis and horseback riding, and beautiful camping and picnicking grounds. During the summer months, major recognized Canadian Equestrian Federation events are held at the Maple Ridge Equestrian Center (467–2413).

At Pitt Lake canoes can be rented. Whonnock Lake has camping facilities, a cooking shelter and a sandy beach. Picnic

among the trees of Ako Park, beside the Alouette River, or in Maple Ridge Park where camping is allowed. At the end of Silver Valley Road in Maple Ridge, visit the UBC demonstration forest (463–8148). It's open daily from dawn to dusk.

10 km (8 mi) north of Maple Ridge is Golden Ears Provincial Park and Alouette Lake. Here camping facilities include space for RVs, and a naturalist conducts nature walks and talks during the summer. If you are there in May, you can join in the Maple Ridge community's Mountain Festival. For detailed information contact the Maple Ridge-Pitt Meadows Chamber of Commerce, 22238 Lougheed Highway (463–3366).

Albion. 5 km (3 mi) east of Maple Ridge, a car ferry shunts back and forth across the Fraser River between Albion and Fort Langley. Here you can choose to cross to the south side of the river to explore the fort, or continue along Highway 7 to Mission.

Mission. Westminster Abbey (1–826–8975), a Benedictine monastery, stands on the highest point of land here with a good view of the Fraser Valley. Visitors are welcome and guided tours of the Abbey's treasures are conducted between 1:30 and 4 pm weekdays, Sundays 2 to 4 pm. Picnic on the Abbey grounds (but only with permission from the monks) or at nearby Rolley Lake.

8 km (5 mi) west of Mission is Storyland Trails, 9314 Hayward (826–6480), where storybook characters and scenes crop up along wooded pathways. This five-acre park includes a trout-stocked lake, a picnic area and a gift shop.

Harrison Mills. Look into the Acton Kilby General Store and Museum (796–9576). This turn-of-the-century historic gem (well-preserved) was built in 1904 when Harrison Mills was a booming sawmill town. To get there turn south from Highway 7 at the east end of the Harrison River Bridge. Kilby Park surrounds the store and you can picnic there.

North of Harrison Mills, about 11 km (7 mi) on the Morris Valley Road, there's the Chehalis Fish Hatchery (796–2281). You can visit this example of B.C. fish farming, but phone ahead to make arrangements.

Further north on Morris Valley Road, is Hemlock Valley, a popular winter-time ski area and summer resort.

Agassiz. This town is located at the junction of Highways 7 and 9, and visitors can stop at the Agricultural Research Station with its arboretum and picnic area.

Harrison Hot Springs. 125 km (78 mi) from Vancouver and 6 km (4 mi) north of Agassiz, Harrison Hot Springs is a total year-round resort. Boating, sailing, camping, picknicking, fishing, golf, and hiking are all available. In summer, you can swim in the cool waters of Harrison Lake, laze on the sandy beach or join in the sandcastle-building or kite-flying contests. If the lake is too cold for your liking, relax in the warm mineral waters of the public pool which are piped from the nearby hot springs. Call Chilliwack Chamber of Commerce Tourist Centre, 1–792–4231, for more information.

Sasquatch Provincial Park. A few kilometres north of Harrison Hot Springs, you can visit the park named after that huge, elusive, hairy, man-like creature which is so much a part of the Agassiz-Harrison area folklore.

Ruby Creek. On Highway 17 towards Hope, 26 km (16 mi) from Harrison Hot Springs. Sightings of Sasquatch footprints have been reported near here.

Fraser Valley — South Side

The south side of the Fraser River Valley can be reached in two ways. The TransCanada Highway (1) crosses over the Fraser River by way of the Port Mann Bridge and continues up the south side of the valley to Hope. The alternate route, Highway 1a through Surrey, crosses the river from New Westminster via the Pattullo Bridge. Take either Kingsway or Canada Way from Vancouver to New Westminster. This second route takes you through the back roads and small towns of Surrey where you can bid in a local auction or browse in the numerous antique stores. In season, there are plenty of road signs directing you to farms where you can "pick-your-own" fresh berries.

Whalley/Newton Area, Surrey. On the south side of the Pattullo Bridge, along the King George Highway (which is also 136th Street as well as Highway 99a), you can look through the collectibles, glass and china in many of the excellent antique shops of the area.

Cloverdale, Surrey. At the junction of Highways 10 and 15 the town can be reached either from the King George Highway or from the Fraser Highway (1a), or the 176th Street exit south from the TransCanada (1). Visit the Cloverdale Fairgrounds or the Surrey Museum, at 60th and 176th. Join in an auction or visit more antique stores. Except on Mondays, peruse the Valley fresh produce and other goodies at either the Cloverdale Village Market (179th and Highway 10) or the Surrey Public Market (64th and King George Highway). If you are there over the Victoria Day long weekend in May, join in the "Cloverdale

Rodeo'' celebration. Further south, Redwood Park and Arboretum will be off to your left at 180th and 20th. How about exploring the Ste-Michelle Winery (576–6741)? It's just west of Cloverdale, at 152nd Street and Highway 10. Tours are available, but phone first to make arrangements.

Langley. At the junction of Highway 10, the Fraser Highway (1a) and Glover. From the TransCanada Highway (1), take the 264th Street, Glover Road exit south. On Saturdays, year round, the Fraser Valley Livestock Auction (534–3241) begins at 9:30 am at 21801 56th Avenue.

Fort Langley. Go north via the Glover Road (264th Street) exit from the TransCanada Highway to historic Fort Langley, the original capital of the Crown Colony of British Columbia and the oldest building (1839) in the province. A visit to the fort (888–4424) and to Langley Centennial Museum (888–3922) provides insight into some of the province's history. The Fort itself is open daily, 10 am to 6 pm during the summer months, 10 am to 4:30 pm Labour Day to June 1. Admission is adults $1, children 50¢, families $3. The Langley Centennial Museum is free and open Tuesday through Saturday 10 am to 5 pm, Sunday 1 pm to 5 pm. Near the Fort, the B.C. Farm Machinery Museum is open Monday to Saturday, 11 am to 5 pm, Sundays 1 to 5 pm. Admission is adults $1, children 25¢ (free with an adult), and seniors 50¢. In the National Exhibition Centre, you will find exhibits of contemporary arts and crafts.

From Fort Langley you can take the free car ferry across the Fraser River to Albion and head back to Vancouver along the river's north side.

Bradner. In April, join in the Daffodil Festival. Take 264th Street south from the TransCanada Highway.

Aldergrove. East of Langley, via the Fraser Highway or just off the TransCanada on 264th, is the Vancouver Game Farm (856–6825). Its 120 acres can be explored—by car or on foot—any day, from 8 am until dusk. Try the ride on the baby elephant.

Abbotsford. The fantastic Abbotsford Air Show is on and over the Abbotsford Air Field every August. There are delightful picnicking spots at Matsqui, just north of Abbotsford on Highway 11.

Chilliwack. Located north of the TransCanada Highway via the Yale Road. The Canadian Military Engineers Museum near here has items dating back to 1610. In mid-May, experience the two-week long ''Country Living Festival.'' In August, look out for the Raft Race. Besides the numerous annual events, you can enjoy hiking, fishing, cycling, golf, horseback riding, and auctions in the area. Nearby, on the TransCanada Highway (#1) at the Harrison Hot Springs exit, the Minter Gardens, 52892 Bunker Road in Rosedale (794–7191), are open April through October from 9 am until dusk daily.

Sardis. The Salish Indian Weavers Shop is south of the Trans-Canada Highway on Wells Road. For information, contact the Salish Weavers Guild, Box 370, 7201 Vedder Road, Sardis B.C., V2R 1A7 (858–7933), or ask at the Chilliwack Tourist Information Centre.

Cultus Lake Park and Cultus Lake Provincial Park. South of Sardis and Vedder Crossing, these parks offer picnic and camp sites, hiking, climbing, golf, water skiing, boating, swimming, water-slide, fishing, and riding.

Bridal Veils Falls. 15 minutes east of Chilliwack on Highway 1 at Bridal Veils Falls is Flintstone Bedrock City (794–7361), open from late spring to early fall. Nearby, you can hike in the alpine meadows of Mount Cheam.

Hope and Beyond

Gateway to the Fraser Canyon and Manning Park, Hope is situated at the junction of Highways 1 and 3. In town you can see samples of unspun Chinese silk, historical photographs, and Indian jade tools in the Hope Museum (869–7322) in the Municipal Hall. Open daily during the summer, 8:30 am to 4:30 pm. In winter, Monday through Friday, 8:30 am to 4:30 pm, by appointment only. Christ Church, at Park and Fraser, was consecrated in 1861, and many of the original furnishings are still in the sanctuary.

The surrounding countryside offers all sorts of recreational activities. Kawkawa Lake and Lake of the Woods are accessible from Highway 3. Jones Lake and Silver Lake can be reached from Highway 1. Trails lead up and down the slopes of Mount Ogilvie, Mount Hope, Holy Cross Mountain, Dog

Mountain and Silver Tip Mountain. Hang-gliders launch themselves from nearby peaks to float precariously down the air currents between the cliffs.

In September, the Hope Brigade Days celebrations turn the town into a carnival. The Hyack Canoe Race begins in Hope on Victoria Day in May.

East of Hope, Highway 3 winds through Manning Park en route to Princeton. Alpine meadows, hiking trails, winter skiing and spectacular views of mountain peaks await you in Manning Park. Just 21 km (13 mi) along Highway 3 from Hope is the site of the disastrous Hope Slide of January 1965—the largest earth and rock slide in B.C.'s history. It destroyed about two miles of the Hope-Princeton Highway, filling the valley with rock and mud to depths of up to 200 feet.

North along Highway 1 from Hope takes you into the beautiful Fraser Canyon. **St. John the Divine** church in Yale, built in 1859, is one of the oldest churches on the mainland of southwestern B.C. Further north at Boston Bar, an aerial car ferry takes one car at a time across the Fraser River to North Bend. 11 km (7 mi) south of Boston Bar is **Hell's Gate Canyon** where the waters of the Fraser River rush through a narrow gorge at volumes of up to 200 million gallons a minute. In 1914, Canadian National Railway blasting caused a massive landslide that further restricted the already narrow channel.

Here, **Hell's Gate Airtram** descends from the highway and over the gorge for a closer look at the Fraser River, the salmon ladders, and informative exhibits. If you are lucky, you may see a raft of people ''shooting'' the perilous rapids of this turbulent gorge. The Airtram (867–9277) across the gorge is open 8 am to dusk, June 1 to September 15. Closed November through February. For the remainder of the year, the tram operates from 10 am to 4 pm daily. Adults $5.50, children $3.25, seniors $5, families $16.

WHISTLER

An absolute must for the skiier has, of course, been Whistler Mountain, a 90-minute drive north of Vancouver along Highway 99 from Horseshoe Bay. (See Chapter 17 for details on skiing at Whistler and Blackcomb Mountains.) Now, however, the town of Whistler and its surroundings appeal to both skiier and non-skiier alike. A wide selection of accommodation, restaurants, facilities for warm weather fun and the magnificence of Whistler's mountain-valley setting more recently stay open on a year-round basis.

Until five years ago, "Whistler" referred to the mountain or its town at the base of the gondola lift. Today the hub of activity is the European-flavoured Whistler Village Town Centre 3 kilometres up the road. Built around a central square are hotels, restaurants and shops. Here you can stay in one of the more than 15 hotels or condominiums—often with fireplace. Many complexes have a swimming pool (open even in winter), saunas, hot tubs, jacuzzis, and kitchen suites. You will also find a concentration of restaurants, a grocery store, post office, pharmacy, and liquor store. And there are plenty of places to go in the evening—lounges, discos, pubs and the movies.

Both Blackcomb and Whistler Mountains converge on the Town Centre. For skiers, this means easy access to the lifts. But even after the snow has gone, the lifts still operate taking visitors to skiing heights and wonderful views. If you didn't get your fill during the winter, you can attend a **Summer Ski Camp** (932–3434) on Whistler Mountain.

Considerably more expensive, another way to reach the heights without too much effort is by helicopter. Located in the Crystal Lodge, **Whistler Heli Hiking and Sightseeing** (932–4105) lifts off for hiking, glacier skiing and glacier-tour excursions.

Back down on the valley floor, you can tee off on the 18-hole (par 72) **Arnold Palmer Championship golf course** (932–4544). Open 6 am on weekends, 8 am weekdays, and always in demand, you can book your tee-off time up to five days in advance.

Near the base of Whistler Mountain's gondola lift, south of Whistler's Town Centre, **Gondola Golf,** the 18-hole mini golf course, is open 10 am daily during the warm weather.

If tennis is your game, there are public courts at Myrtle Philip School across from the Town Centre, Alpha Lake Park near the base of the gondola, Meadow Park in Alpine Meadows, and Emerald Park in Emerald Estates. You can book a court by calling the **Whistler Resort Association** at 932–3928. **Whistler Creek Lodge** (932–4111) has one tennis court as well as raquetball courts and you can rent equipment for either game.

The lakes and rivers of this area afford excellent opportunities for canoeing, kayaking, windsurfing, river rafting, swimming and fishing. Although there are no lifeguards, there are beaches at Alpha Lake, Lost Lake and Wayside Park and Lakeside Park on Alta Lake. Being mountain-spring fed, the water is usually quite refreshing.

At **Whistler Windsurfing** (932–3389) on Alta Lake, you can rent a canoe, a rowboat or a windsurfer. Wetsuits and windsurfing lessons are also available. **Whistler Whitewater** (932–4763), also on Alta Lake, will rent you a kayak, give you a lesson or take you out for half- and whole-day kayaking trips.

If you've never tried river rafting, a 2-hour, 3-hour or full-day outing with **Whistler River Adventurers** (932–3784) might just wet your appetite.

Fishermen in B.C. are required to have a licence. These can be obtained from either **Whistler Village Hardware** (932–3863) or **Whistler Village Sports** (932–3327). Licensed fishing guides for half, full or more day-outings can be arranged by calling the **Leisure Connection** (932–5850).

Numerous hiking trails surround the area, many of them starting right from the Town Centre. If you want to explore the area by bicycle, remember it is a mountain region. Bicycles can be rented from **Summit Cycles** (932–1912), **Whistler Village Sports** (932–3327) and **Whistler Sports Stop** (932–5495).

Or leave the work to a horse. One- and two-hour trail rides leave **Layton Bryson Outfitting & Trail Rides** (932–4487), one mile (oops again! 5/8 km) north of the Village. Day-trips, over-night outings and extended trail-rides can be arranged.

For organized sightseeing of the Valley, call **Whistler Community Transit** (932–3290). They offer two-hour Valley Tours and day trips to Cheakamus Lake, Black Tusk and Callaghan Lake. Day trips aboard **British Columbia Rail** (984–5246) from Whistler to Lillooet let you view more of the region's scenic beauty.

For information on accommodation or any of the activities in the Valley, contact the **Whistler Resort Association** (932–3928). For reservations, call 932–4222.

To get you to Whistler, Maverick Coach Lines runs scheduled service to and from the area, departing from the Vancouver Bus Depot, 150 Dunsmuir Street (662–3222). For visitors arriving in Vancouver by plane, **Perimeter Transportation** (261–2299) connects the airport to Whistler, daily except Tuesdays and Thursdays. On those days, they have a connecting bus from the airport to the Vancouver bus terminal. Daily scheduled service is also provided from North Vancouver by **British Columbia Railway** (984–5246).

From Whistler, you can catch the northbound train for Lillooet (and Prince George), Wednesdays, Fridays, and Sundays. Trains return Mondays, Thursdays, and Saturdays. On Saturdays and Sundays, **BC Rail** (984–5246) may be offering one-day excursions with sightseeing in Lillooet and travel by train in one direction and bus in the other.

During the winter months, the drive up Highway 99 (the Squamish-Whistler highway) must be undertaken with great care. At any time of the year nonetheless, the scenery is spectacular. Even a short run up Highway 99 from Horseshoe Bay will let you savour the beauty of British Columbia's coastal mountains. From Horseshoe Bay to Squamish the road winds along the mountainsides of Howe Sound, over creeks, past hidden lakes and beside the shoreline railway tracks. At **Britannia Beach,** the **B.C. Museum of Mining** (688–8735) has taken over the site of the former Anaconda Mines. They will outfit you in a yellow slicker and hard hat, roll you through underground tunnels, and even let you pan for gold. Just a few kilometres up the road, you can picnic in Murrin Provincial Park.

At Shannon Falls Park, there are trails to climb up the heights beside the waters of Shannon Falls which cascade 313 metres down the rocks. Across the highway at its base is the Klahanie Inn (892–5312) for a meal or coffee. The **Carling O'Keefe Logging Museum** and its locomotive sit in the woods here.

Just before Squamish, you will pass the famous **Stawamus Chief**—a perpendicular and sheer rock face. You may see some brave (or foolhardy) types testing their rock-climbing and rappelling skills there.

If you haven't already smelled Squamish or seen the smog from its pulp plants settling over Howe Sound, the next left turn will take you into the town. Loggers Day, held here the first Saturday in August, is educational as well as fun.

Between Squamish and the beginning of the Cheakamus Canyon, signs direct travellers to Diamond Head, Brackendale, and Alice Lake. Hikers love the challenge of Diamond Head, and campers take their families to Alice Lake.

The drive through the Canyon is beautiful, but don't let the scenery distract you. While constantly being upgraded, in spots the road is very narrow, the shoulders almost non-existent and the curves sharp.

On the other side of the Canyon, before arriving at Whistler, signs point the way to Lucille Lake, Garibaldi Provincial Park, Black Tusk and Brandywine Falls Provincial Park—all favourite haunts for lovers of the outdoors. At Black Tusk, a two-hour hike gets you to the base of the tusk. Brandywine Falls, on its part, is reputed to be one of the highest in B.C.

SUNSHINE COAST

A short ferry ride (50 min) from Horseshoe Bay to Langdale, and you're on your way up the Sunshine Coast as the Sechelt Peninsula and Powell River area is known. Turn right on leaving the ferry, and 14 km (9 mi) along, you can tour a pulp plant, but only on Thursdays at 1 pm. Phone ahead to make sure the tour is on (Industrial Relations Officer, 884–5223).

At Gibsons, location of CBC's television show, "The Beachcombers," the arts are active in the area all summer long. Beachcomber Tours (662–7511) will take you there by yacht from the Westin Bayshore Hotel. Their day-long tour includes attendance at the filming of the show. During the first weekend in August, there's plenty to do at Gibsons' Sea Cavalcade Festival—water sports, broomstick races, greased pole climbing, log burling, a "war of the hoses," and fireworks.

At Roberts Creek Provincial Park further along, you can swim, camp, picnic and fish (in fresh or salt water). Near here is the town of Sechelt.

At Pender Harbour, former home of the killer whales in Vancouver's Aquarium, there are marinas and lakeside resorts. You can fish for salmon or trout, pick oysters, dig for clams, or charter a boat to go up the waters of Skookumchuck Rapids.

To reach Powell River, where visitors can tour one of the world's largest newsprint mills, you have to take another ferry between Earls Cove and Saltery Bay. From Powell River, you can ferry to Comox on Vancouver Island, or to Texada Island.

For a rustic holiday in the Georgia Strait, you might try

Rabbit Island (604–669–0840), 7½ miles (12 km) by water taxi from Secret Cove. They have lovely cabins, each with a spectacular view and fireplace.

VICTORIA, VANCOUVER ISLAND

It is fairly simple to make a day trip to Victoria. Inter-city buses—downtown to downtown—leave the Depot at 150 Dunsmuir (at Cambie), usually every hour on the hour, daily, between 6 am and 9 pm in the summer. They also leave from Victoria on a similar schedule. The ferry fare is included in the price of your ticket.

For that all-inclusive approach, **Pacific Coach Lines** (PCL)

Horseshoe Bay, West Vancouver

(662–3311), and **Gray Line** (872–8311), offer motor-coach re-turn day trips to the province's capital, Victoria, including stops at the world-famous Butchart Gardens near Brentwood Bay, a tour of the Inner Harbour, the legislative Buildings and plenty of time to explore the shops or enjoy tea at the Empress Hotel.

PCL's tours depart from the Bus Depot, 150 Dunsmuir Street, and pick-ups at selected downtown hotels are available. For information, reservations and pick-up locations, call 662–3311 or 662–7575.

Gray Line's day excursions leave from the Hotel Vancouver. They also provide over-night and two-night trips to Victoria with the option of returning to Vancouver or continuing on to Seattle aboard Air B.C. For times, prices, reservations and hotel pick-up, phone 872–8311.

If you prefer to travel in smaller groups, **Scenic Line Tours,** (879–0288), 680A Leg-in-Boot Square, on the south side of False Creek, runs day-return trips to Victoria in mini-buses, with pick-ups arranged in Richmond and Delta (on route to the ferry). For groups of six or more, they will also custom-tailor a guided tour to wherever you want to go for as long as you want to stay. For further info, call 879–0288.

All tour prices include the cost of the ferry crossing from Tsawwassen to Swartz Bay, and there is usually a reduced fare for children.

For $95 or thereabouts, **Air BC** will fly you from Van-couver's harbour to Victoria's. For information and reserva-tions on this float-plane service, contact Air BC, 4680 Cowley Crescent, Richmond, B.C. V7B 1C1, or call (604) 688–2573 or 1–800–663–0522. Air BC flights also take off from the Van-couver International Airport South Terminal bound for Vic-toria's main airport.

Skylink Airlines (946–1316), flying both from Vancouver International and from Boundary Bay, and **Burrard Air** (278–7178), with 50 flights a week from Vancouver Interna-tional Airport, offer the best rates. Flights connecting with PWA and Air Canada flights are operated by **Time Air** (1–800–661–1484).

W. M. Aviation Inc intends to offer helicopter service be-tween Vancouver and the province's capital in the near future.

During the summer especially, motorists should be prepared

for car line-ups (which buses avoid) at the ferries. You could ferry from Tsawwassen to Swartz Bay, visit the gorgeous Butchart Gardens, explore lovely Victoria, with its "olde England" style, and then return by way of the beautiful Malahat Mountain Drive on the road to Nanaimo for the return ferry to Vancouver. Or do this circuit in reverse.

For reaching Butchart Gardens, motorists please note: when travelling north from Victoria, turn left at Keating X Road off Highway 17—but if coming south from Swartz Bay, you *cannot* make a right turn here. Take the earlier turn right at West Saanich Road, drive south to Keating Road and turn right to get to the Gardens. There are plenty of signs.

You'll likely want your Victoria stay to be longer than a day, for the city offers a relaxing atmosphere, fine restaurants, excellent shopping—and **Afternoon Tea and Crumpets** in the Empress Hotel's lobby! This grand regal hotel is a *must* for every visitor, as are The Pacific Undersea Gardens, The Legislative Guildings, the marvellous Provincial Museum, Heritage Village, and the refurbished Crystal Garden. All are close to the Inner Harbour.

Further afield are such attractions as Sealand of the Pacific, The Olde England Inn and the Fable Cottage Estate. Get a copy of *The Victoria Guide Book* by Betty Campbell for details on visiting Victoria and Vancouver Island. An excellent contact is the office of Tourism Victoria, 812 Wharf Street, victoria, B.C. V8W 1T3—telephone 382–2127.

If you wish to travel up-island from Victoria, the **train to Courtenay** will take you through the Malahat Pass and Vancouver Island's beautiful mountain scenery. The trip takes 4½ hours one way. For information fares and schedules, call VIA Rail, 1–800–665–8630. While in Courtenay, you might eat at **The Old House,** an experience in interiors as well as a fine restaurant set on the river.

Further north in **Campbell River,** you'll find fishing expeditions, bushpilot tours, lodges, and access by ferry to Quadra and Cortez Islands. Burrard Air (278–7178) will fly you here either from Victoria or from Vancouver, and arrange sightseeing, fishing or other activities.

THE GULF ISLANDS

If you are planning to take in some of the quiet of the Gulf Islands, you will probably need more than a day. Saltspring, Pender, Galiano, Mayne (and from there Saturna) are all serviced by car ferry from Tsawwassen. You can also travel to them from Swartz Bay near Victoria. Gambier Island is reached by taking the ferry to Sechelt and then water taxi to the island. For schedules, routes and fares, call B.C. Ferries, 669–1211. Lodges on these islands are listed in the B.C. Tourist Accommodation Guide, available at the Vancouver Visitors Bureau (main branch in the Royal Centre Mall) or at Tourism B.C. in Robson Square.

Other lovely islands in the Georgia Strait such as Thetis, Denman and Hornby, and Texada are also serviced by B.C. Ferries. Call them for scheduled sailings.

PARKS

Marine Parks

British Columbia's marine parks, provided by the Parks Branch of the Ministry of Recreation and Conservation, are intended to provide essential facilities for the enjoyment of the boating public, keeping in mind the need to maintain the natural surroundings of the area. Not all have safe anchorages and mooring-buoys. Depending on the park, facilities might include landing buoys, campgrounds and picnic-grounds. Sanitary facilities are located at all developed parks and provision is made for collection and disposal of refuse. At times, fresh water is difficult to obtain. Marine park installations are usually some distance from anchorages. Replenishment at marinas and fuelling stations is recommended.

Plumper Cove Marine Park is the closest to Vancouver. It provides a snug anchorage, protected from most winds, on the northwest side of Keats Island in Howe Sound. Good gravel beach, floats, camping, picnicking, and drinking-water.

At the northern end of **Bedwell Bay** on the eastern side of Indian Arm is another very close park on two tiny islands— Racoon and Twin. In back of the islands are some sheltered waters. This park has beaches, scuba-diving, and a very small-boat wharf, washrooms and camping facilities but no fresh water.

Porteau Cove on Howe Sound about two-thirds of the way to Squamish has a 57-hectare provincial park attached with water, washrooms, camping facilities and a boat-launch ramp. Boat moorage is poor, but good road access and three ships sunk in the bay by Provincial Parks make this a good scuba-diving venue.

For complete information on B.C.'s marine parks and for maps, write Provincial Parks Branch, Dogwood Building, 1019 Wharf Street, Victoria, B.C. V8W 2Y9 or contact Tourism B.C., 800 Robson, Vancouver (660–2300).

Regional Parks

The Greater Vancouver Regional District is a federation of municipalities and electoral areas whose purpose is to protect and enhance the quality of life in the metropolitan area. A key element in this programme is the provision of regional parks. Over 5,000 acres (of 40,000 designated) have been purchased at eleven sites. Some areas have been developed, others have not. Some private lands exist within, and adjacent to, sites not yet in the development stage. Please respect the rights and privacy of the people who reside in these areas.

For information on park sites contact Greater Vancouver Regional District Parks, 4330 Kingsway, Burnaby, B.C. V5H 4G8 (432–6200).

Provincial Parks

In British Columbia, there are literally hundreds of provincial parks. They range from rugged wilderness and glacier areas to developed shoreline beaches and campgrounds. They are organized into three regions, each managed by its own office. For brochures, maps and details, contact the appropriate office.

South Coast Region, 1610 Indian River Drive, North Vancouver, B.C. V7G 1L3 (929–1291).
Southern Interior Region, 101 - 1050 West Columbia Street, Kamloops, B.C. V2C 1L4 (1–828–4501).
Northern Interior Region, 1011 - 4th Avenue, Prince George,

Alouette Lake, Garibaldi Provincial Park

B.C. V2L 3H9 (1–565–6245).

The South Coast Region is divided into four districts — Fraser Valley and Garibaldi on the mainland, Strathcona and Malahat on Vancouver Island — all of which are administered by the South Coast Region's office, 1610 Indian River Drive, North Vancouver, B.C. V7G 1L3. Telephone: 929–1291.

In the Vancouver area, **Cypress** and **Mount Seymour** Provincial Parks are in the mountains of the North Shore in West and North Vancouver, respectively. **Apodaca** Provincial Park is on Bowen Island, reached by ferry from Horseshoe Bay.

The **Sunshine Coast,** considered by many to be one of the finest sport fishing areas in B.C., has four parks with water frontage—Roberts Creek, Porpoise Bay, Skookumchuck Narrows, and Saltery Bay—in addition to a number of marine parks. Skookumchuck means "turbulent water" and refers to the fascinating and dangerous tidal rapids that churn daily through the narrows. At the other parks, the shores reveal their clam and oyster beds, when the tide it out. The waters of Saltery Bay are especially interesting for scuba divers, and road access is good.

Huge **Garibaldi** Provincial Park, 37 km (23 mi) north of Squamish, is one of the most spectacular regions in the Pacific northwest. Within the Park are Whistler and Blackcomb mountains, Black Tusk, and Diamond Head, a volcanic pinnacle, as well as glacier-fed Cheakamus Lake. The park is a wilderness area—no supplies are available there. The Garibaldi area also includes **Alice Lake** Provincial Park, 13 km (8 mi) north of Squamish, which has campgrounds.

Golden Ears Provincial Park, which borders on Garibaldi Park's southern boundary, is in the Alouette region of Lower Mainland parks. It has good hiking trails. Also in the Allouette district, the small **International Peace Arch** Park straddles the Canada-U.S. border on Highway 99 amidst gorgeous scenery.

East of Vancouver, **Cultus Lake** Provincial Park, 13 km (8 mi) south of Chilliwack, provides extensive camping facilities in four campgrounds, and lots of water frontage. The Cultus Lake Motel (1–858–3334) provides recreational facilities and lodging near the Park's boundary.

Furthest from Vancouver (224 km or 140 mi east) in the lower mainland region is **Manning Park.** This large mountain park provides numerous hiking trails, nature programmes, campgrounds and a lodge (Gibson Pass Resort Lodge, Manning Park, B.C. V0X 1R0, tel: 1–840–8822). In winter there is alpine and nordic skiing. A good paved road, open July through October, leads to the Lookout north of the highway. If driving through on your way to or from Vancouver, it is well worth a quick visit.

B.C.'s provincial parks are for everyone's use. Please respect the natural environment by camping only in designated areas. Clean up your litter, and be particularly cautious with fire. If you see a forest fire, dial "O" for the Operator and ask for ZENITH 5555 (a free call for such an emergency).

Tourism B.C., 800 Robson (660–2300), has free brochures and maps of the provincial parks. You could also contact the Parks and Outdoor Recreation District Office, 1610 Indian River Driver, North Vancouver, B.C. V7G 1L3 (929–1291) or the Provincial Parks Branch, 1019 Wharf Street, Victoria, B.C. V8W 2Y9.

HIKING
by Fedor Frastacky

Stawamus Chief

It's hard to miss this sheer rock face over 2,000 feet high—in fact, straight up—that looms over Highway 99 just south of Squamish. Unless you are an expert rock climber or have a determined death wish, you might be interested in how to get the exhilarating feeling of standing on top of this rock without scaling its face.

The back trails to the summit (actually summits, since there are three distinct destinations) begin about 1.2 km (¾ mi) north of Shannon Falls on the Squamish Highway. Turn off to the right on what remains of an old road. Another right and about 400 metres (¼ mi) south will bring you to a small quarry and parking lot. The trail starts by the stream at the south end of this cleared area.

The trail climbs steeply up the rocks beside the stream and then along a well-marked path through shady stands of large timber.

Hikers have a choice of three peaks, with round-trips of 6½, 9½ and 11 kilometres respectively (that is 4, 6, or 7 miles). The longer trails present some additional obstacles and include the need for some rock climbing without offering a notably superior view.

To reach the first peak, follow the trail until it forks and then veer off on the left fork. A series of switchbacks will eventually give way to the open rock summit and an impressive view of Howe Sound—as well as a frightening look down the face of the Chief.

Each of the bald, granite peaks provides plenty of room to walk around, picnic or just lie down and enjoy the view and the warm sun.

Black Tusk/Garibaldi Lake

One of the most interesting and spectacular examples of local geological formations and forces is in the western part of Garibaldi Park. The dominant black volcanic plug of Black Tusk and the emerald green lakes of the area are accessible in a long day's hike, but an extended stay for a climb of the peak itself is certainly worth considering.

To reach the starting point, drive north on Highway 99 about 37 km (23 mi) from Squamish, and turn right at the sign for ''Black Tusk Recreational Area.'' Follow the road to a parking lot and the signs directing you uphill. Although the trail is well-maintained, the seemingly endless switchbacks through wooded slopes do become tedious. Do not despair. After several hurs the trail forks, with the right path leading past Barrier and Lesser Garibaldi Lakes and then along a creek to Garibaldi Lake and the campsite at Battleship Islands.

The campsite is maintained by the Provincial Parks authorities, and is particularly popular. At the far end of the lake is Sphinx Glacier, which provides a spectacular backdrop to the calm and colourful lake.

The left fork takes hikers past a ranger's cabin and to the alpine meadows below the Tusk. Those lucky enough to be in the area in late July or August, will be treated to the annual blooming of the alpine flowers.

If you have an extra day, camping equipment and some climbing experience, you may wish to spend the night at the camping area around the ranger's cabin, and then climb to the

Black Tusk, Garibaldi Park

top of the Tusk. *Not* for the uninitiated, this 11-km (7 mi) round-trip will take six to seven hours.

Follow the path toward Mimulus Lake for about 2.4 km (1.5 mi), and then turn left toward the two ridges which hide the view of the Tusk. Head toward the almost perpendicular wall on the south side and a group of rock chimneys. The last one is highly recommended as the most convenient, although it still involves a couple of hundred feet of climbing. Not unexpectedly, reaching the summit affords the climber a 360° panorama of some of southern B.C.'s most beautiful geography.

Petgill Lake

We have used this trail as a warm-up walk for the beginning of the season. The round-trip shouldn't take more than five hours and provides an easy hike through the woods.

It is reached from Highway 99 approximately 5 km (3 mi) north of Britannia Beach, south of Squamish. Turn left off the highway at the parking lot for the picnic grounds at Murrin Park. The walk's starting point is across the road and about 350 metres north. It is marked by signs, but keep your eyes open.

Don't be discouraged by the walk's decidedly steep beginning. This gives way quickly to the partially-marked trail through the woods. From then on, the rest of the 11 km (7 mi) trek winds past occasional lookouts from which Murrin Lake, Howe Sound, and Stawamus Chief are clearly visible.

The lake itself is pretty and a quiet spot to picnic and offer a few tidbits to the ever-present and always persistent whiskey jacks.

Cheakamus Lake

If a pleasant walk in the woods towards a highly rewarding destination, comfortable for the uninitiated and suitable for smaller children, is what you are looking for, then Cheakamus Lake fills the bill.

About 10 km (6½ mi) past Brandywine Falls Park on Highway 99, a sign indicates the turnoff for Cheakamus Lake. Stay to the left of any forks and drive for about 8 km (5 mi). Where the road ends at some fallen trees, there are signs showing the trail to the lake. The 3 km (2 mi) easy walk changes only slightly in elevation as it winds through tall timber stands and thick lush vegetation.

The lake itself, where some fishing is reported, is a rich emerald colour common to mountain lakes. For my money there's better fishing in the streams passed on the way to the parking area.

Cheakamus is an easy hour-and-a-half walk and an excellent family outing.

Whistler Mountain

It probably shows my personal bent to suggest walks that are easily accessible, but rewarding nonetheless. This walk would probably be dismissed by hiking zealots, but riding the chairlift and then exploring the top of Whistler Mountain seems to me to give the best of both worlds.

Whistler Mountain is about 64 km (40 mi) past Squamish along Highway 99. You will arive at the base of the gondola lift which will carry you to mid-station. From there a chairlift will complete the journey to the Round House situated below the ridge and summit of the mountain.

Once off the lift, head to the right toward the top of the T-bar, along the ridge. The sights are impressive and give some hint of what is to come. Once past the T-bar, begin to climb the slope directly in front of you. Give the edge of the cliffs the cautious respect they deserve. On the top of the ridge, the view is breath-taking. Several bowls known only to the more adventurous skier are plainly visible as are Alta and Alfa Lakes, Cheakamus Valley and, to the south, Black Tusk.

The route is often snow-covered until late summer—and sometimes even then. Depending on conditions and on your own capacity, the 6½ km (4 mi) round-trip could take three to four hours.

Both the lifts and Round House are subject to ever changing summer schedules, and visitors are strongly advised to call Whistler Area Information Center (1–932–5528) or the Whistler Mountain Ski Corporation offices in Whistler (685–0521) before starting on the day's outing.

No Pain, Just Gain

Contrary to some, getting there is not necessarily half the fun. While a good multi-hour slog up a mountain is wonderfully exhilarating experience and thoroughly purifying, it can also be beyond the capacity of many. For those of limited strength or inclination, Heli Hiking has arrived at Whistler. You are deposited to lofty scenic heights in civilized comfort—walk, climb, lunch or just feast your eyes. For further information, contact the Whistler Resort Association (932–3928) or the Village Ski Shop (932–4105) in Crystal Lodge in the Whistler Village.

The Lions

Lest any reader begin to believe that we wish to highlight only the more unchallenging hikes and walks, we offer this submission. The elevation gain along the new Lions Trail is recorded to be 4,000 feet. It is likely to take even the more hardened enthusiast about six hours.

The Lions are clearly visible (assuming it's not raining), from elevations in downtown Vancouver. Simply look in a north-west direction over West Vancouver. To reach the starting point, take the Upper Levels Highway, past Horseshoe Bay and along Highway 99 towards Squamish. About 11 km (7 mi) north of Horseshoe Bay, you will approach Lions Bay and cross Harvey Creek. Right after the Creek, turn right on Centre Road, then left on Bayview which is all part of the Lions Bay subdivision. Keep on Bayview until the pavement ends and you come to an old logging road. It's about a mile from the point where you left the highway.

Now (assuming you are not already lost), park the car and start up the switchback trail keeping to the right at any forks. You will find yourself heading southeast for Harvey Creek after clearing the switchbacks. You will also see that the trail becomes well-marked and leads through Harvey Creek Valley before rising up to a ridge. A good camping spot for those planning an overnight stay is here and, as if it need be repeated, the views of neighbouring mountains, the Strait of Georgia, Bowen Island, the Sunshine Coast, as well as those down the Capilano Canyon to Vancouver, are a real treat.

The base of the West Lion is north along the ridge and difficult to ignore. However, no one—except those with extensive rock climbing experience—should attempt to climb either of the Lions.

B.C. Centennial Hiking Trail

Along the routes followed by early explorers of the area, the Canadian Hostelling Association and other local climbing clubs have cut and marked a 240 km (150 mi) trail. It runs from Simon Fraser University in Burnaby, along the dikes of the Fraser River, behind Sumas Mountain and into the Coast Range. The Skyline Trail which leads into Manning Park travels the ridges of this range, and is only free of snow from mid-July to the end of September.

The trail is accessible at several points for one-day hikes. Those interested should get a copy of the *B.C. Trail Guide Book,* available from The Pack & Boot Shop, 3425 West Broadway (738–3128).

Hikers — Who, What and Where

For information on any of the local hiking and mountaineering clubs, contact The Federation of Mountain Clubs, 1200 Hornby Street, Vancouver, B.C. V6Z 1W2 (687–3333). They can put you in touch with the co-ordinators of the Alpine Club, B.C. Mountaineering Club, North Shore Hiking Club or the Sierra Club, all of which welcome non-members on their outings.

Outward Bound, 206 - 1656 Duranleau Street, Vancouver B.C., V6H 3S4 (669–9196) offers programmes, summer and winter, in mountaineering, rock climbing, mountain rescue, white water kayaking, ocean kayaking and sailing.

The Outdoors Club, an affiliation of the Canadian Hostelling Association, welcomes non-members on their hikes. For scheduled hikes, contact 736–3116.

Three city outlets stock hiking supplies along with literature on the area and the subject as a whole:

Mountain Equipment Co-op, 428 West 8th Avenue (872–7858).

The Pack & Boot Shop, 3425 West Broadway (738–3128).

Coast Mountain Sports Ltd., 1822 West 4th Avenue (731–6181).

Taiga Works-Wilderness Equipment Ltd., 1675 West 2nd Avenue (736–0422).

19 *Survival kit*

EMERGENCY TELEPHONE NUMBERS

The area code for all telephones in British Columbia is 604.
Information is 411
Telephone repair, 611.

Fire/Inhalator

911	in Vancouver
228–4567	on the University Endowment Lands
291–1234	in Burnaby
985–5323	in North Vancouver
922–2345	in West Vancouver

Police

911	in Vancouver
228–4567	on the University Endowment Lands
224–1322	in Burnaby
988–4111	in North Vancouver
922–9111	in West Vancouver

Ambulance

911	in Vancouver
228–4567	on the University Endowment Lands
872–5151	in Burnaby, North Vancouver, and West Vancouver

Forest Fire Sightings

Dial "O" and ask for
ZENITH 5555   anywhere in British Columbia

Persons Missing on the North Shore mountains

985–1311   North and West Vancouver Emergency Programme

Tourist Alert

Newspapers, provincial campgrounds, ferries, radio and T.V. announcements are made for people on vacation who are needed in urgent circumstances. If your name appears on a "Tourist Alert" bulletin, contact the nearest Royal Canadian Mounted Police (R.C.M.P.) office or the local police where you are. R.C.M.P. headquarters are at 37th and Heather Street (264–3111).

MEDICAL SERVICES

If you should get sick or be injured while in British Columbia, there are a number of excellent hospitals with emergency and health unit facilities. Please note that to be covered by insurance, you must have an insurance plan in your home country. Travel insurance will cover emergency treatment necessary to get you well enough to travel home, but does not cover pre-existing conditions and diseases that flare up while you are on vacation.

In Vancouver, you can consult M. H. Ingle Insurance Agency, 1055 West Georgia Street (685–0144), about hospital and medical plans for visitors to Canada.

Hospitals

Children's Hospital, 4480 Oak Street	875–2345
Grace Hospital-The Salvation Army, 4490 Oak Street	875–2424,
Lions Gate Hospital, 239 East 13th Street, North Vancouver	988–3131
Royal Columbian Hospital, 330 East Columbia Street, New Westminster	520–4253
St Paul's Hospital, 1081 Burrard Street	682–2344
Shaughnessy Hospital, 4500 Oak Street	875–2222
Vancouver General Hospital, 855 West 12th Avenue	875–4111
University of British Columbia Hospital, Wesbrook Mall, UBC	228–7121

CLINICS AND OTHER EMERGENCY SERVICES

Pine Street (Free) Medical Clinic, 1985 West 4th Avenue, specializes in the needs of young people and helps people without medical coverage	736–2391
Seymour Medical Clinic, 1530 West 7th Avenue, between Granville and Fir Streets, open 24 hours	738–2151
AIDS Vancouver	687–2437
VD Control, 828 West 10th Avenue	660–6161

Salvation Army	
Family Services, 3213	
Fraser	872–7676
	683–0371, for emergencies after 5 pm
Grace Hospital, 4490	
Oak Street	875–2424
Doctor	683–2474
Dentist	738–4110
Poison Control Centre	682–5050 or 682–2344
Crisis Centre	733–4111
Rape Relief	872–8212
Alcoholics Anonymous	434–3933 or 873–8466
Freeway Patrol	666–5343
Crime Reporting, Non-Emergency	665–3221

During Expo, the major hotels will have access to physicians whom they can contact if you are ill. In addition, a Medi-Centre (683–8138), 1055 Dunsmuir, Bentall Centre Tower # 4, will be set up to take people with or without appointment. Dr. Ian Morgan will be supervising a Travel Medicine Office at # 420–1144 Burrard Street. There will be clinics at both Expo sites to handle emergencies occurring on the fair's grounds, free of charge. Patients treated here for injuries incurred outside the grounds will have to pay for the service.

OTHER SERVICES

ResWest, for booking accommodation	662–3300
BC Marine Reservations, for moorage	687–7447/SHIP
Expo Info, on all aspects of Expo	660–3976/EXPO
The Optimists Club, for problems having to do with the handicapped	731–3178

Granny Y's, for short-term and emergency child care	689–5342
Environment Canada, for the weather	273–8331
Gray Line, for sightseeing tours	872–8311
Vancouver Parks and Recreation Board	681–1141
1200 Hornby, recreation clubs and programmes	687–3333
Provincial Parks and Outdoor Recreation, Lower Mainland Regional Office	929–1291
U.S. Travel Information Centre	669–1446
American Express Office	687–2641
Intercom Inc., Language Consultants (European and oriental languages)	687–2622

LATE-NIGHT PHARMACIES

Kripp's Pharmacy, 994 Granville Street, to 11 pm	687–2564
Carson Midnite Drug Store, 6517 Main Street at 49th Avenue, to 12 midnight	325–3241

TOURIST INFORMATION CENTRES

Tourism BC	
800 Robson Street, Robson Square	660–2300
Vancouver International Airport	273–1648
Greater Vancouver Convention and Visitors Bureau	
Royal Centre Mall, Burrard and Georgia Street	682–2222

Eatons, at the Robson Street
entrance, during the summer
Gastown, Le Magasin Mall,
332 Water Street
Vancouver International
Airport, Level I
Tourism Association of
Southwestern B.C., 1425
West Pender Street   688–3677

AIRLINES

Air BC	685–3211
Air Canada	666–7321, flight arrivals and departures
	688–5515, reservations
Alaska Airlines	1–800–426–0333
American Airlines	1–800–433–7300
Burrard Air, for Vancouver Island and the Sunshine Coast	278–7178
CP Air	685–9166, flight arrivals and departures
	682–1411, reservations
Frontier	276–5920, flight arrivals and departures
	687–2330, reservations
Harbour Air, for Vancouver Island, the Gulf Islands, and the United States	688–1277 or 1–800–972–0212
Japan Air Lines	273–7807, flight arrivals and departures
	688–6611, reservations
Pacific Rim Airlines, for Vancouver Island	224–4398

Pacific Western	669–2412, flight arrivals and departures
	684–6161, reservations
Quantas Air	689–9166, flight arrivals and departures
	684–8231, reservations
Tyee Air, for Vancouver Island and the Sunshine Coast	689–8651
United Airlines	683–7111
Wardair	273–2442, flight arrivals and departures
	669–3355, reservations
Western Airlines	278–3381, flight arrivals and departures
	682–5933, reservations

TRANSPORTATION IN VANCOUVER AND BRITISH COLUMBIA

Airport Hustle-Bus Service, between downtown hotels and the airport	273–0071
City Bus Information, routes and schedules	324–3211
Articles lost on city buses	682–7887
ALRT	683–8401
SeaBus	324–3211
West Vancouver buses	926–4355
North Vancouver buses	324–3211
Bus Depot, Greyhound and Pacific Coach Lines	662–3222
VIA Rail Canada RESERVIA	1–800–665–8630
BC Ferries, information and reservations	669–1211
Schedules	685–1021

FOR THE MOTORIST

BCAA (British Columbia Automobile Association), 999 West Broadway   732–3911

Emergency Road Service in Vancouver   736–5971

B.C. Department of Highways Road Report   277–0112

Seatbelts. Provincial law requires that drivers and passengers use seatbelts while driving or riding in a motor vehicle.

Snowtires and Chains. When a ''Chains Needed'' sign is posted on snowy or mountain roads, do not assume that snowtires are an acceptable substitute. In most cases, they are not.

Drinking and Driving. In Canada, it is a criminal offence to drive with a blood alcohol content which measures over .08%. British Columbia drinking and driving laws are very stiff. If a breath analysis you are asked to take reads over .08%, you will be arrested. Please take a ride with a friend, a taxi, or public transportation if in any doubt at all.

Think Metric. Speed limits on Canadian highway signs are in kilometres per hour.

100 km/hour = 60 mph, the maximum speed on most freeways

80 km/hour = 50 mph, the maximum speed on most rural two-lane roads

50 km/hour = 30 mph, the speed limit on most urban or town roadways

30 km/hour = 20 mph, the speed you will see posted in school zones

Taxis

Black Top	681-2181
McClure's	683–6666 or 731–9211
Yellow Cab	681–1111 or 681–3311

Other companies are listed in the Yellow Pages of the telephone book.

CURRENCY AND BANKING

Currency or travellers cheques can be exchanged at any of the major bank branches at good exchange rates. Deak Perera, International Currency Services, has the most up-to-the-minute rates:

Pacific Centre Mall, 617	
Granville Street	687–6111
Guildford Town Centre,	
Lower Mall near Woolco	584–3338

In Chinatown, Kerrisdale, and the 10th Avenue and Sasamat area, you can find branches of major banks open on Saturdays. The Bank of Montreal and the Canadian Imperial Bank of Commerce also have West End branches open on Saturday.

In addition, The Permanent, 701 West Georgia (689–0611), is open Saturdays from 10 am to 2 pm; Vancouver City Savings and Credit Union, 1030 West Broadway (736–9166), Saturdays from 9 am to 1 pm; and Harbour Savings Credit Union, 1195 Davie Street (688–0436), from 9 am to 1 pm Saturdays. Vancouver City Savings and Credit Union, 898 West Pender Street (683–6521), is open Saturdays from 7:30 am to 5 pm.

Banking Machines

Bank of British Columbia (EXCHANGE)
  1010 Denman Street
  2164 West 41st Avenue
Bank of Montreal
  West Georgia and Seymour Streets
  Granville and West Pender Streets
  Hotel Vancouver
  178 East Pender Street
  958 Denman Street
  2200 West 4th Avenue
  4502 West 10th Avenue
  2102 West 41st Avenue

Bank of Nova Scotia
    5659 Dunbar Street
Canadian Imperial Bank of Commerce
    586 Granville Street
    Georgia and Burrard Streets
    4489 West 10th Avenue
    2251 West 41st Avenue
Harbour Savings Credit Union (CUE)
    1195 Davie Street
Royal Bank
    796 Granville Street
    1055 West Georgia Street
    2395 West 4th Avenue
    4501 West 10th Avenue
    2909 West Broadway Avenue
    370 East Broadway Avenue
    621 Oakridge
    2208 West 41st Avenue
Toronto-Dominion Bank
    700 West Georgia Street
    88 East Pender Street
    2105 West 41st Avenue
Vancouver City Savings and Credit Union (EXCHANGE)
    898 West Pender Street
    1030 West Broadway Avenue

The most widely accepted credit cards are Visa, MasterCard and American Express. Carte Blanche and Diners Club are second. Bank Americard and Barclay cards are accepted in some places.

The American Express Office is at 701 West Georgia Street, Vancouver (687–2641).

COMMUNICATIONS

Telegrammes

CN/CP Telecommunica-
tions, 175 West
Cordova Street   681–4231

Postal Services

First class (up to 30 gm) letter in Canada	34¢
First class (up to 30 gm) letter to the United States	39¢
First class (up to 20 gm) letter to other foreign destinations	68¢

For information on rates for special delivery, registered mail, parcel post, postal money orders, call Customer Information (24 hours)	662–7222

Vancouver Main Post Office, 349 West Georgia Street	662–5724

Post Offices open on Saturday:
Vancouver Main Office, 349 West Georgia Street
Postal Station A, 508 West Hastings Street
Bentall Centre, 595 Burrard Street

For other post office listings, see the White Pages of the telephone book under ''Canada Post Corp.''

Courier

Priority post, overnight delivery from main postal stations of Canada Post, at modest rates. For pick up call	666–2008

CP Air Express,
   overnight delivery
   from Cargo Terminal
   at the Vancouver
   International Airport,
   at moderate rates.
   For information call   278–2131
   For pick up call (8
      am to 4:30 pm)   270–5108

Air Canada Express,
   overnight or same day
   delivery.
   For information call   276–7200
   For pick up call   276–7186

Atlas Courier Ltd, 32
   West 5th Avenue   875–1111

Newspapers

The Globe and Mail (national, daily)
The Vancouver Sun (daily, evenings)
The Province (daily, mornings)
The Westender (local, weekly)
The Vancouver Courier (local, weekly)
The Georgia Straight (local, weekly,
   entertainment)

Magazines

Asia Pacific Business Magazine
Boating News
B.C. Outdoors
Canada Guide Magazine
Chinatown News Magazine
Collector's Guide
Common Ground Directory
Diver Magazine
Fine Art and Auction Review
The Hosteller (at Pack & Boots, 3425 West
   Broadway)
Pacific Yachting

Ski Canada
Vancouver Magazine
Vancouver Living Magazine
Westworld Magazine

Radio

CBC 6.90 AM
CBC 105.7 FM
CBUF 97.7 FM (in French)
CFMI
CFOX 99.3 FM (Rock)
CFUN 14.10 AM (Lite Rock, Less Talk)
CHQM 13.20 AM and 103.5 FM (easy listening)
CISL 650 AM (the last 30 years in rock)
CJAZ 92.1 FM (Jazz)
CJOR 60 AM
CJVB 14.70 AM (cosmopolitan)
CKLG 73 AM (Top 40)
CKNW 98 AM
CKO 96.1 (all news)
CKWX 11.30 AM
CO-OP RADIO 102.7 FM (popular music and public affairs)
Vancouver Co-op Radio 97 FM

Television

Channel 2, Cable 3	-CBC (Canadian national)
Channel 4, Cable 3	-ABC (American)
Channel 5, Cable 5	-NBC (American)
Channel 6, Cable 6	-CTV (Canadian independent)
Channel 26, Cable 7	-CBC (French-language)
Channel 7, Cable 8	-CBS (American)
Channel 9, Cable 9	-PBS (American public broadcasting)
Cable 10	-BCTV (local, weather and airport information after regular programming)

| Channel 8, Cable 11 | -CTV (Canadian independent) |
| Converter 18 | -KNOWLEDGE Network |

Books

Vancouver Public Library,
750 Burrard Street   665–2280
Hours of opening   665–2276
Reference services by department and branches listed
   in the White Pages of the telephone book under
   "Vancouver Public Library"

Bookstores
Duthie Books
    919 Robson Street
    4444 West 10th Avenue
    Arbutus Village Square
Blackberry Books
    Granville Island, 1663 Duranleau Street
    2206 West 4th Avenue
Banyen Books (an unusually large selection on
    spiritual and psychological subjects)
    2685 West Broadway Avenue
University Bookstore
    UBC Campus, across from the bus loop
Hager Books
    2176 West 41st Avenue
Vancouver Kidsbooks
    2868 West 4th Avenue
    Granville Island, 1496 Cartwright Street

Some Useful Publications
Exploring by Bicycle and *More Exploring by Bicycle*,
   by Tim Perrin
Exploring Vancouver's North Shore Mountains, by
   Roger and Ethel Freeman
Granville Island Guidebook, by Neil McDaniel and
   David W. Griffiths
A Guide to Neighbourhood Pubs, by Ian Kennedy,

Vern Simpson and Gordon R. Elliott

109 Walks in B.C.'s Lower Mainland and *103 Hikes in Southwestern British Columbia*, by Mary and David Macaree

Backroads Explorer, Vol I, Thompson-Cariboo, by Murphy Shewchuk

Rainy Day Guide, by Paula Brooks

The Vancouver Book, by Chuck Davis

Vancouver Recreation Guide, by Dona Sturmanis and Karl Bergmann

Vancouver Secrets, More Vancouver Secrets and *Ethnic Vancouver*, by Anne Petrie

The Victoria Guide Book, by Betty Campbell

The Westcoast Trail Guide, by David Vincent-Jones

Gordon Soules Book Publishers, 355 Burrard Street, has a number of other publications on matters having to do with British Columbia   688–5466

FAST PHOTO PROCESSING

Action Reprographics, 2166 West 4th Avenue	731–6313
Broadway Camera, 676 West Broadway Avenue	873–3836
Customcolor Photo Labs, 1110 Robson Street	681–2524
CX Photo Lab, 1616 West 4th Avenue	736–1413
Helen's Photo Service, 1628 West 4th Avenue	731–2550
1 Hour Photo, 701 West Georgia Street, Pacific Centre Mall	681–2511

LATE OPENING LIQUOR STORES

1120 Alberni Street	Mon to Sat til 9 pm
4255 Arbutus Street	Thurs & Fri til 9 pm

2020 West Broadway Avenue	Mon to Sat til 11 pm
1155 Bute Street	Fri til 9 pm
5555 Cambie Street	Mon to Sat til 9 pm
1520 Commercial Drive	Fri til 9 pm
3610 West 18th Avenue	Fri til 9 pm
2060 West 41st Avenue	Fri til 9 pm
3740 West 4th Avenue	Mon to Sat til 11 pm
8495 Granville Street	Mon to Sat til 11 pm
2933 Granville Street	Fri til 9 pm
Harbour Centre, 555 West Hastings Street	Thurs & Fri til 9 pm
2769 East Hastings Street	Mon to Sat til 11 pm
Kingsgate Mall	Mon to Sat til 9 pm
3406 Kingsway	Mon to Sat til 11 pm
4423 Main Street	Mon to Sat til 9 pm
1716 Robson Street	Mon to Sat til 11 pm
6399 Victoria Street	Mon to Sat til 11 pm
1655 Davie Street	Mon to Sat til 9 pm
3415 Cambie Street	Fri til 9 pm

CHURCHES AND TEMPLES

Christ Church Cathedral, 690 Burrard Street	682–3848
First Baptist Church, 969 Burrard Street	683–8441
Holy Rosary Cathedral, 646 Richards Street	682–6774
Central Presbyterian Church, 1155 Thurlow Street	683–1913

Seventh-Day Adventist Church, Central, 5350 Bailie Street at West 37th Avenue, Oakridge	266–1168
Kitsilano Lutheran Church, 2715 West 12th Avenue	738–5323
Chinese Mennonite Church, 375 East Pender Street	688–0877
St. Andrew's Wesley United Church, 1012 Nelson Street	683–4574
Schara Tzedecic Congregation, 3476 Oak Street	736–7607
Temple Sholom, 3476 Oak Street	731–9251
Beth Israel, 4350 Oak Street	731–4161
Vancouver Buddhist Church, 220 Jackson Street	253–7033
Sikh Temple, 8000 Ross Street	324–2010
Hindu Temple, 3885 Albert Street	299–5922

THE METRIC MILIEU

Distance
1 centimetre (cm) = .39 inch (in)
1 metre (m) = 39.4 inches = 3.3 feet (ft) = 1.1 yards (yd)
1 kilometre (km) = .62 miles (mi) = ⅝ mile

1 inch = 2.54 centimetres
1 foot = 30.5 centimetres = .31 metre
1 yard = 91.4 centimetres = .91 metre
1 mile = 1609.3 metres = 1.6 kilometres = 8/5 kilometres
1 nautical mile = 1.9 kilometres

Quick conversion formula for kilometres to miles: Kilometres divided by 2, plus ¼ of the result of that division. E.g. 80 km divided by 2 = 40; ¼ of that = 10; 40 + 10 = 50 miles.

Weight
1 gram (gm or g) = .04 ounce (oz) = .002 pound (lb)

1 kilogram (kg) = 35.3 ounces = 2.2 pounds

1 ounce = 28.35 grams
1 pound = 453.6 grams = .45 kilograms

Volume
1 litre (l) = 1.8 pints (pt) = .88 quarts (qt) = .2 gallons (gal) = .3 US gallons

1 fluid ounce = 28.41 millilitres (ml)
1 pint = .57 litre
1 quart = 1.14 litres
1 gallon = 4.55 litres
1 US gallon = 3.8 litres

Air Pressure
This now comes in kilopascals. Thank goodness service stations have conversion decals on their air meters so putting air in your tires won't be completely mind-boggling.

Temperature
The metric version of temperature is Celcius. Two formulae will help you convert from either Fahrenheit to Celsius or Celsius to Fahrenheit.

(Fahrenheit Degrees – 32) × 5/9 Celsius Degrees, e.g., (68 F – 32) × 5/9 = 20 C
(Celsius Degrees × 9/5) + 32 = Fahrenheit Degrees, e.g., (20 C × 9/5) + 32 = 68 F

	Fahrenheit/Celsius		Celsius/Fahrenheit	
	20	–6.7	–5	23
Water freezes	32	0	–5	32
	50	10	5	41
	60	15.5	10	50
	65	18.3	15	59
	70	21.1	20	68
	75	23.9	25	77
	80	26.7	30	87
	90	32.2	35	95
Water boils	212	100	100	212

THE WEATHER

The climate of Vancouver is best described as mild and moist. Despite the city's northerly latitude, the mountains of the Coast Range surrounding Vancouver form an effective barrier against most polar air, and the waters of the Strait of Georgia moderate temperatures in summer as well as in winter. Vancouver therefore enjoys a climate with winters that are not too cold and summers that are not too hot.

January, the coldest month, has an average daily temperature of 37° F (2.7° Celsius) with an average minimum of 30° F (–1.1° Celsius). July, the warmest month, has an average daily temperature of 64° F (17° Celsius) and an average maximum of 74° F (23° Celsius). Prevailing winds in winter are east to southeast, in summer west to northwest.

Annual precipitation (mostly rain with very little snow in the city itself) varies from an average of 1,070 mm (42 in) at the Airport to 1,520 mm (60 in) in the downtown area. It ranges from 1,900 mm (75 in) to 3,680 mm (145 in) in the Greater Vancouver watershed above the populated areas on the North Shore mountains (more snow is included here). Most precipitation occurs between October and March. Accordingly, the winter months are cloudy and wet, while summer is relatively sunny and dry.

Vancouver City Forecast	273–8331
General Weather Information	276–6109
Marine Weather Forecast	270–7411
Aviation Weather Forecast	273–1151
Mountain Weather Forecast (winters)	276–6112
Road Conditions	277–0112

A CALENDAR OF EVENTS

January
> Polar Bear Swim, English Bay Beach, Vancouver
> Auto Show, Exhibition Park, Vancouver
> P.N.E. Home Show, Exhibition Park, Vancouver

February
> Vancouver International Boat Show, B.C. Place
> Stadium, Vancouver

B.C. Home Show, B.C. Place Stadium, Vancouver
Variety Club Telathon, Queen Elizabeth Theatre, Vancouver
Vancouver Spring Gift Show, Exhibition Park, Vancouver
Chinese New Year Spring Festival, Gastown, Vancouver

March

Recreation Vehicle and Outdoor Show, B.C. Place Stadium, Vancouver
Antique Car Easter Parade, New Westminster

April

Vancouver Sportsmen's Show, B.C. Place Stadium, Vancouver
Bradner Flower Show, Bradner
Canadian Alpine Master Skiing Championships, Whistler

May

Children's Festival, Vanier Park, Vancouver
Timber Days Festival, Sechelt
Labatt's Rugby Cup, Brocton Oval, Stanley Park, Vancouver
Cloverdale Rodeo, Surrey Fairgrounds, Cloverdale
May Days, Whistler
PoCo May Day Celebrations, Port Coquitlam
Pioneer Mayday Celebrations, Memorial Park, Ladner
Hyack Festival Parade, New Westminster

June

Captain Vancouver Day Festival, Vancouver Maritime Museum, Vanier Park, Vancouver
Bullhead Fishing Derby, Steveston
Sea Festival, White Rock
Antique Fair and Auction, Fort Community Hall, Fort Langley
Greek Day, Vancouver

July

Canada Day Celebrations, English Bay, Vancouver
Steveston Salmon Festival, Steveston
Sea Festival, English Bay, Vancouver
Annual Nanaimo to Vancouver Bathtub Race

Invitational Hang Gliding Championships, Grouse Mountain

Summer Showcase of Local Arts and Crafts, Sunshine Coast Arts Centre, Sechelt

Folk Music Festival, Jericho Beach, Vancouver

Canadian Open Sand-Castle Competition, White Rock

August

Squamish Days/Logger Sports, Squamish

B.C. Summer Games, Nanaimo

Annual Fraser River Raft Race, Mission

Abbotsford International Air Show, Abbotsford

Powell Street Festival, Oppenheimer Park, Vancouver

Pacific National Exhibition, Exhibition Park, Vancouver

September

Pacific National Exhibition, Exhibition Park, Vancouver

Coho Festival, Park Royal, West Vancouver

Coho Festival, Ambleside, North Vancouver

Okanagan Wine Festival, Okanagan Valley

October

Okanagan Wine Festival, Okanagan Valley

Oktoberfest, B.C. Place Stadium, Vancouver

Vancouver Home Improvement Show, Exhibition Park, Vancouver

Annual Bazaar, Old Hastings Mill Store Museum

November

Hadassah Bazaar, Exhibition Park, Vancouver

Douglas Day Ceremonies, Fort Langley

December

Christmas Craft Fair, B.C. Place Stadium, Vancouver

Christmas Carol Cruise, New Westminster

Traditional Heritage Christmas, Century Park, Burnaby

Christmas Carol Ships Parade, English Bay, Vancouver

INDEX

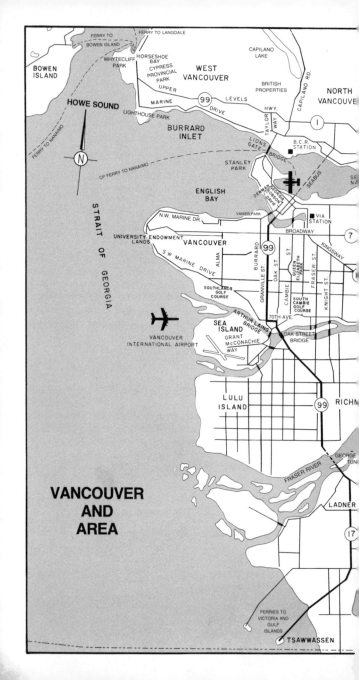

VANCOUVER AND AREA